CUTTHROAT TEAMMATES
ACHIEVING EFFECTIVE TEAMWORK AMONG PROFESSIONALS

Donald F. Heany, Ph.D.

BUSINESS ONE IRWIN
Homewood, Illinois 60430

To my children
Mary Donna and Tom

© RICHARD D. IRWIN, INC., 1989

Sponsoring editor: Jim Childs
Project editor: Karen Smith
Production manager: Ann Cassady
Jacket design: Sam Concialdi
Compositor: Weimer Typesetting Company, Inc.
Typeface: 11/13 Times Roman
Printer: R. R. Donnelley & Sons Company

Library of Congress Cataloging-in-Publication Data

Heany, Donald F.
    Cutthroat teammates : achieving effective teamwork among professionals / Donald F. Heany.
        p.   cm.
    Includes index.
    ISBN 1-55623-171-7, Paper ed. 1-55623-882-7
    1. Work groups.   2. Professional employees.   I. Title.
HD66.H43   1989   89–1240
658.4'036—dc19   CIP

Printed in the United States of America

1 2 3 4 5 6 7 8 9 0 DO 6 5 4 3 2

PREFACE

People in the business community rarely take the time to write their memoirs. When they retire, they take their gold watches and/or warm handshakes and fade away. No one debriefs them or attempts to extract any intellectual capital they have accumulated. Certainly most retirees do not compose for their successors reflective essays on "things to watch out for" or "some tools and techniques of analysis you can count on when the going gets rough." Rather than draw on the wisdom of personal experiences, the business community seems determined to repeat the mistakes of the past and allow tools and techniques of analysis to go out the door with retiring employees as well as those individuals who are promoted within the firm, leave for greener pastures, or are fired.

This book documents some real-life experiences bearing on a serious problem confronting U.S. businesses: *the absence of teamwork among professionals in various lines of business and in multibusiness firms.* It draws on my own experiences as well as those of many friends, colleagues, and clients.

Robert P. Ottman, formerly of the Dexter Corporation, was the source of some of the vignettes in the Introduction. Joseph M. Patten, a senior vice president of the Strategic Planning Institute, provided some of the illustrations in Chapters 1 and 6.

William D. Vinson, for three decades a consultant on GE's corporate staff, lavishly supported this attempt to document "institutional memory." He is the source of the methodology described in Chapter 2, most of the material in Chapter 3, and parts of Chapters 6 and 9.

W. Robert Stone drew on his many years of managerial experience at GE, IBM, A. B. Dick Company, and E. F. Johnson Company to provide source material for Chapters 5 and 6 as well as many helpful suggestions throughout the book.

Dr. James F. Sarver, president of Anderson Physics Laboratory, Inc., and formerly general manager of the engineering department in GE's Lamp Products Division, provided source material for Chapter 6, as did Tom Herlevi, Dr. Sarver's manager of human resources, and Bill Vinson.

David Krabacker, president and chief executive of American Car Car Company, Inc., was the primary source of the material in Chapter 7, and he labored over many drafts of that chapter.

Herbert B. Slate, a former manager and consultant with GE, and Adrian J. Grossman, once a vice president of the New York Stock Exchange, and a member of the corporate offices of GE and Borden, released GE material to help me illustrate the importance of team play between the architects of business strategy and of functional tactics in Chapter 8. They helped tremendously. Their interest in teamwork, like my own, was sparked by two GE executives: the late Harold F. Smiddy, chief architect of GE's decentralization policy, and the late Melvin H. Hurni, manager of GE's OR&S Consulting Service. Both men funded programs to help professionals improve the quality of team play and encouraged business researchers to analyze business and functional decisions.

Inputs to Chapter 9 came from various sources. Bill Vinson shared his files on the ribbon machine project. Jim Sarver reviewed my descriptions of this work. Bernard H. Rudwick, professor at the Defense Systems Management College, was the source of the material on weapon systems acquisition. Filomena P. Lupo shared her files on a systems project for one of the eastern states. David Van Lear, Jack W. Kent, and I were intimately involved in the project to link EDP work more closely to business strategy described in Chapter 9.

Chapter 10 was fashioned from several sources. Walter J. Maurer, a manager of an investment banking unit, provided information on customer sharing. Gerald Weiss, a senior vice president of The Chase Manhattan Bank, N.A., made available material on sharing private files. Ann Steers contributed material on probing

a contiguous market, and Donald S. Holmes, the president of Stochos, Inc., shared information on implanting modern process control techniques in businesses with severe quality problems.

Chapter 11 was another team effort. Jim B. Haag, Edwin L.
DeVilbiss, and Sally Huzyak were the consultants described in
the Box company case. Jodi Harpstead provided the material for
the illustration on how to persuade line managers to support an
innovation spawned by a corporate staff component. The material
on product sections in Chapter 11 was built on inputs from a
client and colleague, the late Robert Finholt, who was a general
manager of a GE product section. Joel Rosenfeld, formerly a manager with GE and now president of the PIMS Associates–North
America, offered insights on how division managers can encourage a free flow of technical information across business borders.
Robert L. Saslaw, TRW's former director of planning, shared information about his firm's procedures for reviewing capital
appropriations.

Charles M. Neul and Deborah A. Smith, both vice presidents
at The Chase Manhattan Bank, N.A., were the sources of the
productivity-profit grid in Chapter 12. They were lavish in their
support of this endeavor. The other tools germane to top-down
team play were based on work a number of us did while members
of GE's planning development staff.

It was no simple matter to find a structure that would accommodate material on team play from so many sources and pertaining to so many organizational echelons. Bernard H. Rudwick, my
close friend and colleague for thirty years, made many penetrat-
ing suggestions on how to organize my case material and link together the lessons to be learned. Ralph Sheridan, president of
HEC Energy Corporation, helped immensely on matters of content and style, as did John Rhode, a former vice president of Com-
bustion Engineering, and William F. Gearhart, a management
consultant in the Midwest.

Other friends and colleagues read early drafts of this book
Thanks are due to John M. Hobbs and Robert G. Blick of GE;
Thos. E. Dolan, Jack W. Kent, and Joseph Kapolka of Norwest
Corporation; Randy L. White and James G. Walters of Reynolds
Metals Company; Donald E. Battis, president of Profile Metal
Forming Company; and Gloria Pennington, the executive director

of Juvenile Diabetes Foundation, International, and her staff. Robert Chilton, John Guiniven, Philip Thompson, Berta Spiesman, and Tina Yurgelon-Dion (all of the Strategic Planning Institute), Andrew Lee (Booz, Allen and Hamilton), Shirley Grossman, G. E. Walker, and R. H. Spencer also commented on early drafts.

The book also benefited from discussions with Arthur J. Ballard, Brian Keidan, C. Alan Larsen, Norman Nordeen, Bill W. Sorenson, Thomas Malarkey, Professor Jackson E. Ramsey of James Madison University, and Professor Ben Branch of the University of Massachusetts.

My agent, Michael Snell, put his mark on early drafts of this material, and Jim Childs, sponsoring editor at Dow Jones-Irwin, continued in the same fashion. Both were avid champions of the subject matter of this book. I am very much in their debt.

Karen Smith, project editor at BUSINESS ONE IRWIN, and copy editor Nancy Maybloom did much to clarify this account of team play among professionals.

It goes without saying that the above-mentioned individuals bear no responsibility for any possible errors of omission or commission in this book. I hope the reader realizes that it was impossible to approach each and every member of the teams cited in this book. Should these professionals wish to document *their* perspectives of the events I described, I will be the first to applaud.

Donald F. Heany

CONTENTS

Introduction   1

PART 1 TUNNEL VISION OF THE FUNCTIONAL TYPE: WHAT CAN BE DONE ABOUT IT?

CHAPTER 1   PROMINENT BARRIERS TO INTERFUNCTIONAL
             TEAM PLAY   13

CHAPTER 2   FUSING THE TALENT ON A MULTIFUNCTIONAL
             TEAM   31

CHAPTER 3   EFFECTIVE MULTIFUNCTIONAL TEAMS   41

CHAPTER 4   GROOVES IN THE MIND: SUBMERGED
             BARRIERS TO TEAM PLAY   64

PART 2 BUSINESS STRATEGY: EASY TO CONCEIVE BUT HARD TO EXECUTE

CHAPTER 5   TEAM PLAY WITHIN NEW BUSINESSES   89
             • Functional Havoc Caused by a Gyrating Strategic
               Compass
             • Evolving Market Boundaries: How to Cope
               without Going Broke

CHAPTER 6   A CONSENSUS: THE BEDROCK OF STRATEGY
             AND TACTICS   105
             • Is It a "New Product" or a "New Business"?
             • Who Builds a Structure for a New Service
               Business?
             • Business Definition: A Job for a Top-Level Team

CHAPTER 7   "MAKING THE NUMBER": HOW TO GUT A
            BUSINESS AND STILL BE A HERO   122

CHAPTER 8   TIME OUT! WE HAVE TO RESTRUCTURE THIS
            BUSINESS   135

CHAPTER 9   VENDORS: FOES OR PARTNERS?   146
            • Giving an Old Plant a Facelift
            • Weapon Acquisition: A Joint Effort of Users and
              Providers
            • Customer Buy-In: A Challenge for System
              Designers
            • EDP Support for Business Strategy from a
              Captive Vendor

PART 3 INTERBUSINESS TEAM PLAY: THE IMPOSSIBLE DREAM

CHAPTER 10   TRANSFERRING EXPERTISE: A FORWARD
             PASS FROM ONE COMPONENT TO ANOTHER   173
             • Customer Sharing: A Duty of Established
               Business
             • Turning Private Files into a Business Asset
             • Getting Broad-Based Support for a Probe of a
               Contiguous Market
             • Infusing New Techniques into a Backward
               Business
             • Moving Know-How around within a Portfolio
             • Packaging and Sharing Managerial Wisdom

CHAPTER 11   THE ODD COUPLE: LINE AND STAFF   196
             • A Team Effort to Put Teeth into a Corporate
               Quality Policy
             • Innovation: A Challenge for Both Staff and Line
               Managers
             • The Left Hand versus the Right Hand: Linking
               Capital Appropriations to Business Strategy

CHAPTER 12   THE LACK OF TOP-DOWN TEAM PLAY: A
             PROBLEM THAT DEMANDS A SOLUTION   216
             • Coping with Voluminous Financial Data: Tools
               from Chase Manhattan
             • Strategic Data: Too Much and Too Little

- How Inter-Business Relationships Complicate Top-Down Team Play
- Call for Action

APPENDIX A   THE CONTRIBUTIONS OF A QUALITY MAP TO TEAM PLAY DURING NEW-PRODUCT DEVELOPMENT   241

APPENDIX B   AN OPERATIONAL BUSINESS CHARTER, BUSINESS STRATEGY, AND FUNCTIONAL GUIDANCE   245

References   249

Index   255

LIST OF EXHIBITS

3–1   ONE STRAND IN THE QUALITY MAP DEVELOPED BY THE BRIGHT STIK TEAM

3–2   PORTION OF A GRAPHIC MODEL OF SOME DETERMINANTS OF MOTOR NOISE

4–1   SPI QUALITY PROFILE

4–2   TWO VIEWS OF CUSTOMERS' DETERMINANTS OF QUALITY—CUSTOMERS VERSUS MANAGEMENT

4–3   RELATIVE QUALITY FOR THREE COMPETITORS, BY ATTRIBUTE

4–4   THE LEVEL OF A PRODUCT

7–1   ACTIVITIES IN A REGIONAL SERVICE CENTER

12–1   A PRODUCTIVITY GRID

12–2   REGIONS WITHIN THE PRODUCTIVITY GRID

12–3   RETURN ON INVESTMENT AND OPERATING EFFICIENCY FOR FOUR PRODUCTIVITY PATTERNS

12–4   A FRAMEWORK FOR LINKING CORPORATE STRATEGY, BUSINESS STRATEGY, AND FUNCTIONAL TACTICS

12–5   FRAGMENT OF A STRATEGIC MAP FOR THE HEALTH CARE ARENA

A–1   FRAGMENT OF A QUALITY MAP DEVELOPED BY A MULTIFUNCTIONAL TEAM CHARGED WITH COMMERCIALIZING A NEW PRODUCT (BRIGHT STIK)

B–1   A NEW CHARTER FOR AATD

B–2   PLANKS IN THE PROPOSED BUSINESS STRATEGY

B–3   STRATEGIC CONSTRAINTS ON FUNCTIONAL MANAGERS

INTRODUCTION

To my mind, the performance of a manager is measured by how well that manager can organize a large number of people and how effectively he or she can get the highest performance from each of the individuals and blend them into a coordinated performance. That is what management is. It does not start at the bottom line of the balance sheet.

—Akio Morita, *Chairman of the Board, Sony Corporation*[1]

When a helicopter plummeted into Manhattan's East River, two rescue teams sped to the scene. One came from the fire department, the other from the police department. On arrival, each team protested the other's presence. In each case, the argument was "We have jurisdiction!" This cross-departmental feud had a fatal consequence—a passenger on the helicopter died.

The mayor of New York City heard about the tragedy, summoned the department heads to his office, and gave them his own view of their deportment: "This defies common sense!"[2]

* * * * *

Intermodal transport is a concept that intrigues transportation tycoons. Passengers on the Montreal to New York City Express were less impressed. Their train had completed most of its journey when they were forced to get off and transfer to a bus. The driver pulled out of the station, drove 200 yards, pulled up in front of a diner, stopped the bus, and got out to have coffee and a doughnut.

* * * * *

A health maintenance organization made a contract with a well-known Boston hospital to share that hospital's facilities. A doctor from this HMO went over to meet his new colleagues and to work out mutually acceptable procedures for accommodating HMO patients. The reception he got was less than cordial; he was told that he could have access to the hospital's equipment *only on weekends!*

* * * * *

1

THE COST OF A NARROW PERSPECTIVE

Are these merely three isolated examples of unusual behavior patterns? Hardly! Anyone who has spent more than a few days inside a business has encountered professionals who display an equally narrow perspective. They are determined to do things their way. They prefer jousting to collaboration and devote a considerable amount of their time and energy to fussing and feuding with their colleagues in other organizational components.

For example, HC, Inc., a prominent manufacturer of health care equipment, enjoyed spectacular sales growth for more than 15 years.[3] In fact, growth was so fast that the company's CEO set up an elaborate financial system for accelerating customer payments and dealing promptly with delinquent accounts. This system called for the finance department to challenge the credit rating behind every order.

In the early 1980s, the federal government and insurance firms set out to cap the rate of increase in the cost of medical care. Their programs had a dramatic impact on hospitals and their vendors. Hospitals responded by postponing purchases of capital equipment. Those which did buy equipment settled for lower-priced models or rebuilt equipment.

HC, Inc., was hurt by these dramatic changes in purchase patterns. Recently its vice president–sales stormed into the office of his executive vice president and lodged a complaint about "those imbeciles in finance." Apparently his sales team had worked for weeks to win an order from a leading hospital. When the purchase order arrived, a specialist in the finance department refused to process it on the grounds that the hospital's credit rating was "too low." When the hospital's purchasing agent learned about this incident, he became irate and informed the HC sales representative that he intended to redirect his order to another vendor.

The following week, a similar unilateral decision by a financial specialist infuriated HC's vice president–sales. When another customer called to ask why he had not received his equipment, the order service department investigated and discovered that a clerk in finance had stopped delivery. Why? Because the invoice covered the cost of the equipment but *not* the cost of the instruction manuals. This glitch was enough to hold up the order!

The customer was indignant about this unreasonable behavior. He already had written a check for $40,000 to cover his purchase, but he decided to leave it in his desk drawer until HC learned how to process requisitions properly.

WHY IS TEAM PLAY SO RARE?

These incidents have their counterparts in many businesses. The executive vice president of HC, Inc., investigated the above incidents and concluded that they had a common taproot: His managers and specialists were operating with *an outdated mind-set,* acquired at their parents' knees, in college, or from the days when growth and profits came automatically to HC. Specifically, the financial specialists were *not* "imbeciles"; they were merely apt pupils of an accounting system that had developed when HC faced a fast-growth market. No one had taken the young specialists aside and explained that they should interpret their accounting rules loosely when market demand was slack. No one had authorized them to adjust the rules of this system to take into account the level of effort required to sell in a depressed market.

Indeed, the reverse was true. The manager–finance had instructed his staff to ignore what was going on in other functions. They were to give their full attention to financial work. Only in that way could they support his efforts to protect HC's cash flow and preserve the integrity of the data underlying financial decisions. If a rigorous interpretation of the current accounting conventions made financial specialists unpopular with professionals in other functions, so be it. After all, financial specialists were not running for public office. Like other "police officers," good accountants could not expect to be loved by the people they disciplined. Their job was to enforce financial policies, *not* to bend them. They should always remember that no outside auditor had ever faulted a financial specialist for being "too strict."

The bottom line was: Professionals in *all* functions had to *unlearn* lessons they had mastered only a few years earlier when

HC, Inc., was on its upward roll. Now, however, all professionals in HC had to go back to school and learn this new lesson:

> We can survive if, and only if, we begin to work together, each and every day. No exceptions. No more dominant functions. No more jousting. No more infighting. We either learn how to collaborate or we will go down the tubes together.

Why must professionals learn this basic lesson so late in life? Are they not all working for the same business? Indeed they are. But this does *not* ensure that harmony will prevail. Ask any professional, in any function. For example, ask Joe, a marketing specialist. He will quickly explain that many of his colleagues are:

- Slow to understand.
- Narrow-minded.
- Difficult.
- Quick to take offense.
- Opinionated.
- Hard of hearing.

When Joe observes two of his colleagues feuding, he does not intervene. To him, peacekeeping is not part of his job. In fact, he has virtually concluded that most professional relationships have an adversarial quality. A plaque on his desk summarizes his cynical response to calls for joint integrated performance: "If I were not surrounded by all these turkeys, I would soar like an eagle."

Nonetheless, Joe would be the first to agree that somebody should create a climate that favors interfunctional collaboration. In his opinion, X is the ideal person to do so. Why? Because X has a managerial position two levels higher than Joe's. And Joe firmly believes that only people with a great deal of political clout can prevent professionals from feuding with one another.

Joe's managers are less cynical. They have not abandoned hope that professionals *can* be motivated to work together. In fact, they make these three points:

1. We think teamwork is *very* important. Indeed, it is the glue that holds a business together. Without it, we cannot create, let alone sustain, a competitive advantage.

2. We urge our people to act as members of a closely knit team at every opportunity.
3. The quality of teamwork in our own business is far lower than what we would like it to be.

CHALLENGING THE STATUS QUO

This book challenges Joe's cherished belief that conflict among professionals is inevitable and only senior managers can foster team play. The fact is, professionals at *every* organizational level can do much to lessen conflict and promote teamwork—not every day, not in every situation, but certainly sometimes. Thus, the ideal change agent is *thee and me*. We know where the skirmishes are taking place; we are on the scene; we can intervene before the conflict grows serious. To wait for senior managers to intervene would be like waiting for Godot.

Many professionals see the futility of interfunctional feuds. The problem is that *they do not know how to prevent them from breaking out*. They are waiting for someone to show them how to work together more effectively.

Such is the purpose of this book.

Why Should Anyone Care about High-Quality Team Play?

Today U.S. firms can find several compelling reasons to view conflict among professionals as a time-consuming "luxury" they can no longer afford. The following items are samples of the penalties a business pays when professionals feud among themselves.

Item: Friction on the borders that separate functions diverts attention from important business goals (e.g., rebuilding a competitive advantage).

Item: In businesses where adversarial relationships are the norm, professionals feel compelled to protect themselves from "the system." While they are busy protecting their own positions, business effectiveness plummets.

Item: The corporate office responds: A plague on your functional houses! We can find professionals offshore who will do the same work without all this friction.

Item: In many companies, the corporate guillotine has been rolled out in order to remove "excess fat" from the payroll. This has left a smaller cadre of professionals to handle a larger workload. For the professionals who remain, teamwork is not a luxury; *it is a necessity.*

WHO SHOULD READ THIS BOOK?

This book is not for everyone. Read no further if:

• Your name is Hatfield or McCoy. Individuals who have sprung from such stock delight in internecine warfare. They are adept at infighting and have no interest in ways to promote team play.
• You are planning to move out of the war zones in your business and into Shangri-la, a place where professionals never fight, never raise their voices in anger, never bury a hatchet between the shoulder blades of a colleague.
• You are convinced that conflict among professionals is so pervasive and intense that no mere mortal can deter the combatants from mutual destruction. Hence, you direct all your energy at résumé preparation.
• You are a business Eskimo—that is, you reside in an igloo that buffers you from all interpersonal conflicts. From this igloo you observe your colleagues' foibles with scholarly detachment. You find the risks incurred by peacemakers excessively high. Therefore, you have resolved *not* to return to the field of battle, either as a combatant or as a peacemaker. Better a long-lived cynic than a short-lived martyr.
• You are a rugged individualist, convinced that a solo performance is a better way to call attention to your own considerable talents.

Therefore, this book must be for those individuals who are appalled by the cost of friction among professionals, be they managers or specialists. They realize it is counterproductive to operate from isolated, tightly sealed compartments. They have seen too much jousting in manufacturing and service businesses, in startup and mature businesses, in profit and nonprofit organizations. They know there must be an alternative.

OUR SOURCE MATERIAL

There *are* alternatives. Most of the illustrations cited in this book come from managers and consultants who have discovered ways to help professionals work together. The reader is invited to look over their shoulders and profit from their team-building methods.

PLAN OF THIS BOOK

This book offers team-building tools that can be applied by professionals in every type of business, at every organizational level. In the course of illustrating how these tools have been used, we occasionally insert an author's commentary to draw attention to a generic point that might otherwise be lost. These commentaries are printed in *italics*.

Part 1 deals with *interfunctional team play at the line-of-business level*. It offers tools that managers in other U.S. businesses have developed, tested, and found useful in lowering the Chinese-type walls that isolate professionals from one another.

Part 2 focuses on *team play between professionals who conceive business strategies and those who carry them out*. By their own admission, managers in U.S. firms have *not* excelled at strategy implementation. Therefore, we describe team-building tools valuable both to general managers and their staffs and to middle managers and their specialists. Part 2 also recognizes the value of team play between a business and its vendors.

Part 3 emphasizes *interbusiness team play within a multibusiness portfolio*. Instead of exhorting managers to "wear" their corporate hat, we show them *why* and *how* to do so. Part 3 also examines the lack of *top-down team play*, namely that between executives and the line managers in charge of different profit centers. The obstacles to top-down team play are formidable, particularly in firms that measure their planning horizons in months rather than years. Nonetheless, we believe modest improvements in this type of team play are possible if firms use the team-building tools at hand.

WHY NOT BE PATIENT?

Some say: Give professionals a little more time and they will learn to work together. However, there are two arguments against waiting for adversarial relations to yield to collaboration.

First, professionals emerge from academe, the citadel of specialization. Peter Drucker aptly refers to a university faculty as a group of anarchists united by a parking lot. Given their abysmal performance at team play, we can hardly expect their intellectual offspring to be predisposed to becoming team players.

Second, U.S. firms do not have time on their side. They must conform to the tempo set by world-class competitors operating in a culture that emphasizes team play over adversarial relationships. Those who call for a level playing field and tariff barriers must bear in mind that the most formidable obstacle facing U.S. firms lies within themselves. If they got their act together, if their professionals exchanged collaboration for feuding, U.S. companies would have a chance to retain their former preeminence. Meanwhile, their world-class competitors are *not* waiting on the sidelines.

NOTES

1. Akio Morita, Edwin M. Reingold, and Mitsuko Shimomura, *Made in Japan: Morita and Sony* (New York: E. P. Dutton, 1986), p. 154.
2. Richard Levine, "At City Hall, More Than the Usual Ill Will," *New York Times,* May 8, 1988, sec. E, pp. 1, 6.
3. This is not the real name of this firm.

PART 1

TUNNEL VISION OF THE FUNCTIONAL TYPE: WHAT CAN BE DONE ABOUT IT?

The Boston Celtics are one of the most successful sports franchises in the world. Why? Because year after year they put on the court five players of star caliber who *play as a team*. They play with great intensity, and they win with great frequency.

Business managers sit in the stands and watch with amazement. They ask themselves: Why can't we get professionals in *our* organization to play as members of a closely knit team? Why are we always required to arbitrate feuds between specialists working in the various functional areas? Why has turf defense become a fine art in our companies? Why do we dedicate so much energy to politicking and so little to new-product development and customer service?

This sad state of affairs is no secret. When Lee Iacocca became chief executive of Chrysler, he found

. . . thirty-five vice presidents, each with his own turf. There was . . . no system of meetings to get people talking to each other.

> I couldn't believe . . . that the guy running the engineering depart-
> ment wasn't in constant touch with his counterpart in manufactur-
> ing. But that's how it was. Everybody worked independently. . . .
>   Nobody at Chrysler seemed to understand that interaction
> among the different functions in a company is absolutely critical.[1]

Peter F. Drucker would not have been surprised by the behavior of professionals at Chrysler. He was one of the first to note
the appearance of a new breed of worker—the "knowledge
worker."

> The knowledge worker must be focused on the results and per-
> formance of the entire organization to have any results and per-
> formance at all. This means that he has to set aside time to direct
> his vision from his work to results, and from his specialty to the
> outside in which alone performance lies.[2]

Unfortunately, there is a big difference between what *ought
to* happen and what *does* happen. Managers did not rush to implement Drucker's sage counsel. Drucker himself offered professionals little specific guidance on how to become less narrow in their
vision, skills, and loyalties.[3]

Instead, managers resorted to exhortation. They urged their
subordinates to mend their ways, to become team players, to
think of "the good of the firm." Professionals listened to such
sermons with rapt attention—and then went back to their desks
and their traditional adversarial behavior patterns.

In recent years, executives of firms in the United States have
rushed to Japan looking for a formula that might enable them to
match the performance of their Japanese competitors. There they
were converted to the importance of targeting "zero defects" and
forming "quality circles." They concluded that basic changes were
needed in the outlook of their blue-collar workers. However, they
conveniently overlooked the need to motivate their *professional
workers* to work together. They also failed to redesign the managerial practices that had fostered adversarial relationships among
their professionals.

Today it is much easier to get people to think about ways to
help professional workers work more effectively *and together*.
Akio Morita has defined the challenge succinctly:

> There is no secret ingredient or hidden formula responsible for the success of the best Japanese companies. . . . The most important mission for a Japanese manager is to . . . create a familylike feeling within the corporation, a feeling that employees and managers share the same fate.[4]

The word *family* conjures up bonds, trust, mutual respect, shared values, and mutual cooperation. However, the new breed of U.S. manager does not project these values.[5]

The intent of this book is not to advocate an ideal world but to suggest that professional workers have a key role to play in any drive to help U.S. businesses recover their competitive advantage.

Part 1 describes both the visible and the hidden obstacles to team play among professionals in the various functions. It also offers answers to two fundamental questions:

- How can professionals take responsibility for results?
- How do knowledge workers integrate their own output with that of other professionals?

The methods we present have been developed, tested, and validated by managers in many U.S. businesses.

We recognize that some of the friction registered on the borders separating the various functions is traceable to flawed strategic decisions made at a *higher* organizational level. These remote causes of interfunctional feuding will be addressed in Part 2.

NOTES

1. Lee Iacocca and William Novak, *Iacocca: An Autobiography,* (New York: Bantam Books, 1984), pp. 152–53.
2. Peter F. Drucker, *The Effective Executive* (New York: Harper & Row, 1967), p. 30.
3. Peter F. Drucker, *Management: Tasks, Practices, Responsibilities* (New York: Harper & Row, 1973), p. 561.
4. Akio Morita, Edwin M. Reingold, and Mitsuko Shimomura, *Made in Japan: Morita and Sony* (New York: E. P. Dutton, 1986), pp. 130ff.
5. Steven Prokesch, "Remaking the American C.E.O.," *New York Times,* January 25, 1987 (Sunday business section).

CHAPTER 1

PROMINENT BARRIERS TO INTERFUNCTIONAL TEAM PLAY

. . . the central problem of economic policy becomes how to create the kinds of organizations in which people can pool their efforts, insights, and enthusiasm without fear of exploitation. . . . This is far from a simple task.

—Robert B. Reich[1]

Our culture does not place a premium on collaboration except in sports (e.g., basketball, hockey, rowing, polo). In many U.S. businesses, team play is conspicuous by its absence. Perhaps professionals ought to collaborate with their colleagues working in another area of the business. The fact is, they do not.

The rhetoric in favor of team play goes on relentlessly. Managers exhort their professionals to unite.

- We must make this into a single-punch organization.
- Everyone must join forces to make this business the low-cost, high-quality vendor.
- If we pull together, we can become the industry leader, or at least a quick follower.
- All of us must be more market driven.

Why do these exhortations fall on deaf ears? What is blocking collaboration? Why do highly intelligent professionals prefer feuding to team play? Why do adversarial relationships persist? Why do professionals insist on solo performances rather than a group performance? These are questions that professionals in for-profit and not-for-profit institutions alike must ponder.

CUTTHROAT TEAMMATES: THE CLASSIC EXPLANATIONS

There are five popular explanations for the failure of professionals at the line-of-business level to work harmoniously with their colleagues in other functional areas:

1. Specialization.
2. Organizational structure and organizational flux.
3. Managerial ego trips.
4. Tension between personal goals and business goals.
5. External changes.

Specialization

The late publisher Frank Sheed left us an apt definition of a specialist: "A specialist lives, not in a rut but in a hole. A brilliantly lighted hole, but a hole unmistakably."[2] Members of the business community may agree, but they are still convinced that Adam Smith was correct when he pointed to the economic advantages of organizing work around specialties. You certainly will find Smith's imprint on the organization charts of many firms, charts filled with boxes containing semantic labels such as "Marketing," "Sales, " "New-Product Development," "Customer Service," "Finance," and "Human Resources."

Managers who adopt this type of functional organization assume that each cluster of professionals will derive their functional objectives from *business* objectives. They also presume that individuals in each cluster will take the next logical step: Develop personal objectives that support both functional and business objectives.

That is easier said than done.[3] Managers still complain about professionals who are:

- Too wrapped up in their own disciplines to care about what is happening outside their own bailiwick.
- Indifferent to the negative impacts of their technical decisions on business profitability and business effectiveness.

- Overzealous in lobbying for the goals of their respective functions.

If these managers had paid more attention to what was going on in the universities they attended, they might have anticipated these side effects of excessive specialization. After all, universities took specialization to its limits:

> Few laymen realized how tightly compartmentalized the scientific community had become, a battleship with bulkheads sealed against leaks. Biologists had enough to read without keeping up with the mathematical literature . . . molecular biologists had enough to read without keeping up with population biology.[4]

Habits encouraged in a university environment have been carried into the business world and have contributed to functional disharmony. Some examples follow.

Professionals No Longer Share a Common Language

Today we are confronted with a modern version of the Tower of Babel. Terms like *product, quality, business,* and *strategy* take on different meanings when one moves from function to function.[5] Here is an example.

A start-up business in California developed a new electrostatic printer to enhance the productivity of product and process designers and draftspeople in very large companies. In due course, the director of marketing visited Detroit to learn how a leading auto manufacturer was employing the new printer.

His customer gave him a frosty reception. For a full hour, he had to listen to a litany of complaints about the quality of service his firm rendered when installing the new printer. Then his customer began to enumerate the deficiencies in the manuals provided with the printer. The marketing director meekly recorded each of his customer's complaints and promised to address them promptly.

By the time the manager arrived back in California, he had formulated an action plan that would mollify this important customer. Much to his surprise, he discovered that his colleagues in R&D and engineering were unmoved by his report of customer dissatisfaction. Their concept of "product quality" did *not* extend to things like instruction manuals and installation service. They were annoyed that any customer could fail to be impressed by their state-of-the-art hardware.

The director of marketing persisted. He knew his colleagues in R&D worked in a quasi-academic environment and rarely met customers, but he also realized that his firm was unlikely to win additional sales in the Detroit market as long as the first electrostatic printer in that market had not been enthusiastically received. For these reasons, he persuaded his general manager to support his effort to mount a multifunctional response to his customer's legitimate complaints.

This effort succeeded. On his next trip to Detroit, the director of marketing had the satisfaction of hearing a once irate customer give an unsolicited endorsement for the new printer at an important professional gathering.

The Cult of the Elite
Colleges and universities attempt to convince their graduates that they are "different" from—indeed, clearly superior to—their friends who matriculated at less prestigious institutions. The business culture to which these young professionals attach themselves amplifies these perceptions. For example, do not be surprised if new entrants into your engineering function look down their noses at those "engineering dropouts" who had to settle for jobs as manufacturing engineers. In another six months, you may find these same recruits transmitting orders, not information, to their colleagues in manufacturing:

> Just conform to these specifications and you will have quality products to ship. Deviate from them and *you* (not we) will have quality problems to deal with.

The definition of "dominant function" varies. In businesses that produce packaged goods, marketing probably claims functional dominance. In mature businesses operating with razor-thin margins, the financial function typically dominates strategic decisions. In businesses that produce high-tech products or software, R&D usually claims top honors.

Fortunately, functional dominance is not eternal. But while it lasts, professionals who perceive themselves as being in the dominant function will be undisposed to collaborate with the less fortunate mortals who work in other functions.

The Urge to Be a Solo Performer

Another by-product of all those years in an academic environment is the inclination of many professionals to render solo performances and thereby draw attention to their *individual* contributions.

This habit has been institutionalized in the sales department. Each salesperson has a quota. Bonuses go to those who exceed their quotas. The honor of being "best salesperson in the territory" assures the winner of a free trip to Las Vegas. In the insurance industry, agents vie for membership in the "President's Club," an honor reserved for the most productive salespeople in the company. In banks, the reward takes yet another form: The most productive loan officer is automatically judged to be the one best qualified to manage the department!

This managerial emphasis on individual performance goes unchallenged because group performance is much more difficult to measure.

The Perks of Stars and Superstars

Specialists see themselves as members of a select community with the right to set their own standards and to police performance against these measures. While acknowledging the need for performance reviews, they insist that it be a "peer review." This attitude explains, for example, the resistance of medical practitioners to attempts by the government and insurance firms to cap the fees charged for surgical procedures.

In this they are not alone. In all probability, the specialists in your EDP facility believe they are in the best position to define the "quality" of service rendered to their captive clients. In their opinion, if their mainframe computer has an uptime of 95 percent, the pursuit of excellence is over. Who could ask for more?

Some of their clients, however, might demur. What about the impact of that missing 5 percent on the quality of service that other components of the firm render to their customers?

Instead of sitting down with their captive clients and searching for a mutually agreeable measure of performance, EDP professionals simply assert that the quality of their systems is "good—indeed, it exceeds industry standards." To discuss "our" standards with nonprofessionals would make the latter equal to "us." This is a perk no professional is willing to surrender without a fight.

Functional Turf Is Like One's Native Soil: It Must Be Defended

Managers have been warned about the limits of functional organization:

> . . . used beyond fairly narrow limits of size and complexity, it [functional design] creates emotional tensions, hostilities, and insecurities. People will then tend to see themselves and their functions belittled, besieged, attacked. They will come to see it as their first job to defend their function, to protect it against marauders in other functions, to make sure "it doesn't get pushed around."[6]

These perceptions prompt political maneuvers and power plays. A party line emerges. In meetings attended by professionals from other areas of the business, each member of the "fraternity" is expected to adhere to and advance that party line.

One politician begets another. If your staff meetings are characterized by interminable debates, you are witnessing the wake of specialization.

Organizational Structure and Organizational Flux

While the functional form of organization is highly favored, in some businesses it spawns behavior patterns that inhibit collaboration across functional borders:

> At its best, functional organization works with high economy. . . . But, at its fairly common worst, functional organization is grossly uneconomical. As soon as it approaches even a modest degree of size or complexity, "friction" builds up. It rapidly becomes an organization of misunderstandings, feuds, empires and Berlin-Wall building. It soon requires elaborate, extensive, and clumsy management crutches—coordinators, committees, meetings, troubleshoot-

ers, special dispatchers—which waste everybody's time . . . without solving much.[7]

The obstacles to interfunctional team play soar still higher when frequent changes occur in the organizational structure. Just ask the office comics, "Who is the general manager of this business?" Do not be surprised if they answer, "We're not sure. But we will take a look!"

This kind of humor is very revealing. It signals that organizational flux has bred cynicism.

Like death and taxes, some managerial turnover is inevitable. At times, it is even quite healthy. But in many U.S. firms, managerial turnover has reached a ridiculous level. The reasons are familiar. Executives are vigorously seeking to

- Restructure their corporation.
- Shift the mix from manufacturing to service businesses.
- Experiment with matrix management.
- Shift manufacturing work to offshore sites, and so on.

These corporate policies often have produced a "revolving-door" effect at the line-of-business level. The temporary resident of the corner office will not bother to get familiar with the work his or her professionals are doing or seek their counsel. This person is content to manage the business with the help of a generic financial model. Since he or she expects to be moving on, why get immersed in the details of the business? This individual is committed to neither the organization nor its people.

Some organizational changes are not imposed by corporate executives; rather, they originate with general managers of lines of business. Newly appointed managers like to tinker with the organizational structure they have inherited. First, a change in this structure sends a clear signal to all employees that there is a new hand on the tiller. Second, it forwards a message to the corner office: Things are beginning to happen already.

Regardless of the reasons behind these changes in organizational structure, they have implications for the quality of interfunctional team play. Each amendment severs established relationships. New relationships must be forged. Since there are new people "in the loop," this takes a little time and much effort.

More important, each change prompts professionals to ponder their own vulnerability. Will their decades of service in the business be recognized as a plus or a minus? Does the new manager have a retinue of retainers in the wings waiting to be assigned to key positions? Is a change in strategy to be announced? Will the new boss scuttle previously approved investments in this business so that he will be an "instant hero?"

When questions like these shuttle back and forth on the office grapevine, productivity falls and discussions on how to improve the quality of interfunctional team play move to the back burner: "Yes, interfunctional teamwork is important, but it will have to wait until stability returns to the organization."

Managerial Ego Trips

Much has been written about the "new breed of manager." We need only note that team play appears to be a low priority for managers whose role model is Napoleon or Attila the Hun. These managers project the image that they have all the answers. Any professionals brash enough to question their "wisdom" will quickly find themselves in the arms of an executive search firm. The reason for their dismissal? "Disloyalty and incompetence!" From such a verdict, there is no appeal.[8] Witnesses on the sidelines decide to keep a low profile. They will not draw attention to themselves by leading a drive to foster interfunctional team play.

Tension between Personal Goals and Business Goals

In any collective undertaking, one expects a degree of tension between personal and organizational goals. Yet colleges and graduate schools invest little time teaching their students how to harmonize personal and collective goals. Perhaps they presume that students will acquire this skill via extracurricular activities like sports, orchestra, glee club, and so on.

This is a heroic assumption. The evidence is right there in the measurement systems that encourage managers to steal orders from the next fiscal year in order to assure their bonuses in the current fiscal year. In extreme cases, some executives continue to pay dividends even when income is declining![9]

External Changes

We must make a passing reference to the effect of external changes on the quality of interfunctional team play. Momentous events like an unfriendly takeover attempt, a major antitrust suit, or a plant catastrophe do more than absorb the attention of people in the corner office. They also affect professionals at the line-of-business level. For example,

- Some profitable businesses are (regretfully) sold, and the funds thus obtained are applied to the "crisis."
- Other businesses are ordered to make a greater contribution to corporate profits—somehow.
- Budgeted capital projects are put on hold.
- New products are scrapped in favor of less expensive product line extensions.

One might think that such decisions would stimulate rather than discourage team play. Theoretically, they might. But draconian measures spawned by external changes such as those listed above rarely do. The bottom line is fewer people, more work, and higher revenue expectations.

To professionals in an integrated firm, "external change" includes the arrival of a new chief executive officer, a shift in corporate strategy, and a corporate reorganization. For example, should a newly installed chief executive officer embark on an aggressive acquisition strategy, the more established businesses are likely to be asked to provide the funding. In plain English, this means deferring their own aggressive strategic moves, postponing their own R&D programs, and abandoning plans to modernize their own plants. A blanket of austerity descends on the businesses that made up the corporate portfolio before the pursuit of acquisitions began in earnest. The most mobile professionals depart for greener pastures and a higher quality of life.

After the targeted businesses have been acquired, there is an aftershock: Management discovers structural flaws that escaped detection during the courtship. When this is the case, a business transfusion is arranged. Personnel and/or technology from established businesses are sent to the new arrivals to cover up the bad news. The published reasons may sound perfectly logical, but professionals in the donor business will remain convinced that "they robbed Peter to pay Paul." They realize that they must produce more profit with fewer resources.

NEGLECTED OBSTACLES TO TEAM PLAY

There are other, less publicized deterrents to interfunctional team play. Following are four illustrations.

The Absence of a Strategic Context

Interfunctional team play is a lot easier when general managers offer their professionals a vision of the kind of business they wish to create and a clear understanding of what it takes to be successful in their market/industry. Unfortunately, some general managers fail to provide this vision and instead, focus exclusively on technique. Fascination with technique begins in college.

An engineering graduate returned to his alma mater 25 years later. Since he had become a manager at a well-known New England firm, he received a royal welcome. The dean of the engineering school jumped at the chance to tell him about the curriculum changes that had taken place since his student days.

After listening patiently, the graduate began to suspect that the new curriculum ignored material pertaining to business strategy, e.g., market scope, market segmentation, and product quality. When the dean paused for breath, the graduate asked about these topics. The dean's answer was very revealing: "We do not include marketing subjects in our curriculum. But we do give our students a broad exposure to statistical process control."

For the next 60 minutes, the dean listened to a lecture about the need to give engineering students some understanding of market forces. Then and only then would they be able to utilize statistical techniques *with understanding*.

You might not need this lecture, but this dean certainly did. His new curriculum had evolved from the perspective of a *single function*. It failed to inform students of the need to examine the market context before rushing into a statistical analysis.

Failure to See the "Critical Issue" Facing the Business

Professionals in *all* functions need help in seeing how their respective contributions relate to business goals. If managers fail to offer such help, needless friction will spring up along the functional borders. But executives *can* provide a clear understanding, as the following case makes clear.

Recently a medium-size company appointed a new group executive to head its industrial products division. The businesses comprising his group were earning attractive rates of return. He felt that with a little tightening up here and there, he would have no trouble convincing his CEO that he had assigned the right person to this important position.

One of his first steps was to call for a strategic audit of his businesses. To his chagrin, the consultant who conducted this audit informed him that the long-term profit prospects for his portfolio of businesses were rather dim.

The following dialog summarizes the ensuing exchange between the group executive and his consultant:

EXECUTIVE: I can't believe those findings of yours. There must be a bug in the model you used to arrive at those conclusions.

CONSULTANT: I wish that were the case. Unfortunately, there is no bug. Your group has a severe productivity problem.

EXECUTIVE: That's ridiculous! We have a highly motivated labor force and very high labor productivity.

CONSULTANT: I meant that you have a *capital* productivity problem.

EXECUTIVE: But that is even more preposterous. Our plants are the most modern in this industry.

CONSULTANT: No doubt they are. But you still have a problem. You are committing too much investment in order to generate a dollar of value added.

EXECUTIVE: Prove it!

CONSULTANT: I think I can. I have been searching the PIMS database for businesses that resemble those you have inherited. I found 84 that were definitely "look-alikes" to your businesses. All are established businesses. All have strong competitive positions. All offer quality products.

EXECUTIVE: Get to the point.

CONSULTANT: I will. Would you like to hazard a guess as to the average return on investment (pretax, preinterest) your look-alikes earned?

EXECUTIVE: I don't know why I should humor you, but okay. Such businesses probably reported an ROI of 30 percent.

CONSULTANT: I'm sorry to have to take your money. Only 30 percent of them earned more than 18 percent return on investment, pretax and preinterest.

EXECUTIVE: Impossible! Did you really limit your attention to businesses with high market shares and high product quality?

CONSULTANT: Yes. But these businesses were similar to your businesses in another respect: They required a lot of investment to produce a dollar of value added. In short, they also had a *capital* productivity problem.

EXECUTIVE: The way you are talking, I should throw in the towel.

CONSULTANT: By no means. I am suggesting that capital productivity is one of your major management challenges. More important, this problem is likely to become more serious in the short term.

EXECUTIVE: What circumstances are you talking about?

CONSULTANT: I am talking about OSHA and EPA. Your plants will undoubtedly have to add new emission controls. Your investment will go up, not down, thanks to Uncle Sam.

EXECUTIVE: Stop being so negative. Where's the silver lining in the dark sky you just painted?

CONSULTANT: There are obvious ways to boost investment per dollar of value added. For example, you might survey your customers to identify ways to increase your product differ-entiation. Vendors who deliver high-quality products and services have the option of raising their prices and thereby increasing their value added.

EXECUTIVE: That will take time.

CONSULTANT: If you need a quicker response, why not search for ways to reduce your investment in working capital?

This dialog closed on an issue critical to this business's success. The consultant's job was over. His client took on the task of communicating to his functional managers what now had to be done. Together they orchestrated a multifunctional, integrated response to a problem that they all shared. Their individual responses were simplified because they operated from a *shared strategic context*.

Flawed Strategic Decisions that Create Functional Havoc

Part 2 highlights the linkage between business strategy and functional tactics. Here it is sufficient to call attention to the fact that many functional feuds have a strategic root. Think, for example, of general managers who cause unnecessary confusion when they cloak their strategic decisions in slogans and clichés:

We ought to invest more in our core businesses.

We must play to our strengths.

From now on we will strive to be the low-cost producer in our niche.

Perhaps the editors of *Business Week, Fortune,* and *Forbes* can tolerate this type of loose language. But if multifunctional action programs are to support strategy implementation, general managers must express their strategic decisions in more precise terms.

Functional feuds may also be spawned by heroic assumptions underlying business strategies. Take the following example.

Tension had erupted on the border between sales and manu-facturing. Manufacturing had just moved into a new, highly automated facility and therefore was hungry for high-volume orders. Unfortunately, people in the district sales offices were unable to generate the kind of order mix that the designers of this modernized facility had in mind. Instead, the sales force sent in a stream of orders for "specials" and for low-margin products. Small wonder that the manager–manufacturing was displeased and turned a deaf ear to their pleas to shorten the production cycle.

The sparring between these two functions was a symptom of a deeper problem: Their CEO had made a flawed strategic decision. He had shifted from a job shop to an automated factory just before his market began a sharp decline.

Grooves in the Mind

Each of us has a mind-set that influences how we perceive events. Historians have searched diligently to discover the "grooves in the mind" that shaped the strategies of famous military commanders. For example:

- Admirals who stubbornly rejected their subordinates' suggestions to invest in new weapon systems (e.g., the airplane) or safeguard messages transmitted over the airways (by employing a cipher).
- Generals who rested their plans on the horse cavalry while their future opponents were investing in armored divisions.
- Admirals and generals who refused to permit forces under their command to form combat teams that would operate under a unified command.

The above are familiar examples of the folly of resting plans for the future on past experience and traditional tactics.

Business historians would have no trouble citing equivalent examples of grooves in the mind that have led managers to adopt unsound business strategies. For example, Henry Ford, Sr., belatedly reacted to the emergence of a used-car market and customers' interest in car styling. Likewise, his successors were slow to recognize their customers' concerns about product quality and fuel economy. Why? Grooves in the mind. By the time these grooves were challenged and eventually erased, Japanese competitors had captured a major slice of the U.S. automotive market.

We grant that no one is totally free from the conventional wisdom of the day. But there are ways to illuminate those grooves in the mind that inhibit interfunctional team play. This topic is so important that Chapter 4 covers it exclusively.

HOW HIGH ARE THE BARRIERS TO TEAM PLAY IN YOUR BUSINESS?

Businesses do not maintain barometers to record the quality of their interfunctional team play. But you can construct your own barometer. Attend a meeting of professionals from the various functions. Sit back and listen carefully to the content and tone of the information exchanged.

Here is a checklist that will help you uncover clues about the extent of interfunctional team play during a meeting on product/ service innovation:

1. Do the attendees view their work as a set of stand-alone tasks? ("We will now hear a report from marketing. Reports from other functions have been scheduled for this afternoon.")
2. Is the work proceeding as though product innovation were a relay race, that is, one function moves before another begins? Are tasks performed in series rather than in parallel?
3. Do representatives from one function refrain from commenting on work underway in another function?[10]
4. Do you ever hear questions that begin: How do *we* solve the following problem . . . ?

When you leave the meeting, continue your search for information on the quality of collaboration among functions. For example, ask:

- Are written memos the favored method of communicating among functions?

- Does information take the great circle route from one function to another? (When specialist A wants to give specialist B a piece of information, he sends it upward to his own manager, who then sends it to specialist B's manager, who then shares it with specialist B.)
- Does anyone monitor the speed of transmission of interfunctional messages? ("It takes as long as it takes!")
- Do quality problems ignite a search for the "guilty" party?
- Are finger pointing and raucous debates common occurrences?
- Do professionals appear more interested in avoiding criticism than in accelerating the race to the marketplace?
- Do the potential "downstream" effects of technical decisions generate little interest?
- Does the marketing representative complain that "our new products always arrive on the market *after* the competition's products"?

If you listen on this frequency, you will get a good fix on the quality of interfunctional team play within your product development area.

SUMMARY

The obstacles to interfunctional team play are numerous, formidable, and deeply ingrained in our corporate culture. They are rooted in our love affair with specialization and our propensity to try to solve all problems by making quick changes in our organizational structures. The emergence of the "new breed" of manager has cast a long shadow and complicated the efforts of individual professionals to build intellectual bridges over functional boundary lines. Finally, there is the ever present tension between personal goals and business goals.

Most assuredly, professionals cannot call a halt to changes from the outside. As the saying goes, "These things go with the territory." Fortunately, however, professionals do have many opportunities to reach out to their colleagues in other functional areas. In the next three chapters, we will suggest a number of tools they can use to seize these opportunities.

The important thing to remember is that *someone must take the first step*. Nothing will be gained by merely grousing about the obstacles to team play. It is futile to wait for the "higher-ups" to remove these barriers or for the "system" to reform itself. Each professional is a component of the "system." Drucker's classic challenge to professionals remains as fresh as the day he penned it:

> The knowledge worker does not produce something that is effective by itself. . . . He produces knowledge, ideas, information. By themselves, these "products" are useless. Somebody else, another man of knowledge, has to take them as his input and convert them into his output before they become any reality.[11]

*   *   *   *   *

> The knowledge worker must be focused on the results and performance of the entire organization to have any results and performance at all. . . . He must . . . direct his vision from his work to results, and from his specialty to the outside in which alone performance lies.[12]

Regardless of the obstacles, it is time to lay siege to the Chinese-type walls that have sprouted up around our disciplines. This is *not* a task we can assign to a new breed of specialist. To effect any improvements in adversarial relationships, the specialists already in place must see the need to call time out and admit that their behavior *has* been counterproductive, childlike, and perhaps even a little irresponsible.

NOTES

1. Robert B. Reich, *Tales of a New America* (New York: Times Books, 1987), p. 246.
2. Frank Sheed, *The Church and I* (New York: Doubleday & Co., 1976).
3. The level of effort dedicated to testing the linkage between business and personal objectives has plummeted in recent years.

4. James Gleick, *Chaos: Making a New Science* (New York: Viking Penguin, 1987), p. 131.
5. Technical jargon merely amplifies the communication problem. We will examine other obstacles to information interchange in Chapter 4.
6. Peter F. Drucker, *Management: Tasks, Practices, Responsibilities* (New York: Harper & Row, 1973), pp. 560ff.
7. Ibid., p. 560.
8. Philip Shenon, "Weinberger Says Bribery Inquiry May Show Reforms Are Necessary," *New York Times,* June 20, 1988, sec. D, pp. D1, D4.
9. John J. Curran, "Companies That Rob the Future," *Fortune,* July 4, 1988, pp. 84–89.
10. Jacques Barzun, *Science: The Glorious Entertainment* (New York: Harper & Row, 1964), pp. 26–27.
11. Peter F. Drucker, *The Effective Executive* (New York: Harper & Row, 1966), p. 4.
12. Ibid., p. 30.

CHAPTER 2

FUSING THE TALENT ON A MULTIFUNCTIONAL TEAM[1]

QUESTION: What's the difference between a "committee" and a "team?"

ANSWER: A *committee* is made up of professionals, each of whom has a personal agenda and strives to advance it. A *team* consists of professionals who operate from a shared agenda and a common view of their assignment.

The occupant of the corner office faces many challenges. But none are more awesome than ill-defined business problems—those whose root systems seem to branch into every corner of the organization. Who is supposed to solve them?

There is no easy answer to this question. General managers are reluctant to tackle these problems on their own. The reasons are obvious: lack of time, inadequate knowledge, insufficient data, and lack of expertise in dealing with poorly defined problems.

It is equally obvious that this type of problem cannot be assigned to a single function for resolution. Professionals at the functional level lack breadth of experience. They are, in essence, specialists—very good at their specialties but inept at solving poorly defined problems. Further, other functions would look askance at their recommendations. True, there are creative individuals in the R&D function who have proven their ability to push back the frontiers of knowledge, but few of them are also knowledgeable about business problems.

In desperation, many general managers turn their business problems over to a committee or task force. They choose a few professionals from each function, divert them from their regular duties, and tell them to come up with an answer.

To an outsider, the logic behind committees appears impeccable. Clearly several heads are better than one. A broad perspective is better than tunnel vision. Those selected have high IQs. Their assignment offers them a chance to grow and to prove they are ready to manage an entire business.

No one keeps statistics on the performance of ad hoc committees. No doubt some turn in creditable performances. Others labor long and hard but produce only an analysis of the problem, *not* a solution. Still others have been known to:

- Solve the wrong problem.
- Analyze pieces of the assigned problem but leave it to others to integrate their recommendations.
- Offer a compromise or cosmetic solution that leaves the real problem untouched.
- Present an outline detailing what the various functions might do to resolve the problem.

When the committee's analysis fails to result in action, the members return to their regular assignments, consoling themselves that "we tried our best." They are happy to be home again, working on well-defined problems clearly suited to their expertise.

No wonder managers ask themselves why no one has found a way to convert a committee of highly regarded professionals into a cohesive, problem-solving team!

When George Baker became general manager of a privately held company, he realized that his market and industry would not mark time while he mastered the ins and outs of his new job. But in retrospect, he underestimated the number of change-induced business problems that would pile up in his in-box. Despite his decades of business experience, he was unable to specify how to attack these problems or visualize solutions.

The manager–finance sympathized. He advanced the conventional response to an ill-defined business problem: Appoint a committee and staff it with the "smartest people in this business." Surely five or six savvy professionals from the various functions could find a solution in a reasonable period of time.

Baker, however, had his doubts. In the course of his career, he had served on many committees and task forces. But he could not think of a single instance in which he and his fellow committee members converted a problem into a solution. They may have worked hard, surfaced new ideas, and organized data in an original way. But in each instance, the committee's report went to the central file to gather dust. Very little happened. The business continued on its normal trajectory. Meanwhile the problem continued to fester.

Discouraged, Baker sat down and had a heart-to-heart talk with each of the other functional managers. When he reviewed his notes from these meetings, he got very discouraged:

Marketing Manager: Competition is always beating us! I spend most of my day apologizing to our customers for the boners perpetrated by those screwballs in manufacturing or engineering!

Engineering Manager: Marketing is always calling for new products! We never seem to satisfy them. When we do put a new product in the field, product service is slow to alert us to quality problems. If they *do* pass on information, it's invariably wrong. As for those guys in manufacturing, they seldom do anything right!

Manufacturing Manager: At least 90 percent of the quality problems that surface on the factory floor are due to flawed product designs. Honestly, you wouldn't believe some of the specifications issued by engineering!

Product Service Manager: We get lots and lots of complaints from customers about product quality. We pass them up the line, but nothing happens. It is so discouraging. This business is terribly slow to react to signals from the marketplace. If a world-class competitor chose to enter this market, he would eat our lunch!

At this point, Baker tossed aside his notes, gulped down two aspirin, and drove off for lunch with an old friend. His friend listened patiently while Baker discoursed at length about his new job, the lack of consensus among his functional managers, and the "messy" problems that would be waiting in his in-box when he got back from lunch.

Eventually his friend managed to get in a word: "It seems to me that you need a team, *not* a committee. Professionals need direction. They are not good at organizing a multifunctional attack on an ill-defined business problem. Why should they be? Why not engage an outsider to work alongside your professionals, someone who can help fuse the talent that you bring to bear on the problem? That's what we do—and it works for us."

This was the first positive thing Baker had heard in days. So he spent the rest of that very long and very informative lunch listening to his friend explain all the steps he used to convert a committee into a multifunctional team.

CONVERTING A COMMITTEE INTO A TEAM

A sketch of the above business luncheon has survived. It is labeled "Memo for Record" and bears the title "How to Convert a Committee into a Team." This memo will never win a prize for English literature, but it does capture the main points made during lunch:

1. What type of problem merits a group effort?
Answer: Whenever your business faces an ill-defined problem that

- Affects every functional area and cannot be solved by tinkering with current operating procedures.
- Is symptomatic of a *new* business environment that baffles everyone.
- Has existed for years and been analyzed by lots of smart individuals but continues to recur.
- Divides the entire management team, with each manager lobbying hard for his or her path to an answer and refusing to listen to any alternative approach.

Analytical skills are in short supply within a business and must not be frittered away on trivial problems or on problems that fall in the domain of a single function. There must be a compelling reason for a general manager to commandeer resources under the control of functional managers and direct them to attack a business-level problem.

Ideally there should be a consensus among senior managers that their business faces a problem or issue that is critical to *all* functions and so important that a diversion of functional talent is justified. They must also be persuaded that this particular problem/issue must be assigned to *internal* talent. They must understand that the problem/issue may require a thorough overhaul of practices and procedures that have sustained the business for decades.

2. Which professionals should be picked to work on ill-defined business problems?

Answer: Select those professionals who

- See themselves as *responsible,* at least in part, for finding a solution to the problem.
- Believe their *expertise is relevant* to solving the problem.
- Will *personally benefit* if they solve the problem (e.g., their own jobs will be easier to perform; their own efficiency will increase).
- Know how to *find and "liberate"* data or technical advice that bears on the problem.
- Can be trusted to approach the problem from a *business perspective* rather than a narrow functional standpoint.
- See themselves as *playing a key role when the time comes to move from analysis into action/implementation.*

Pass over those individuals who

- Are acutely conscious of their rank and unwilling to admit that anyone with less than 30 years in the business can register a challenge to the status quo.
- Are likely to echo the political positions and biases of their bosses.
- Lack the patience to tackle complex business problems.

Team selection is a critical step. Too often managers tap individuals to serve on a committee because the latter happen to be idle, underutilized, or awaiting a transfer to another business. Availability is one thing; selection is another.

Obviously the size of the talent pool that a general manager can tap is limited. The very best people have been identified and therefore already have a great deal on their plates. Thus, it comes down to a question of priorities and the cost of allowing the ill-defined problem to fester.

3. How many professionals should be on the team?
Answer: No set number. The size and mix of talent depends on the nature and complexity of the problem to be addressed. This will change as the focus shifts from problem definition to problem analysis and finally to implementation.

Start with a small "core" group of people, perhaps four to eight. Farm out all "well-defined" tasks (e.g., data collection, stand-alone technical analyses). *After* locking on to a solution, augment the group with professionals whose work will directly relate to implementation.

The main point is to select professionals who will see their special assignment as being closely connected with their *regular* jobs. If this perception erodes, the work will not move forward and boredom will set in. This will signal that it is time to review your initial selection.

4. Why include an "outsider?"
Answer: General managers often select an outsider to work alongside their own professionals. This individual performs various roles:

1. A catalyst.
2. A process facilitator.[2]
3. A diplomat who will defuse personal conflicts and convert differences in opinion into positive action.

The *primary* job of this professional is to:

- Concentrate on the problem-solving *process* while other members of the group focus on *work content*.
- Ensure every member of the group a chance to be heard.
- Assume the role of devil's advocate by challenging those who offer cosmetic solutions or whose perspective is warped by the conventional wisdom.
- Offer colleagues a structure—a context or way of thinking about their assignment—that will help each

appreciate where his or her contribution is needed and how it relates to contributions from others in the group. (We expand on the value of a structure in Appendix A.)

The above abbreviated job description challenges the current belief that professionals are self-sufficient. The fact is, few professionals are trained to perform as members of a problem-solving group. Why is it so hard to challenge the self-sufficiency of professionals working in a business environment, yet so easy to acknowledge the value of having a coach on the sidelines of a basketball court, a conductor to lead 100 highly skilled musicians, or a director to oversee performers with years of experience on the stage? But many managers have observed the penalties of *not* adding an outsider to a group of professionals assigned to work on a complex business problem. They have seen groups that "spun their wheels"; ignored attractive though unconventional approaches to their problem; argued over details or wasted time on a topic peripheral to their assignment; and tuned out suggestions from shop people or from younger members of the group.

5. What restrictions should be put on the outsider?

Answer: General managers do *not* want their outsiders to

- Dictate how members of the group should approach *their* assignment.
- Intervene if other members of the group are making progress.
- Comment on the professionalism of any member of the group.
- Act as an informal information channel (i.e., spy) for the senior managers of the business.

6. What skills should the outsider possess?

Answer: An effective problem-solving group requires two distinct types of experts. Look *inside* for people with expertise in the product, processes, systems, and shop practices. Look *outside* for individuals with expertise in group dynamics and group effectiveness. The ideal outsider will:

1. Be a fast learner—someone who can *quickly* learn to converse with the internal experts *using their terminology*.
2. Project an attitude of neutrality with respect to local politics. Members of the group must see the outsider as someone who is *not* "running for office," who devotes full attention to the needs of *the business as a whole*, and is self-confident enough to let all the credit for the work done go to the internal experts.
3. Be a good teacher/catalyst.

These are challenging specifications indeed. Since managers have made no effort to attract and hold professionals of the type described above, they have little choice but to recruit such talent from outside their own businesses.

One caveat: The required talent can *not* be developed in a two-week seminar on process facilitation. The professional we have labeled the "outsider" indeed facilitates the problem-solving process but has other duties, as noted above.

7. Who should sponsor a group of business problem solvers? Answer: A sponsor must have the following:

- Control over the resources needed to launch and sustain a group effort.
- A budget sufficient to cover the cost of the outsider's services.
- An awareness of the seriousness of the problem.
- A personal stake in seeing that the problem is solved as soon as possible.
- The "political clout" to ensure that action is taken when the group has a fix on the real problem and has found a solution.

Clearly a unit manager or subfunctional manager does *not* meet these criteria.

The advantages of having as a sponsor someone at or close to the top echelon of the business are obvious. This sends a signal to the problem solvers, their bosses, and all sources of information. It tells them that the problem is important, that a solution is urgently needed, and that everyone in the business is expected to support the group's efforts to find and implement a solution.

When functional managers get such a signal, they will think twice before denying the group access to data or a pool of expertise. They also will be reluctant to encourage a parallel or competing investigation.

8. What are group sponsor's tasks?
Answer: The group sponsor

1. Appoints the professionals to the group.
2. Contracts for the outsider's services.
3. Designates a team captain to preside over group meetings.
4. Charges the group to find an innovative solution even if it means challenging the conventional wisdom (or the sponsor's earlier pronouncements).
5. Follows the group's progress.
6. Buffers the group from political pressures or crises that otherwise might absorb its energies.
7. Supports implementation of the group's recommendations.

Also note what a sponsor must refrain from doing: He or she *must not tell the group how to solve the assigned problem.* Instead, the sponsor must be content to share his or her own perception of the problem and personal feeling of urgency. When the going gets rough—and it often does—the sponsor encourages the professionals to keep at their task. If they discover that the assigned problem needs to be redefined, the sponsor must listen to their reasons for doing so.

We realize that such restraint is atypical of the "new breed" of manager. But then again, the new breed of manager does *not* invest in solutions to ill-defined problems. Instead, he or she prefers to run away from them or find a way to bury them.

9. How can group effectiveness be enhanced?
Answer: The following well-known (but often ignored) administrative practices make for group effectiveness:

- Limit the duration of group sessions—three to four hours at most.

- Do not let a session end without specifying the action items that have surfaced.
- Let no more than two weeks elapse between work sessions.
- Insist on regular attendance at group sessions. Death or hospitalization should be the *only* legitimate excuses for missing a work session. Group members who claim they are "too busy" to attend are signaling their lack of interest in the assigned problem. Find others to take their places.
- Allow no phone calls or other interruptions during a work session.

The team-building process described above has been tested in many businesses. It is the way to convert a committee into a team capable of solving an ill-defined business problem. Chapter 3 describes how other managers have followed this method and elicited a true team performance from a multifunctional group.

NOTES

1. This chapter reflects the work, experiments, and experiences of William D. Vinson. Vinson began developing this method in the late 1950s and continued to do so during a long and distinguished career in GE's corporate consulting services. Since retiring from GE, he has continued to refine this method with the help of a new set of clients.
2. See Edgar H. Schein, *Process Consultation: Lessons for Managers and Consultants,* vol. II (Reading, Mass.: Addison-Wesley, OD Series, 1987).

CHAPTER 3

EFFECTIVE MULTIFUNCTIONAL TEAMS[1]

There is no "i" in the word "team."

—Bobby Knight (while serving as coach
of the U.S. Olympic basketball team)

The purpose of this chapter is to analyze the performances of seven multifunctional teams and distill the factors that have made them successful.

The first four teams were established to make new-product development more effective. The fifth team was formed to discover how an existing product might be altered to satisfy a key customer's standard of quality. The last two teams focused on existing production processes. Their goal was to improve yield and discover how to adhere to quality specifications consistently.

Each of these seven teams made a distinct contribution to business performance. They visibly affected customer satisfaction, profitability, and shop practices. This chapter gives a partial report on their activities. It focuses on the reasons behind their success rather than on the details of their contributions. We firmly believe that managers of service businesses and non-profit institutions, as well as those in manufacturing, can capitalize on the concepts and principles presented here.

NEW-PRODUCT TEAMS

It is both inefficient and ineffective to allow specialists involved in new-product development to make their contributions in a *serial* fashion.[2] This unduly extends the innovation cycle and needlessly generates friction among the functions.

One alternative is to add an organizational overlay, that is, create a multifunctional team and give it the authority to orchestrate the discrete contributions of functional specialists. Many managers have been pleased with this unconventional approach to new-product development when the teams they formed followed the methodology described in Chapter 2.

Following are excerpts from the files of the four new-product multifunctional teams. Their sponsors gave them the following assignments:[3]

Team	Assignment
1	Orchestrate the many contributions from our new-product specialists working on this innovative lamp system. Make certain there are no surprises.
2	Here is a sketch of a new circular fluorescent lamp designed for open sockets. See if there is both a market for this lamp and a chance for this business to make a profit with it.
3	Determine whether this product line extension will make a good addition to our product line.
4	See whether this new headlamp will boost our sales to original-equipment manufacturers.

Writing a Score for a Team of New-Product Specialists

The first new-product team served for over a year. Their job was to help scores of specialists—such as those in marketing, engineering, manufacturing, sales, finance, and human resources—function as one team.

Earlier, researchers in GE's Lighting Business Group had proven that it was technically feasible to make a fluorescent lamp system that contained its own ballast and fixture.[4] They labeled their innovation "Bright Stik."

Management agreed that Bright Stik might be a useful addition to the group's product line—but could they produce it at a profit? The challenges were formidable and multifunctional. This was GE's first lamp *system,* and it called for materials and manufacturing steps that were new to the group. Clearly there were many opportunities to stumble along the journey from laboratory to market.

These considerations prompted management to appoint a multifunctional team to oversee Bright Stik's progress. This team included professionals from marketing, engineering, manufacturing, and quality control (but *not* sales or finance). Since the schedule for this innovation was tight, the team sponsor added an outsider from the corporate consulting staff.

The first topic on the team's agenda was customer wants. Bright Stik did not resemble conventional fluorescent lamps. It had so many novel features that the professionals on the team could hardly presume that everyone knew who would buy this system or how they would appraise product quality.

> *The team did* not *delegate this task to the marketing function or make it a solo assignment for the marketing representative on the team. Rather, all members of the team jointly compiled a list of customer wants. They needed to reach a consensus on this first— and perhaps most vital— step on the road to the marketplace.*

The team's second challenge flowed from the first: Make an *integrated* response to each customer want.

> *The conventional ways to obtain such a response are:*
>
> - *Exhort all the professionals involved in new-product development to "make it right the first time."*
> - *Insist that specialists work together: "Call specialists in marketing, engineering and manufacturing out of their cubicles. Make them sit down and talk to one another. No more friction—just do it! From now on, act like members of one and the same team!"*[5]

Sounds great. Unfortunately, however, exhortation is rarely effective.

The Bright Stik team took a different approach. They set out to establish an *explicit* link among

- Various customer criteria for a "quality product."
- Various elements of engineering's proposed design logic.

- Various steps in the new manufacturing process which delivers a new product that satisfies both the customers *and* the product engineers.

If the group managed to forge and sustain these links, they would have a lamp with the desired end-product characteristics. But if there was even one weak link, Bright Stik would *not* meet its targets.

The team-building device that this team used to plot these linkages is called a *quality map*. It is so named because it directs engineering's product design decisions and manufacturing's workstations and procedures to the customers' determinants of product quality.

> *Note how the team departed from conventional wisdom on product quality. Instead of orienting product designers toward standards on product/process specifications issued by a group of engineers and manufacturing engineers, this team chose to relate the work of specialists in each function back to customer wants. Each specialist was helped (not exhorted) to be market driven.*

We cannot show a complete quality map for Bright Stik without disclosing proprietary information and possibly confusing the reader with many technical terms. However, the excerpt from the quality map shown in Exhibit 3–1 adequately depicts its function. The exhibit takes one customer criterion of product quality—area lighting—and shows how it impinges on both product design and manufacturing work.

Appendix A at the end of this book explains in detail how a quality map stimulates interfunctional teamwork. Here a brief summary will suffice. A quality map

1. Enables specialists in the primary functions to grasp the connection between their own work and two important business goals: customer satisfaction and business profitability.
2. Dramatizes the impact of technical decisions on the *effectiveness* and *efficiency* of work by professionals in other functions.
3. Helps many solo performers function as one.

EXHIBIT 3–1
One Strand in the Quality Map Developed by the Bright Stik Team

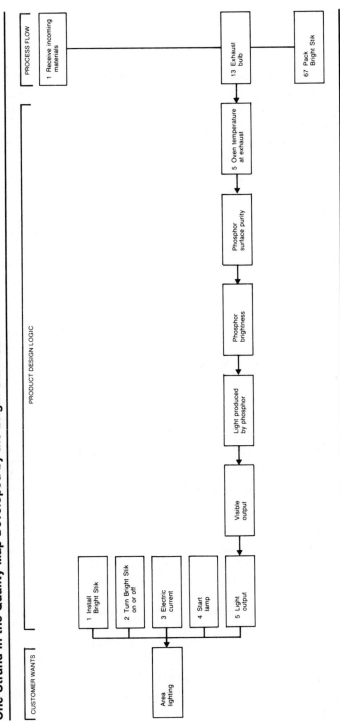

Source: Adapted from William D. Vinson and Donald F. Heany, "Is Quality in Control?", *Harvard Business Review* 55, no. 6 (November-December 1977), p. 117.

Bright Stik has earned itself a solid position in the product line of GE's Lighting Business Group and made a significant contribution to the group's profits—all in the face of formidable technological challenges.

One final excerpt from the Bright Stik file: The members of this team were not aware that many in the district sales offices were unenthusiastic about this lamp system. Sales people pined for a traditional high-volume, low-cost lamp that could be produced in large quantities on automated assembly lines. Instead, the Bright Stik team had produced a technological marvel that

- Carried a price 10 times higher than that for traditional lamps.
- Was made in modest quantities on a production line that necessitated much hand assembly.
- Had many characteristics of a nonexpendable item. (Customers who were disappointed with their Bright Stiks did not throw them in the trash—they returned them! Since the district sales offices were not geared to handling returns, this was a major headache.)

Unfortunately, the anger and resentment of GE's sales force toward Bright Stik came to light in the form of only tepid support after the product came on the market. The cost incurred for such lackluster support does not appear in any financial record.

This is still another illustration of "grooves in the mind" and how they heighten the tension among professionals in different functions. No one bothers to itemize such grooves in the mind.[6] They are never discussed in staff meetings. Nonetheless, they are real and formidable barriers to team play.

The Bright Stik example illustrates three key concepts:

1. The importance of furnishing specialists with a business context that will show them where and how they can support the organization's goals.
2. The value of an organizational overlay that eliminates serial contributions from the individual functions yet does not threaten them.

3. The payoff from inviting specialists in one function to comment openly and freely on the work of professionals in other functions.

Detecting Thin Markets, Early

The second new-product team met only a few times but nevertheless made a significant contribution to business profitability by *recommending that the innovation they were to follow to market be scratched!* What initially had been viewed as a large market was in reality a thin one.

A product designer had unveiled a sketch of a new fluorescent lamp that was quite unusual: It was circular rather than straight. It was designed to fit into an open socket rather than a fixture with an attached ballast. Marketing specialists were asked to estimate how many homes and apartments in North America might find a use for the new lamp system. The answer came back: well over one million.

> *There is nothing wrong with back-of-the-envelope answers to questions about market size, but* they should be labeled as such *lest the user of the information make investments that are out of line with the innovation's market appeal.*

The general manager of this business became interested. He established a new-product team to oversee the commercialization of this product innovation.

After the team had reached a consensus on the standards of product quality relevant for the targeted customers, they turned their attention to product design questions. The engineering representative, who had been itching to flesh out the preliminary product design, posed the first question: What is the ambient temperature and moisture level of the sockets that will hold the new lamp?

Marketing's representative did not have this kind of information at his fingertips, but he promised to obtain it within a few days. He kept his promise, but some of the information he brought back was most upsetting: Many of the targeted open sockets were located in *tenement buildings!*

The team realized immediately that owners and occupants of tenements were unlikely to purchase a state-of-the-art lamp like the one they had been asked to work on. Therefore, they went back to their sponsor and recommended that design work on the innovation be halted at once or at least refocused on the lighting requirements of a more affluent class of customer.

> *The sponsor was greatly relieved that his team had spotted a gap in marketing intelligence early in the product development cycle. He knew that his product designers easily could have made an incorrect assumption about the environment of the new lamp. In the past, erroneous assessments such as this one had unduly lengthened the product development cycle and contributed to cost overruns.*

This brief extract from the file of a new-product team dramatizes the communication problems that can arise when information is exchanged among functions. First, an engineer conceives a new product. Then marketing is asked to make a quick and admittedly rough estimate of market size. After giving a ball-park estimate of market size, *marketing moves to the sidelines.* Months later, marketing returns because it must develop a sales plan. Only then, after so much work and effort, do the product designers hear the numbing phrases:

The market for the product is too thin.

The customer would never buy the product.

The product is overpriced.

A few iterations of this type will crush the spirits of even the most intrepid product designer.

Multifunctional teams therefore offer a safe way to change this sequential thought process and deliver an *early* critique of engineering's preliminary design work *from a multifunctional perspective.*

Trade-offs between Customer Satisfaction and Lower Manufacturing Costs

Innovations that entail only a minor change in the design logic of existing products and are sold to the same market are labeled *product line extensions.*[7] We look at one here because it rated a multifunctional critique that spotted evidence of technical bias.

A manufacturer of steam irons had challenged a product designer to search for ways to lower the labor content of one of its more popular irons. The designer satisfied this goal by eliminating the depressions that had surrounded the steam vents (holes) in the bottoms of earlier models.

A new-product team met to study this designer's work.[8] They found against him. The team rested its verdict on the likely response of shoppers: They would pick up the iron, turn it over to see if it was a steam iron, note that the holes in this model *looked* smaller, and reach the understandable but erroneous conclusion that this iron would generate *less* steam than older models!

The team knew that this model would produce the same amount of steam as older models. Their point was that the average customer would not realize this. Since purchasers of houseware products spend only a minute or two examining the models that retailers display, their first impressions are to be reckoned with, even if they are not in accord with the laws of physics!

The sponsor accepted the team's recommendation: Instruct the designer to alter his original design and restore the traditional depressions.

There are two key points in this illustration that are relevant to all types of businesses:

1. Product innovations are purchased by individuals who base their shopping decisions on *limited* information. Their perceptions are all-important. In the short run, innovators must accept these perceptions as givens.
2. The effect of a "cost reduction" *today* often registers with the customer as a decay in product quality *tomorrow*.

The Error of Getting Ahead of the Customer

Our final illustration concerns functional bias. Many engineers have been programmed from their student days to compete against other engineers, to aspire to produce the most innovative design, and to tackle problems that historically baffled other engineers. The rationale behind such programming is obvious, but at times it leads to imprudent decisions. Some customers are lukewarm toward new products that advance the state of the art.

A firm that sells headlamps to automotive manufacturers was made aware of this bias when one of its young engineers stepped forward with a preliminary sketch of a new headlamp. He was quite proud of the fact that his lamp placed a pattern of light on the road that exceeded government standards both in the United States and abroad. Surely safety-conscious drivers would insist that their cars feature this state-of-the-art headlamp.

A new-product team was established to critique the design. The team members were soon convinced that the new headlamp would *not* generate much enthusiasm in Detroit. They reminded the young engineer that to purchasing agents in the auto centers of the world the "hot" buttons were cost, size, and weight. These professionals were *not* inclined to invest in headlamps that exceeded the government's standards for illumination; they were quite happy with headlamps that met the current standards. This terse pronouncement elevated the product review from the *functional* level to the *business* level.

The team claimed that to arouse Detroit's interest in the new headlamp, their firm would first have to presell the creators of the product specifications on which purchasing decisions rest (i.e., automotive designers). In an industry with a complex process technology and a custom of changing models infrequently, the time lag between preselling auto designers and changes in the standards purchasing agents use when selecting vendors is a matter not of weeks or months but of years.

In the end, business considerations took precedence over the engineer's understandable interest in designing a state-of-the-art headlamp. The team convinced their sponsor to halt further developmental work.[9]

Everyone is calling for an acceleration in the pace of product innovation. As an abstract concept, this is definitely a commendable goal. But managers and product designers must never lose sight of the important distinction between *immediate customer* and *end user*. This is an elementary but often overlooked distinction. If ignored, it can sabotage the profit goals that inspire new-product teams. Before dreaming about the profit potential of the "aftermarket," product designers must deal with purchasing agents who are loathe to score vendors on their creativity.

It is a simple matter to determine whether your own product designers honor the distinction between immediate customers and end users. Merely call for

- A roster of your immediate customers.
- The quality standards these customers use.
- The weights they apply to each criterion of product quality.

Contrast the answers you get. You will be surprised at the lack of consensus. (The standards of quality are not static.)

The preceding four illustrations pertain to product innovation work that yields a new product or product line extension. The following example comes from the files of a multifunctional team that was established to critique an *existing* product. The members of this team were innovative and creative, but in a different dimension: Their goal was to salvage a valued account by improving *perceived* product quality.

A key customer of a prominent manufacturer of fractional-horsepower motors was threatening to run into a competitor's arms. The reason: "Your last shipment included motors that were too noisy." This threat evoked a predictable response: "Impossible! Why, that customer has been using our motors for years, and never once has he complained about motor noise."

The general manager of the business did not echo these sentiments. He had ordered a series of tests of this particular motor, which convinced him that his customer had a legitimate complaint. Therefore, he directed his product designers to find ways to dampen the level of motor noise.

Note that this manager's first response was to seek a solution using conventional *methods and the* existing *organizational structure.*

The designers responded with a number of design changes for the motor. But while they did reduce the noise level somewhat, they did not placate the customer. The customer remained unhappy and reiterated his threat to switch to another vendor.

The general manager realized that all volume purchasers of fractional-horsepower motors are linked by an informal network. If he lost one large account, the chances were that others would become nervous. He also knew that a competitor had just introduced a new, "super-quiet" motor. If this new product was promoted aggressively, his own shop load would shrink dramatically. Clearly it was time to sound "general quarters."

This general manager did not *stand by while his competitor exploited a perceived quality advantage. Nor did he tolerate the time delays inherent in the conventional product overhaul cycle. By his definition, any solution that took a year to reach his desk was no solution at all.*

Therefore, the general manager organized a multifunctional team and ordered it to neutralize the threat to his competitive position. The team consisted of

1. A marketing specialist to ensure that everyone understood the basis of the customer's complaint and how he utilized motors in his own line of products.
2. A product designer to translate the team's insights as to the roots of motor noise into design changes.
3. A process engineer to help the team uncover any links between motor noise and steps in the business's manufacturing and assembly processes.
4. A quality control specialist to incorporate the team's recommendations into the business's quality control system.

The manager urged these professionals to examine every conceivable way to eliminate or muffle motor noise. He also urged them to specify how their business might get ahead of—rather than merely catch up to—the most aggressive innovators in the market.

Since time was essential, the general manager also engaged a consultant from the firm's corporate engineering staff to work with the team. This consultant had worked with many other multifunctional teams and was reputed to be a superb catalyst. Although he lacked expertise with respect to electric motors, this was not viewed as a drawback. After all, the other team members had a combined total of 80 years of experience in the motor business.

The Team's Line of Analysis.   The team began by searching through the business's voluminous files for some clues to the determinants of motor noise. They came up empty-handed. Marketing's records contained no hint as to what this customer regarded as a "permissible" level of motor noise. Engineering's documentation did not distinguish among the various types of motor noise (mechanical? electrical? wow-wow?) or specify the best way to eliminate or abate it.

Manufacturing's files were the most voluminous of all. There were thousands of blueprints, assembly drawings, and parts lists. Each document had an *inward* focus (i.e., within that one function). Their authors were interested in only two things: listing the parts, components, and materials needed to build a motor; and explaining how to assemble these parts and components. They offered no information on the one topic of interest to this team: *What causes a motor to be noisy?*

The team members were stunned by this gap in their business's documentation. Their job was to close it PDQ.

When the consultant from corporate headquarters saw the team's morale plummeting, he suggested that they set down on paper all the steps that engineering had to take to design a motor that would meet this new criterion of product quality—a much quieter motor. Then they could link the end points in engineering's design logic to the steps in the manufacturing process. The consultant predicted that this approach would identify the determinants of motor noise.

> *One of the outsider's jobs was to prevent the team from despairing of finding a solution to the assigned problem. He proposed a novel approach to get them off dead center.*

The other team members agreed to try this approach. They pooled their own ideas about the possible causes of motor noise and recorded them in a treelike structure that was anchored to the single criterion of product quality, motor noise. After a few sessions, they began to realize that they were getting a handle on the causes of motor noise. At that point, they invited other professionals in the business to critique their progress.

Their colleagues did not disappoint them. The information the team had jointly fashioned into a crude map of the determinants of motor noise proved to be an efficient medium for an *intellectual exchange*. It helped their "critics" understand how the team had approached their assignment. It also enabled the critics to draw upon their own personal databases to suggest how to improve on the team's handiwork. The team was open to any and all suggestions. The N.I.H. factor ("not invented here"; used when experts fail to appreciate suggestions from outsiders) was conspicuous by its absence.

> *Note the difference between this oral exchange of views and the conventional mode of interfunctional communication: a* written progress report. *Had the team circulated an internal memorandum describing how far they had come, the amount and quality of the feedback they received would have been far inferior to that obtained in a face-to-face discussion. The readers of the memo had no opportunity to hear the replies of other critics, hear the team's rejoinder to each suggestion or criticism, or comment on subject matter outside* their function's turf.

The team readily incorporated their colleagues' criticisms and suggestions into a graphic model of the determinants of motor noise. Exhibit 3–2 presents a portion of this model.[10]

> *Since this book focuses on team play rather than product quality, we will not give a detailed commentary on Exhibit 3–2. The exhibit contains more information on motor design than we need be concerned with here. Therefore, focus solely on the explicit strand of thought that connects one criterion of product quality—motor noise—to the designers' logic and on to workstations in manufacturing. Exhibit 3–2 is* not *an exhortation to professionals in manufacturing ("Meet the specs! Let's have zero defects!"). Instead, it furnishes these specialists with a* business context *for their work. It shows them how and why their contributions are linked to those of the marketing and engineering functions. That is one of the major reasons why a team builds a structure: to forge a shared vision of their* joint *endeavor. Finally, note how this particular structure terminates with information pertinent to the manufacturing function.*

EXHIBIT 3–2
Portion of a Graphic Model of Some Determinants of Motor Noise

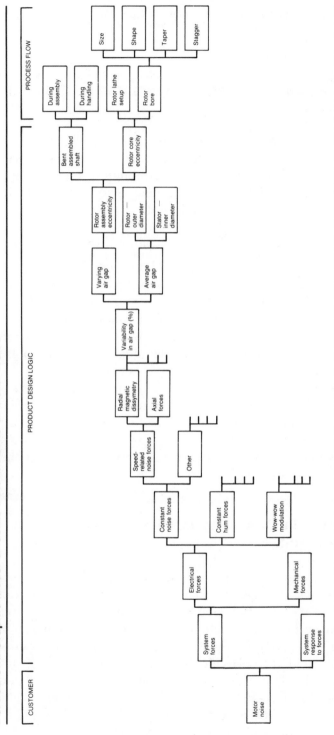

On the far right, our attention is drawn to a remote cause of motor noise—the size and variability of the air gap between the rotor and the stator.

The End Result.   Within several months, the team was able to report to the general manager that *the level of motor noise had dropped by 50 percent*. This was enough to convert an angry customer into a satisfied one. The team also influenced the design of motors still on the drawing board.

The key points of this illustration are:

1. The team sponsor should be content to pose the assigned problem *without* specifying the approach.
2. The team must set aside sufficient time to arrive at a shared perspective of their assignment. They must resist the temptation to break down a poorly structured problem into subproblems for individual specialists to grapple with on their own.
3. If the team needs to build a structure from scratch rather than using an existing structure, the team captain (or an outsider) must ensure that *all* members participate in its development.
4. The team should disband *after* it has solved the problem, not before.

PRODUCTION AND ADMINISTRATIVE PROCESSES

New products usually require new production processes and sometimes changes in distribution and service systems.[11] The close connection between *product* and *process* is obvious to every employee in a manufacturing firm. However, managers of service businesses do not always appreciate this. For example, when banks decided to provide depositors with access to their funds 24 hours a day from several remote locations, they realized that they had to do more than buy a few automatic teller machines. They also had to develop, test, and implement new information systems and make many changes in their communications systems.

The emergence of worldwide telecommunications systems,

sophisticated mathematical models of the type required for program trading, and customized software has caught the attention of executives in service industries. These professionals now appreciate the infrastructure on which their services depend. They see that their "back offices" have become vitally important to their firms' profit and productivity. They marvel at American Express's new billing system. It is not only a boon to customers, but it also slashes personnel costs and opens up the possibility of more effective marketing to small market segments. Airlines, hospitals, banks, and travel firms are scrambling to clone this system.[12]

In light of these advances, this chapter closes with two illustrations from the files of multifunctional teams that were established to scrutinize complex production processes. Both teams faced the same challenges:

- What process characteristics have the greatest impact on product quality and/or throughput?
- How can one use such information to exert tighter control over throughput and product quality?

Dealing with the Defenders of the Status Quo

Our first illustration emphasizes that multifunctional teams can find opportunities to improve process yield even when the custodians of those processes insist that yield is already at a maximum level.

The general manager of a business with a continuous production process desired to improve productivity and to reduce work-in-process inventory. He was reluctant to make either goal a topic for discussion at his next staff meeting lest he spark a debate as to which functional manager was to blame.

Instead, this manager appointed a multifunctional team and instructed the members to address both problems. The professionals on this team came from marketing, engineering, manufacturing, and quality control. An outsider was engaged to help them coalesce their impressive talents.

At their first meeting, the team members inquired about the current quality control procedures. They learned that a specialist took samples from every batch run, calculated the average particle size, and studied the distribution around that average. If the samples fell within specified limits, the specialist rated the entire batch "acceptable." If they fell below specifications, he routed the material to another location in the plant. At some later date, this material would be combined with the output from an earlier run that had been rejected because it exceeded specifications. For example, an equal part of "average" 1.0 particle size and 1.5 particle size would be combined to produce an acceptable quality level of 1.25 average particle size. Theoretically, all "out-of-spec" material could be disposed of in this fashion, and in due time work-in-process inventory would drop to zero.

People in all the functions were comfortable with this procedure. There were no demands to amend process control procedures to make every run conform to specifications.

When interest rates began to rise, however, investment in work-in-process inventory became a matter of concern. The team felt obliged to search for a way to alter their process or shop practices to meet output specifications more consistently. If they were successful, work-in-process inventories would drop automatically.

The manager in charge of this production process did not encourage their search. He had been in charge of the process for more than a decade. He was certain that he had mastered all of its secrets and wanted no "outsiders" poking around "his" area.

In an attempt to divert the team's attention to other areas of the business, the production manager played them a tune: "If It Ain't Broke, Don't Try to Fix It."

It's a waste of time for you fellows to look here for a solution to this business's high inventory. I have had many years in this business. Trust me when I tell you the solution lies *upstream.*

Sure, something must be done to improve yield. But let's face it: In this business, the key to process yield is the distribution of the crystalline compound *we begin with.* Nine times out of ten, when we are forced to reject a batch run, it is due to the low quality *of our input.*[13]

What we need is a scientific breakthrough that will provide us with *quality input.* Why don't you go back to our boss and persuade him to put some talented chemists and chemical engineers to work investigating ways to improve our input? In the meantime, give me a break. I have my hands full keeping this process running. I really can't spare my time or that of my people to field your questions.

Since the team had been instructed to look into every nook and cranny of the business, they could hardly bypass its core: the production process. They conceded that some talented researchers might find a way to improve input quality. But basic research takes time—and time was one thing they lacked. Their general manager had *not* asked them to define long-term research projects.

With patience and persistence, the team overcame the production manager's objections and got access to all of his experts as well as to the practical wisdom of the blue-collar workers who attended "his" process. Within a short time, they identified a number of shop practices that needed changing.

We need not examine the shop procedures earmarked for revision (e.g., how material entered into the furnace, the amount of material in each container, etc.) Suffice it to say, the general manager heeded the team's recommendations. Within 60 days, yield shot up and work-in-process inventory dropped 75 percent—and with no change in the quality of the input.

> *A team of professionals has the prestige and political clout to stand up to defenders of the status quo. They have been handpicked by the general manager. They occupy positions of power in the business's organizational structure. They have the general manager's ear. In short, when they speak as a team, they are likely to be heard. In contrast, it is easy for the defenders of the status quo to intimidate a lone critic.*

Two key points in the above illustration are applicable to every type of business:

1. Production systems are not self-reforming. Every business has a cadre of professionals who stoutly defend the status quo. They overwhelm casual observers who spot flaws in their standard operating procedures.
2. A multifunctional team gives managers a tool for accelerating reform of practices and work rules that have acquired an undeserved halo of respectability.

Obsolete Specifications

Managers have waged a relentless campaign to get professionals in manufacturing to conform to product and process specifications. Behind this effort is a perception that if defective products or materials are being produced, *the professionals and/or blue-collar workers in manufacturing must be doing something wrong.* This is certainly a possibility, but it is not a certainty, as our final multifunctional team discovered.

A business that produced a component used in the manufacture of personal computers found itself swamped with orders. Its production process seemed to be approaching its upper limit. Managers had two options:

- Invest in additional capacity.
- Reexamine the practices and procedures followed by the crew attending their process.

The general manager chose the second option. He assembled a team of professionals from engineering, marketing, and manufacturing and gave them the job of finding a short-term way to increase yield. He also hired an outsider to function as a catalyst for the team.

The team members went immediately to the quality control station at the end of the production line. Piled up behind that station were products that had failed to meet specifications. Attached to each was a sticker on which had been scrawled "walls too thick."

The conventional response would have been to instruct attendants of this production line to "conform to engineering's specifications." But the manufacturing representative on the team convinced his colleagues that it was futile to lecture the production crew about conformance quality. The (aging) equipment in place simply could not hold to tighter tolerances on wall thickness. Then one team member asked the pregnant question "Do we have any customers who would be willing to accept components with thicker walls than our engineers have specified?"

The marketing representative had always taken it for granted that engineering had chosen their specifications with one eye on customers' wants. He had never contemplated the possibility that the specifications underlying quality inspections at the end of the line did not mirror the needs of certain customers.

One week later, there was another team meeting. The marketing representative claimed the floor. He had two pieces of good news. First, indeed there were customers who would accept components with thicker walls than specified. Second, these customers would pay full price for the "flawed" components!

Needless to say, this report was a cause for rejoicing. It opened up an unanticipated path to higher yield: Just redefine the standards the quality control specialists were using.

How could any business have overlooked the existence of distinct segments within its served market? How could engineering have ignored variations in customer requirements? Hadn't anyone read any of the numerous published articles citing the many reasons for segmenting a market and collecting quality standards for each segment?

Yes, there is much knowledge about market segmentation. But in many industries, there is also a strong tradition that favors *forecasting total demand.* Why invest time and energy in market segmentation when your business has never remotely approached the rated capacity of its process? Why bother to incur the costs of market segmentation when your business has been meeting its budget year after year and generating an acceptable rate of return?

The engineers stoutly defended their product specifications. They pointed out that marketing had given them no information on market segments. Surely no intelligent person would urge engineering to second-guess the experts who were in daily contact with customers.

This example makes two points that are important to professionals in any type of business:

1. Product and process specifications reflect someone's perceptions about the customers' standards of quality. Like other perceptions, these deserve to be updated periodically.
2. A multifunctional team has the motive and political clout to challenge existing specifications. People in manufacturing would be charged with "making excuses" if they launched an equivalent challenge.

SUMMARY

We have looked at seven multifunctional teams, each of which was assigned a poorly structured business problem. Each team operated under the auspices of a responsible manager who was already convinced that a solution was needed. Therefore, these teams included professionals who had a stake in finding those solutions. Each team was told the nature of the problem but not how to solve it. To facilitate team play, the sponsor invested in an outsider to monitor the problem-solving process while the other team members focused on content.

The nature of the contributions these teams made varied considerably. Some unearthed "glitches" in a proposed product design. Others pointed to flaws in conventional operating procedures. Still others identified new products aimed at the wrong market or an excessively thin market.

In each case, the team members took the time to reach a consensus on the nature of the assigned problem. They recovered some of this time because they developed and shared a framework that helped each specialist bridge the chasm between business goals and functional goals.

No minority reports were filed. Each team returned to their sponsor with a real solution rather than a laundry list of suggestions as to how others might ameliorate the problem.

NOTES

1. Every line of this chapter reflects inputs obtained from William D. Vinson. Mr. Vinson is also the source of the illustrations. He deserves the accolade as GE's best process facilitator, particularly when there was a need to bring a new product to market, to solve stubborn quality problems, or to enhance the yield of existing production processes.
2. For example, the new-product teams that worked on the 1988 Lincoln Continental shipped the first cars to rental car firms. These firms identified a number of quality problems, which they diagnosed and remedied. Then the other cars held in inventory were retrofitted *before* being shipped to dealers. These 1988 models were quickly sold out. One can hardly rate this new-product team as turning in a "superior" performance (at least on the first try). See Marshall Schuon, "Ford's Luxurious Drive into the Future," *New York Times,* May 8, 1988.

3. The sponsors of these teams charged them to investigate additional topics, which we will not deal with here.
4. Normally the lamp, the ballast, and the fixture are viewed as three distinct products.
5. John R. Hauser and Don Clausing, "The House of Quality," *Harvard Business Review,* May–June 1988, pp. 63–73.
6. Chapter 4 expands on the subject of grooves in the mind.
7. Donald F. Heany, "Degrees of Product Innovation," *Journal of Business Strategy* 3, no. 4 (Spring, 1983), pp. 3–14.
8. This was *not* the team's sole assignment.
9. A few years ago, design errors of this type might have been detected by a "mentor," that is, an experienced designer who doubled as a technical leader for young engineers. Today mentors are a vanishing species.
10. The final version of this quality map contains proprietary information as well as product and process specifications. We must be content with an excerpt.
11. When cash registers were replaced by point-of-sale devices with a link to a network, the product service team had to acquire additional skills.
12. John Markoff, "American Express Does Hi-Tech," *New York Times,* July 31, 1988, Sec. 3, pp. F1, F6.
13. Professionals in most of the other functions shared this view.

CHAPTER 4

GROOVES IN THE MIND: SUBMERGED BARRIERS TO TEAM PLAY

Human beings are perhaps never more frightening than when they are convinced beyond doubt that they are right.

—Laurens Van der Post

Many a functional feud has been caused by *grooves in the mind*— a mind-set that the feuding parties acquired long ago. Each party is comfortable with his or her way of looking at the work going on in other functional areas. This definitely affects their behavior toward colleagues.

Here are a few examples:

- Our "core" businesses may not be profitable, but they are the flagships of this portfolio, and we will never walk away from them.
- Our business is different!
- That's a small project, so we can allow our most junior engineer to handle it.
- That [disaster] could never happen here!
- Such problems may plague businesses in the North, but never in the South.
- The boss would never go for that idea.

The mind-set of one functional area may have devastating effects on other functions and on the quality of interfunctional team play. For example, for many years a high level of capacity utilization was viewed as the proper—and only—way to sustain a textile mill's profitability. The watchword was: Keep the looms covered!

Senior managers gave each member of their sales force a sales quota. If these quotas were met, no one quibbled about the types of textiles sold or the terms of trade agreed to. Salespeople concentrated their efforts on the large retail chains, because these customers were able to place large orders. In return, retail customers demanded price concessions, custom patterns, and rapid delivery.

The profit consequences of these demands were visible in other functional areas. For example, a large rush order might require the mill to (1) delay orders already in process, (2) authorize a second shift, and (3) invest in unusual designs and patterns.

No one reprimanded the sales force for bringing back low-profit orders. They had met their quota. They had kept the looms covered.

Today's textile firms are much more aware of the perils posed by capital-intensive plants. But for decades, marketing personnel were allowed great latitude in selecting their customers and in defining the terms of trade. The same held true for commercial bankers and salespeople for large, integrated paper companies.

Can anything be done about such grooves in the mind? This is a touchy topic. Managers have been very leery about stepping into the role of psychiatrist, and we do not recommend that they do so. However, this chapter demonstrates that professionals indeed operate from distinct mind-sets, and it offers tools to help those brave enough to challenge perceptions that obstruct inter-functional team play.

PRODUCT QUALITY: WHO'S IN CHARGE?

It is hard to identify a business goal that depends more heavily on high-quality team play than product quality. Virtually every employee in the business is in a position to boost (or destroy) product or service quality.

This point has been made many times. But no doubt each of us has an inventory of horror stories proving that many businesses lack a broad commitment to product quality.

For example, a New England branch of a company that promised its customers to come to their rescue if their vehicles required road service failed to respond to five requests for aid over a seven-hour period. (It was a lovely fall day; weather was *not* a factor!) One customer wrote an angry letter, terminated his policy, and detailed his reasons. In reply, he received a form letter that totally ignored the details of his complaint. It ended with the pious sentiment "We hope you will some day rejoin our family."

As another example, one of the new communications companies that emerged following the breakup of AT&T sent its subscribers a toll-free customer service number. But it did not alert them to the fact that that number was likely to ring 50 or 60 times before anyone thought of answering it. Meanwhile, customers listened to canned music and smoldered.

THE STANDARD APPROACH TO QUALITY CONTROL

The large volume of literature on product and service quality might make one expect that every established business has convinced its employees to make a firm commitment to quality. This is not the case, although manufacturing businesses have spent vast sums in an attempt to "inspect quality into their product." They have delegated responsibility for product control to their quality control units and assume these professionals will address any quality problems that surface within their plants.

Until a short time ago, managers of service businesses might have agreed that service quality was important, but this did not mean that they clearly understood the determinants of service quality. Rarely did one find even a passing reference to quality in their strategic plans.

In the late 1970s, senior managers began to think seriously about product quality. They watched with dismay as American customers began to express a strong preference for products made in Japan. Some managers rushed to Japan to discover how Japanese firms produced nearly flawless products. They came home espousing the concepts of "zero defects" and "quality circles." Within weeks they launched an advertising campaign promising that quality was Job Number 1.

However, professionals in U.S. firms were *not* impressed by corporate statements about the importance of product quality. Slogans and slick advertisements used to promote "quality consciousness" turned them off. They echoed the mind-sets of their engineering managers: "If only manufacturing would adhere to our product and process specifications, our quality problems would vanish."

A NONSTANDARD APPROACH TO PRODUCT/ SERVICE QUALITY

For many years, the Strategic Planning Institute (SPI), headquartered in Cambridge, Massachusetts, has argued for a broader approach to quality enhancement. We will describe its approach with the help of an illustration from the health care industry, a firm we will refer to as Health, Inc.

When the chief executive officer of Health, Inc., reviewed the replies he had received from his MBO (Management by Objectives) program, he realized that his recently launched quality enhancement program lacked broad support. Only a handful of professionals had listed quality enhancement as one of their personal objectives—and all of them worked in quality control units! The executive silently wondered how his new corporate policy on product quality would ever be implemented if most of his professionals felt no personal obligation to improve product quality. In an attempt to answer his own question, the executive ordered his line managers to (1) develop a set of realistic quality objectives for their components (organizational units within the corporation) and (2) specify how they intended to realize these objectives.

The line managers could not ignore such an edict. But before they could develop their quality objectives, they had to reach some agreement on the meaning of the term *product quality*.

Some of the managers advocated the conventional concept of "conformance quality."[1] But eventually the firm derived its quality enhancement efforts from the Strategic Planning Institute's concept of "relative quality."

Relative Quality

SPI reminds managers that their customers are the proper judges of product quality. Customers make judgments about quality using standards that would mystify members of a quality control unit. For example, many customers reserve their highest quality rating for businesses that offer service(s) along with their products.[2] They are acutely sensitive to such matters as

- Availability of credit.
- A manufacturer's willingness to help with installation.
- Scope and duration of the warranty offered.
- Expertise of the individuals who sell, deliver, and/or install the product.
- Speed with which vendors respond to their requests for product maintenance.

None of the above criteria of product quality falls within the purview of a quality-control unit. Nor is any found among the product specifications that engineering sends to manufacturing.

In addition, SPI emphasizes that customers think of quality in relative terms. It reserves a high quality rating for businesses that *outperform their competitors*. This has serious implications for firms. A manufacturing firm that has achieved "zero defects" within its factories cannot expect applause from its customers if competitors offer products or services that meet customer wants more effectively.[3]

A Quality Profile

How does one help professionals in *all* functional areas focus on their customers' view of relative quality? SPI answers: Encourage them to construct a quality profile for their lines of products and/or services, such as that shown in Exhibit 4–1.[4]

A quality profile distinguishes between *product-related* and *service-related* attributes. Column 1 of Exhibit 4–1 is reserved for the *customer's* perceptions of the degree of importance, or "relative weight," of each attribute. Column 2 records the customer's rating of the product line, attribute by attribute. Columns 4–7

EXHIBIT 4–1
SPI Quality Profile

Quality: From the customer's viewpoint							
Key Purchase Criteria		Rel. Weight (%)	Performance Rating (scale 0-10)				
Product-Related Attributes			Our Business	Comp A	Comp B	Comp C	Comp D
Performance	1						
	2						
	3						
	4						
	5						
	6						
Style/ Packaging/ Attractiveness of Customer Outlet	7						
	8						
	9						
	10						
	11						
	12						
Service-Related Attributes							
Associated Services/ Warranties/ Delivery	1						
	2						
	3						
	4						
	5						
	6						
Brand & Company Image	7						
	8						
	9						
	10						
	11						
	12						
Totals		100%					

Market Share					
Price (relative to ours)	100				
Direct Cost (relative to ours)	100				
Technology (relative to ours)*	3				

*Codes
1 - Very inferior
2 - Inferior
3 - Equivalent
4 - Superior
5 - Very superior

Importance of quality vs. price in purchase decision

Quality	
Price	
Total	100%

Source: Reproduced with permission of the Strategic Planning Institute.

contain the customers' ratings of the attributes of products or services offered by four of the business's competitors.[5]

A Profiling Procedure

How does one counter the natural tendency of professionals to be complacent about their own efforts to enhance quality and denigrate the quality of products and services their competitors offer? SPI's answer: Conduct *two* surveys.

The first survey targets managers and specialists *within the business*. It asks them to identify what their customers regard as the key determinants of relative quality. Then it asks each professional how he or she thinks customers rate (1) the attributes of the business's products or services and (2) the attributes of products or services marketed by its leading competitors.

The second survey targets immediate customers (e.g., purchasing agents and specifying engineers) and/or end users. It asks respondents to

1. Identify and weigh each of the key determinants of quality.
2. Assess the quality of the business's products and services attribute by attribute.
3. Assess the quality of products or services from the business's *competitors*, attribute by attribute.

SPI then organizes this information into a second quality profile.

Rarely do the *internal* and *external* views of relative quality coincide. Managers and specialists within a business often operate from a perspective of relative product or service quality that differs from that of their customers. Some are unaware of their customers' quality standards altogether. Small wonder that corporate-inspired programs to enhance product quality often fall short of their goals!

Exhibits 4–2 and 4–3 exemplify how SPI draws attention to the differences between internal and external views of relative quality. Specifically, Exhibit 4–2 contrasts customers' perceptions of the relative weights to be assigned to product- and service-related attributes and those of Health, Inc.'s managers and specialists. The solid bars reflect information obtained from cus-

EXHIBIT 4–2
Two Views of Customers' Determinants of Quality—
Customers versus Management

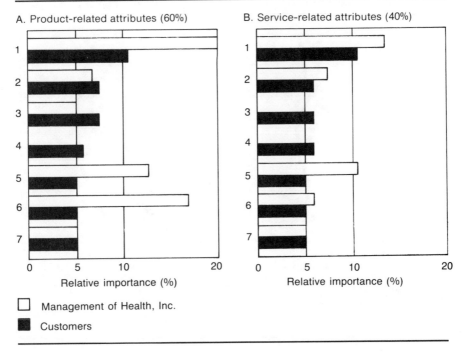

A. Product-related attributes (60%)   B. Service-related attributes (40%)

Relative importance (%)   Relative importance (%)

☐ Management of Health, Inc.

■ Customers

tomers; the unshaded bars show information acquired from managers and specialists within the business. The exhibit shows that

- Customers identified one product attribute (attribute 4) and two service attributes (3 and 4) that were *not* mentioned by in-house managers.
- Customers viewed product attributes 1, 5, and 6 as less important than their suppliers did.

Customers weighted the service-related dimensions of relative quality as 40 percent, while professionals within the business thought their customers assigned a weight of only 30 percent to services.

EXHIBIT 4–3
Relative Quality for Three Competitors, by Attribute

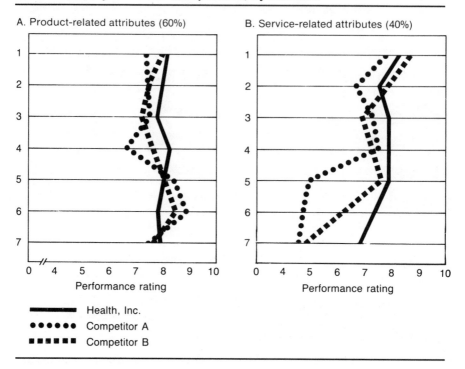

A. Product-related attributes (60%)   B. Service-related attributes (40%)

Performance rating   Performance rating

━━━━━ Health, Inc.
●●●●● Competitor A
■■■■■ Competitor B

Exhibit 4–3 contrasts the customers' view of the quality of Health Inc.'s product line with the quality of the product line of two of its competitors (A and B). The solid line links the attribute ratings of Health, Inc.'s product line, the dotted line links the attributes of Competitor A's product line, and the dashed line records the customers' ratings of Competitor B's product line. Where the three lines coincide, the quality race is a dead heat. In Exhibit 4–3A, we see that Health Inc. and its competitors are matched with respect to product-related attribute 5. It lags behind them with respect to attribute 6. Fortunately, Exhibit 4–3B records an edge with respect to service-related attributes 6 and 7.

The information in Exhibits 4–2 and 4–3 is extremely important for any executive who wishes to launch an effective quality enhancement program. It provides the grist for that rarest of planning documents: a quality plan.

Financial records track how much money *some* functions spend on *internal* quality control activities. They do *not* inform managers whether

- Any quality enhancement programs are being concentrated on product attributes that are of little importance to customers.
- One function is failing to take full advantage of customers' high regard for a product or service attribute.
- Programs for enhancing relative quality are incomplete or unintegrated.
- How much relative quality will improve if the efforts to enhance quality succeed.
- There is a risk that a competitor will neutralize their own quality enhancement programs.

Health, Inc., prepared no formal quality plan, but it did respond to its two surveys of relative quality. Among other things, it

1. Established specific quality goals *for each function*. No longer did the professionals in the quality control unit feel they had sole responsibility for quality enhancement.
2. Converted each quality goal into tasks and assigned them to professionals in the various functions.
3. Began to monitor the steps its competitors were taking to enhance their product quality.

Most important, the chief executive officer of Health, Inc., decided to let his customers tell him how effective his expenditures on quality enhancement turned out to be. He earmarked funds for a new market survey in 12 months and specified that outsiders would conduct it.

Health Inc.'s functional managers were understandably inclined to believe in the effectiveness of their own programs. Furthermore, the customer survey had already raised a question about the accuracy of their perceptions of relative quality.

This illustration points out the following guidelines:

- Recognize your customers as the arbiters of relative product quality.
- Give due recognition to the contributions which services can make to relative quality even if your business elects not to charge for them.
- Admit that outsiders are more likely to produce *objective* information on relative quality than are many internal experts.
- Do *not* presume that your own quality-enhancement programs will always elevate your relative quality. Your competitors may offset or even nullify your quality-enhancing programs.
- Understand that quality enhancement requires a team effort. Each member of each of the functional teams must be made aware of the links between his or her own efforts and those being made by other professionals in the business.

FEUDS OVER PRODUCT VARIETY

The pursuit of product quality is not the only area which calls for collaboration across functional borders. We also need a consensus with respect to product variety.

Henry Ford, Sr., would be the first to agree that product variety is a strategic issue. Recall his willingness to cater to the color preferences of his customers *provided they chose black.* Mr. Ford was not being capricious. He set out to manufacture an automobile which the average American could buy. This meant that the car's purchase price had to be low. He saw no way to offer cars of different colors and at the same time keep his manufacturing costs under control.[6]

In another instance, a manufacturer of watt-hour meters discovered that its functional managers were feuding over a similar difference in viewpoint. Professionals in marketing believed that their business's profitability rested on their willingness to cater to their customers' interest in customized products. In fact, in marketing the phrase "The customer is king!" was taken quite literally. Therefore, when a utility company asked for a watt-hour meter with unique functions and features, marketing hurried to engineering and pleaded that they add such a model to the line.

However, manufacturing had great difficulty delivering on marketing's promises to its customers. Orders for "specials" played havoc with scheduling and purchasing. Shipments often fell behind schedule because the model mix changed from week to week. This meant that expediters from marketing had to rush out on the factory floor, locate their customer's order, and then seek out the manager–manufacturing to lobby for a shop priority.

The manager–manufacturing tried to get his colleagues to recognize the hidden costs associated with excessive product variety (e.g., the need for frequent setups; higher unit costs; the need to pay a premium price when placing rush orders for parts and materials; the necessity of hiring factory workers one week and laying them off the next). But no one seemed to listen. Professionals in manufacturing felt they were being asked to play the familiar game of "crack the whip"—and each time they were assigned a position at the end of the line.

When the plant approached its rated capacity, some managers called for a new, highly automated production facility. Was not this the modern way to keep abreast of demand?

The general manager refused to invest in an automated plant. He was waiting for a report from a team of line managers and operations researchers who were studying, among other things, the department's manufacturing process.

Reframing the Issue

In due course, the multifunctional team stepped forward with a concept of "product" that made the debate between marketing and manufacturing moot. They had analyzed recent orders for watt-hour meters and found that most had been assembled from a relatively small number of common parts and subassemblies. The team displayed a product structure that highlighted the degree of uniformity.

The team recommended that all customer requisitions be translated into "shop language" (i.e., exploded into the common components and subassemblies required to fill a given customer order). They pointed out that their product structure was an efficient bridge between marketing terminology and shop terminology.

Many workers and professionals in this business were aware that the meters listed in the business's sales catalog shared many parts and subassemblies.[7] But prior to the team's analysis, no one had challenged the applicability of marketing's concept of "product" (numbers listed in the sales catalog) to manufacturing's work.[8] More important, no one had proposed a way to take advantage of this commonality and to end the feuding between the two functions.

Once this conceptual shift was made, the friction between the manufacturing and marketing functions ended abruptly. The manager–manufacturing capitalized on the commonality latent in marketing's list of model numbers. Instead of forecasting the demand for individual meters, he instructed his people to forecast the demand for *common parts and subassemblies.* He soon discovered that the now redefined shop load was remarkably stable over time. Last-minute calls to vendors for parts and subassemblies became a thing of the past. Consequently, his purchasing team no longer had to pay premium prices, for there were no more rush orders.

This drastic change in shop orientation benefited other functions as well. The marketing manager was pleased to hear that promises made to customers were now being met 99 percent of the time. Also, customer representatives no longer spent hours on the shop floor expediting orders, and specials orders were no longer a bone of contention. After all, specials also were assembled from common parts and subassemblies.

Even the manager–engineering found a use for the new product structure: He employed it as a weapon in his campaign against product proliferation. He instructed his product designers to maximize use of common parts and subassemblies rather than making each new product a monument to their creativity.

The final payoff from the new product structure took a different form: Calls for a new, automated plant ceased. Once the existing facility had been reoriented around common components and subassemblies, throughput increased!

Solomon hardly could have done a better job. This multifunctional team had provided an intellectual platform that enabled professionals in marketing, engineering, and manufacturing to function as a single team. The positive impact on profitability was "icing on the cake."

The emergence of personal computers, spreadsheets, and shared databases has greatly reduced, though not eliminated, the risk of *purposeless* product proliferation. If your business has a very modern computer center, do not rush to the conclusion that your manager–engineering can quickly spot instances in which product designers have tolerated more variety at the component/part level than is justified.

Why not run a test in your business? Drop in on your product designers, and ask them what constraints senior managers have imposed on them to avoid product proliferation.

DISCRETE PRODUCTS VERSUS SYSTEMS: THERE IS A BIG DIFFERENCE!

Messages sent across functional borders can be garbled if the sender and the receiver entertain different perceptions of the meaning of *product*. This can easily happen if the business's products have "migrated."

Exhibit 4–4 presents a straightforward way to avoid needless debates over the meaning of the term *product*. It locates products on a product spectrum.[9] "Raw material" appears at the lower end and "supersystems" at the upper end. The remaining columns are reserved for customer groups to which the products are offered. Usually these columns are arrayed with "immediate customers" on the left and "end users" on the right.

This tabular display is far from new, but it remains a useful tool for communicating the impact of changes in product technology on a product line. When these shifts are not reported, functional programs may drift apart[10]

The electronic revolution has resulted in many shifts in product level. For decades, cameras were classified "discrete" prod-

EXHIBIT 4–4
The Level of a Product

		Markets*			
Level of Product	*Example*	1	2	3	4

High

↑

Level of Product	Example
1. Supersystem	Disneyworld; Busch Gardens
2. System	All-electric kitchen (all appliances matched and sold as a set) Entertainment system (Radio + TV + turntable + speakers + VCR + amplifier + . . .)
3. Discrete product	Radio
4. Assembly	Clock for an appliance
5. Component	Transistor
6. Part	Screw
7. Raw material	Copper

↓

Low

*Examples: Original-equipment manufacturers; contractors/subcontractors; general contractors/prime contractors; developers

ucts. Today even cameras for nonprofessionals are properly classified as "camera systems." A camera buff buys a highly automated camera body, an assortment of lenses, a bewildering variety of filters, a hood, one or more flash units, and perhaps a camera back.

The same technological revolution has replaced the family movie camera with a "video system" (i.e., a camcorder). Now people routinely film family gatherings, record voices and sounds, and instantly replay the end result on the TVs with no help from a professional photo laboratory.[11]

Affluent families have traded their mundane radios or television sets (discrete products) for "entertainment centers." These may provide sound and/or pictures for a single room (the price tag is from $1,000 to $3,000) or permit the homeowner to program reception into every room in the house. For a few extra dollars, such systems can be modified to monitor temperature, light levels, and security in all parts of the home.

Small businesses are benefiting from the same revolution. They can now order a compact facsimile machine with a built-in copier and a telephone that will transmit the copies over a tele-communications network. The components of this compact system have been available for years as discrete products. Now they are neatly packaged into an integrated system.

The most dramatic shift along the product spectrum took place 30 years ago when Walt Disney recognized the difference between discrete products and a system of products. He designed Disneyland to attract and entertain children using animated characters (Donald Duck, the Seven Dwarfs, etc.) in the Disney inventory. The successors to Disneyland have pursued a broader goal: They feed, house, transport, entertain, and educate both children and their parents. Small wonder that the initial investment for a single center has run into billions of dollars.[12]

Without a high level of service quality, these supersystems would not be profitable. They demand an integrated team effort from the thousands of people who serve the hoards of visitors to entertainment centers.

In other industries, executives have not always been alert to the implications of product migration and, as a result, the requisite level of team play has not been forthcoming. Following are three examples.

Hospital Equipment

The vice president–sales for a health care firm felt justified in telling his sales representatives to "sell what is in the catalog," namely discrete products. His sales training programs explained how to sell such products: Draw the customer's attention to the *technical* merits of each product in the line.

Suddenly, this firm's customers changed their buying habits. Purchasing agents became less interested in product features. Brand loyalty began to erode, and prices softened. Architects and consultants appeared at the customer's side when large orders were being negotiated.

The vice president–sales reacted to these dramatic changes by exhorting his sales team to "sell systems." Alas, people who had been selling discrete products for twenty years found this a formidable transition. Before they could sell systems, they had to "unlearn" sales techniques designed for discrete products.

Videotex

A number of U.S. newspapers, retailers, and banks have flirted with the idea of using telephone circuits to distribute videotex for viewing on home video screens.[13] Banks have targeted a market consisting of young, affluent customers who own personal computers and would welcome the chance to do their banking from their homes.

On the surface, home banking might appear to be a small shift from branch banking. In reality, home banking poses many strategic as well as technical problems. For example,

- Should the bank send its electronic products over a network designed and operated by a common carrier?
- Should the bank merely turn its products over to a systems contractor that would add them to a much broader line of products (informational, educational, entertainment, and transactional)?
- Should the bank take on the role of systems contractor itself and, with the help of retailers, telecommunications firms, and/or firms with databases or time-sharing services, offer all manner of products that appeal to its more affluent customers?

Cogent answers to these questions require that bankers assess the risks that attend any movement upward on the product spectrum from "discrete products" to "systems."

Turnkey Contracts

Product migrations have caused severe profit strains. Think, for example, of those manufacturers of atomic power equipment who allowed themselves to be coaxed into taking on "turnkey projects." Think too of the profit problems that plagued GE's transportation division when it broadened its product line to include subway trains.

PRODUCTS, MODELS, AND SOFTWARE

Interfunctional feuds have also been sparked by a more subtle shift in product offerings, namely the incorporation of microcomputers, powerful software, and mathematical models into a discrete product or system that formerly consisted exclusively of hardware. For example, manufacturers of complex equipment for paper mills and chemical plants have had to respond to their customers' interest in software that would enable them to optimize their existing systems. Such firms have broadened their concept of "product" and recruited professionals with expertise in information systems, operations research, and electronic controls. Managers who have spent decades making and/or selling stand-alone equipment still find it difficult to view these newcomers as teammates in a common cause. The groove in their minds still reads, "We sell hardware."

A different product shift occurred in the power generation industry. Up until the mid-1970s, the idea of "big is beautiful" was an article of faith. Utilities placed orders for larger turbines and generators because these enabled them to push down the cost of electricity. Given this mind-set, professionals in engineering and in manufacturing regarded orders for renewal parts as a nuisance.

Then came the energy crisis. Utilities found it difficult to raise new capital. Interest rates soared. The rate increases that utilities needed to pay for new turbine generator sets were slow in coming.

The utilities found a simple solution: Upgrade the performance of *installed* equipment. As a result, the demand for new turbine generator sets evaporated.

Manufacturers of power generation equipment had no choice but to shift their emphasis from new turbines and generators to renewal parts. No longer did customer service have to plead with engineering and manufacturing to accelerate their response to requisitions for renewal parts. They were the only requisitions in the in-box!

SERVICE THAT PRECEDES HARDWARE

A narrow concept of product generates an interest in cost reduction, particularly in businesses with a mature product line. Chief executives recognize this and send managers with a strong financial background into such businesses.

By contrast, businesses that offer proprietary chemicals operate from a much broader concept of product. Their engineers spend a great deal of time in their customers' plants. In some instances, they have more understanding of what is going on there than their customers! Such knowledge is a prerequisite to identifying how customers might enhance their products by using the supplier's proprietary chemicals.

For example, the late Robert Finholt, who orchestrated the market introduction of GE's Noryl line, showed a potential automotive customer how he could eliminate 24 steps in his production process by replacing metal parts with plastic ones. This demonstration diverted his customer's attention away from the price of Noryl to its potential contributions to the customer's own cost-reduction and productivity-enhancement programs.

Similar examples might be found in the files of other businesses selling proprietary chemicals. They appreciate the need to do solid chemical engineering and industrial engineering on the customer's premises as a precondition to winning his order. They sell "value," not "commodities." Their product line includes engineering *services* as well as proprietary chemicals.

A MIND-SET THAT BREEDS AN INWARD PERSPECTIVE

Functional perspectives of "product" have at times dominated business policy decisions. Think of the current plight of this country's steel manufacturing businesses. Prior to the 1980s, the career path for promising engineers began in the mill. There engineers acquired an *inward* perspective and the belief that the key to business success was a modern production facility that operated at or close to rated capacity. They preferred large, integrated, "gold-plated" plants with a life span of at least 25 years.

Their quest for economies of scale closed their minds to the need to respond quickly and effectively to changes in customer requirements. In this scenario, there was no emphasis on team play between professionals in the mill and those in marketing and sales. The job of the latter two functions was to find orders for whatever the mill produced.

In the early 1980s, customers' needs changed and high-quality steel from new mills located abroad began to penetrate the U.S. market. Local minimills also began to capture orders. To survive, steel companies were forced to diversify and seek out market niches to which they might offer customized, high-grade alloys. This necessitated (1) a redefinition of marketing's traditional role; (2) a greater willingness to anticipate and quickly respond to shifts in customer requirements; and (3) high-quality team play among specialists in all functions.

Every professional has a mind-set. Yours may differ from mine. But if we are to be teammates, we must make a sincere effort to understand each other. A good way to begin is to define our terms and be alert for nuances. When uncertain of the other's meaning, we must press for more information. Most important of all, when others cross-examine us, we must not take offense or privately label them fools or adversaries. None of us has all the answers. We can and ought to learn from our colleagues. To do this we must listen with our intellects, not just our ears. If we do so, Allan Bloom may write a book about us and call it *The Opening of the American Mind.*[14]

NOTES

1. Philip B. Crosby, *Quality Without Teams: The Art of Hassle-Free Management* (New York: McGraw-Hill, 1984).
2. R. D. Buzzell, "Product Quality," *PIMSLETTER* 4 (1978); B. T. Gale and R. Klavan, "Formulating a Quality Improvement Strategy," *PIMSLETTER* 31 (1984).
3. Later sections of this chapter discuss the notion that "services" sold or given away with a physical product are to be considered when studying a business's "relative quality."
4. Exhibit 4-1 also can be used for individual products and services.

5. Some of SPI's member companies reserve columns 4 through 7 for information on competitors that are gaining or losing market share.
6. Mr. Ford was anxious to move away from the mind-set of carriage manufacturers. Their perspective has remained. Communities still place customized orders for fire engines.
7. Earlier, Melvin H. Hurni and Alfred P. Sloan, Jr., had drawn attention to the same phenomenon. Hurni wrote internal publications for GE. Sloan's ideas are found in *My Years with General Motors* (New York: Doubleday & Co., 1964), pp. 156–57.
8. M. L. Hurni uncovered a structure underlying orders for distribution transformers. GE urged its departments to avoid undue product variety with the help of product structuring techniques. Some responded; others did not.
9. It is useful to add services to this spectrum. See Exhibit 12.5 in Chapter 12.
10. An example would be a firm with a line of transportation products offered to railroads that added riding lawn mowers or golf carts. These increments to the line would go to different markets and move through different distribution channels.
11. "Tape Tells the Story in Canon's New System," *New York Times,* July 20, 1986, p. 43.
12. Jennifer Stoffel, "What's New in Amusement Parks," *New York Times,* July 3, 1988, sec. M4, p. 34.
13. *Forbes,* August 13, 1984, p. 34; Peter H. Lewis, "Once More into the Videotex Breach," *New York Times,* May 22, 1988, p. F13.
14. Allan Bloom is the author of *The Closing of the American Mind: How Higher Education Has Failed Democracy and Impoverished the Souls of Today's Students* (New York: Simon & Schuster, 1987).

PART 2

BUSINESS STRATEGY: EASY TO CONCEIVE BUT HARD TO EXECUTE

Part 2 shifts our focus from interfunctional team play to team play between the architects of business strategy and those of functional tactics. Over the last 15 years, managers of U.S. businesses have discovered that it is far easier to conceive a business strategy than to persuade functional managers to develop action programs that will implement it. Some general managers have inferred from this unfortunate experience that formal strategic plans are a poor investment. They conveniently overlook the fact that they themselves have made little effort to orchestrate tactical programs that could give their strategic choices substance.

Part 2 illustrates how general and functional managers can elevate the quality of their team play by arriving at a consensus on the fundamental postulates of their business. Specifically, they must agree on:

- The identity and location of the customers they wish to serve.

- The types of products and services their businesses will offer to customers, and their standards of product quality.
- The businesses they will compete against.
- The type and degree of expertise they must develop in order to differentiate their product lines from their competitors.

If these managers can concur on these points, they will be able to "get their act together." More important, professionals at the middle echelons will operate from a shared strategic context, which will enable them to give consistent, high-quality support to business strategy.

In contrast, when such a consensus is absent, numerous raucous debates over minor tactical issues will break out. The debaters will fail to realize that they differ, not on matters of tactics, but on issues of business strategy. They will not understand that the source of their functional feuds lies at the *next higher echelon*.

This fact is most visible in start-up businesses. Chapter 5 illustrates both low- and high-quality team play between professionals at the top and middle echelons of two fledgling businesses. It shows how a gyrating strategic compass can cause stress and disharmony at the tactical level while a sound and consistent business strategy can preempt functional discord.

Chapter 6 offers additional consensus-building tools for general managers and their functional managers. For example, it describes both successful and unsuccessful efforts to develop an organizational structure for a newly created business. The chapter closes with a systematic, disciplined approach to reaching agreement on a business's market boundaries, its current structural characteristics, and the strategic profile managers wish to impart to their business.

Arriving at a consensus is one thing; sustaining it is another. Chapters 7 and 8 describe two quite diverse responses to outside events that strained the coupling between business strategy and tactics. The illustration in Chapter 7 deals with a middle manager's efforts to persuade his senior managers that it was possible to realize their published goals—high service quality, revenue growth, and profit—even in a depressed market. The manager's chief weapon was a simulation model, a tool that manufacturing businesses had been using for many years. In Chapter 8, the barrier to team play is much higher: An event beyond the management team's control suddenly wiped out a major source of revenue. This forced senior and middle managers to redefine their business and build a new intellectual platform for their strategic and tactical planning.

Part 2 closes with four illustrations of team play between customers and their vendors. In the past, managers of U.S. businesses have not regarded their vendors as partners. In fact, they have viewed themselves as being embroiled in a zero-sum game with their vendors (i.e., for one party to win, the other has to lose). This perception has manifested itself in very aggressive behavior patterns. For example, purchasing agents were expected to do more than "lean on" and "threaten" their vendors. In some firms, purchasing agents were given annual quotas that defined the magnitude of the concessions they were to extract from their vendors!

Such behavior is hardly conducive to team play. Therefore, Chapter 9 describes various methods managers have used to foster more harmonious relationships with their vendors. The illustrations come from the Department of Defense, a multibusiness manufacturing firm, a systems project launched by an eastern state, and a regional bank.

CHAPTER 5

TEAM PLAY WITHIN NEW BUSINESSES[1]

In the orchestra . . . the score is given to both players and conductor. In business the score is being written as it is being played.

—Peter F. Drucker[2]

New-product development resembles a steeplechase rather than a canter around the smooth, oval track at Churchill Downs. But new-business development is a far more difficult order of magnitude. Customers are wary about dealing with vendors without proven track records. They are even more leery of trusting products based on new technology.

Professionals who work in a new business face a host of problems. First, they may never have worked with one another before. Second, their general manager may change strategic direction, *monthly!* This forces professionals at the functional level to respond to a business score which is constantly changing.

In such an environment, functional stress is inevitable. But when new businesses pursue overly aggressive strategies or change their strategic course every few months, the level of functional stress jumps from "acceptable" to "life threatening." By the time the managerial team gets their act together, the window of opportunity may be tightly shut and their financial backers may have lost faith and confidence in the new business.

The purpose of the next two illustrations is to demonstrate how strategic decisions made at the general manager level can affect the quality of team play among professionals at the functional level. All too often we ignore this linkage. We liquidate functional managers whose only mistake was to attempt to implement their boss's flawed strategic decisions.

FUNCTIONAL HAVOC CAUSED BY A GYRATING STRATEGIC COMPASS

A few years ago, a young engineer working in one of the country's largest electronics firms developed a product capable of controlling the level of light from incandescent and fluorescent lamps. He believed that the market would welcome such a device. Thus, he dutifully submitted a request for the corporate funds he needed to commercialize it. He expected that with a little luck, his new line of lighting products would be in distributors' hands within 18 months.

But he was *not* lucky. His chief executive officer recently had chosen a corporate strategy that diverted the firm from lighting markets. Therefore, while the CEO acknowledged the engineer's excellent work, he denied the request for corporate funding.

The Launching of a New Venture

The result was predictable. The young intrapreneur (defined as an innovator on the payroll of an *established* business) resigned and took along a number of colleagues who shared his faith in his product innovation. They soon found venture capitalists who agreed to fund a start-up business resting on the innovation. Within a few months, these "defectors" were at the helm of a new, Texas-based company that we will call Southwest Electronics.

Initially, Southwest Electronics appeared to have found the short road to profitability. It offered a line of lighting control products. Its order backlog buttressed its claim that these products were indeed superior to other control devices. On the surface, at least, the new management team seemed to be following Horatio Alger's script to the letter. Each member of the team expected to see his name on the list of Texas's newest millionaires.

Unfortunately, their expectations were not realized. Within months, they found themselves struggling with the symptoms of a deep-seated problem. Specifically,

• *Razor-thin margins.* The new line of lighting controls was priced below competing products, because the new CEO was in a great hurry to build volume. He was prepared to buy market share. Needless to say, his pricing policy did not add luster to Southwest's income statement. In fact, the red ink there made its financial backers very apprehensive.

• *Unrest in the shop.*   A rash of in-house quality problems produced a surge in work-in-process inventories. The reason? The documentation that engineering had offered to manufacturing was, to put it delicately, downright skimpy.

• *Problems with yield and scheduling.*   As the production lines began to falter, semiconductor yields fell precipitously. Shipments often were late. Daily staff meetings were necessary in order to allocate those devices that did pass inspection. Customers whose orders had been put on hold called to protest and to lobby for special treatment. Privately, they began to wonder if they had made a mistake when they placed their orders with a fledgling business.

• *Distributor unrest.*   In its haste to build volume, Southwest Electronics sold its proprietary components to its competitors! Needless to say, its distributors were upset by this strategic decision. They had hoped to use Southwest's unique products to build a commanding market share. These hopes were dashed when their competitors unveiled equivalent products fashioned from Southwest's components. Silently these distributors asked themselves, "When your supplier is Southwest Electronics, who needs an enemy?"

• *Slippage in R&D Schedules.*   R&D programs and advanced-engineering projects were being completed late. An investigation revealed the reason: Southwest's best engineers were being diverted to work on ad hoc engineering projects *for their customers.* Some of these projects had originated with competitors that had purchased Southwest's proprietary components and incorporated them into competing products! It was one thing to be nice to customers but quite another to aid and abet their efforts to nullify Southwest Electronics' competitive advantage.

• *Incessant firefighting.*   Crises were a routine occurrence. Senior managers spent hour after hour in staff meetings trying to respond to these crises and to arbitrate the functional feuds provoked by their own gyrating strategic compass. Before long, senior managers found themselves mired in day-to-day decisions related to shop loading and distribution. They had no time or energy left to think about strategic issues.

> *It would be ideal to plant stress gauges along functional borders to signal an absence of team play or, worse, functional feuds. To be truly effective, these gauges would have to be able to illuminate the causes of the feuds.*
>
> *Such gauges, of course, are not on the market. General managers are supposed to cope with functional feuds on their own. If your firm selects general managers of high-tech start-up businesses exclusively on the basis of their mastery of technical subjects, functional stress may not be recognized for what it is, namely, evidence of flawed strategic decisions.*

Southwest's financial backers knew a lot about tax shelters but next to nothing about managing a new, technologically-based business. They were understandably slow to detect and decode tactical signals that a major policy error had given Southwest a fast start on a perilous and often changing strategic course.

Eventually the venture capitalists got the message. They conceded to one another that they had picked a technological wizard rather than an experienced manager to head Southwest Electronics. They fired him and imported a replacement from the ranks of one of the country's top 10 companies. Their charge to the new manager was: Turn Southwest Electronics around—*quickly.*

The Diagnosis: A Lack of Clarity in Business Purpose

After one day on the premises, the new manager remarked, "Southwest Electronics exhibits as much order as a tossed salad!" No one offered evidence to the contrary.

After a week on the premises, this manager concluded that most of the daily crises and all of the incessant firefighting were due to Southwest's market orientation. Southwest was *not* serving a single market; rather, it had a toehold in half a dozen markets! Had the venture capitalists not intervened, the manager's predecessor probably would have upped that number to a full dozen.

Small wonder that there was friction along the functional borders. Professionals at the middle echelon had no idea of what sort of business they were trying to create. They operated with no strategic perspective. They could not enumerate their business's long-term goals. They were being pulled in many different directions, hoping against hope to survive another month. Had these professionals been asked to articulate their business's strategy, they would have replied, "Stay loose and build volume as soon as possible." A simple recipe—easy to learn, easy to store—but perilous to follow.

Southwest's new manager concluded that his first task was to provide his team with a clear answer to the question *what kind of business are we trying to create?* Then and only then could he turn his attention to his strategic options.

After innumerable meetings and luncheons with his colleagues, the new manager called the question as to viable strategic options. Should Southwest Electronics strive to become a manufacturer of (1) highly specialized power semiconductor devices, (2) specialized wiring devices, (3) lighting products for professional firms, commercial establishments, and homeowners, (4) devices for controlling heat and/or motor speeds, or (5) some combination of the four?

Clearly, the character of Southwest Electronics would change depending on which of the above options was exercised. As the general manager considered the pros and cons of each option, he bore two questions in mind:

- *Which strategic option will produce a positive cash flow?* Southwest's financial backers had plenty of cash, but they had made it crystal clear that they would put no more money into the business unless and until cash flow turned positive.
- *Which strategic option will produce the least functional stress?*

Morale within Southwest already was at a low ebb. The professionals were beginning to wonder if their firm would survive. Some were convinced that their former general manager had gotten a raw deal. Most doubted the ability of his replacement to succeed where they had failed, namely at extricating Southwest from profit trouble. Finally, they were annoyed with their financial backers who had shown so little understanding of the effort required to launch a high-tech business.

After due thought and interminable discussion, the general manager concluded that it was imperative to pull back Southwest Electronics's market boundaries and to hold to a new, less aggressive business strategy, namely, to offer a line of lighting-control products to the commercial and residential lighting markets.

Southwest's board of directors concurred with this decision. They promised additional capital *provided that* Southwest gave some indication that it had "gotten its act together."

The new manager set out to demonstrate to one and all the wisdom of leading a strategic retreat from those markets where the opportunity to generate positive cash flow in the short term was dim or nonexistent. Specifically, he cut his firm's ties to the theatrical lighting market. It was a thin market at best and much too specialized to justify any product development.

His next step was to cut all ties with original-equipment manufacturers and decline to renew existing contracts.

> *The new head of Southwest Electronics had come from a large firm and was well aware that original-equipment manufacturers (OEMs) employed aggressive and sophisticated purchasing agents who were determined to extract price concessions in return for volume orders. In the same breath, they would demand products of the highest quality and evidence that their vendors were trying to advance the technologies underlying their product lines. Such aims were incompatible with Southwest's. It would never earn an attractive rate of return on its own investment if it continued to deal with such demanding customers. Southwest had to generate cash and profits— the key to its survival—not sales volume. If it failed to do so, its financial backers would become discouraged and throw in the towel.*

When these strategic retreats were first announced, Southwest's functional managers had their doubts. How could a business get out of profit trouble if the boss turned his back on firm orders? Clearly he did not know the first thing about marketing!

But their morale rebounded when they saw their own quality of life improve after Southwest had accomplished its strategic retreat. Finger pointing ceased. Infighting became merely a bad memory. Fewer crises erupted. Positive things began to happen. For example,

1. Southwest's R&D projects began to move ahead once the new manager had concentrated his limited technical resources on lighting-control devices.

2. Engineering improved their documentation, which enabled manufacturing to reduce the level of work-in-process inventories. ROI began to recover.
3. With fewer products in the line, manufacturing engineers had no trouble finding ways to increase process yield with *no* increase in investment—another boost to ROI.
4. Expediters no longer roamed the factory floor. Therefore, the manager–manufacturing could spend his time on the shop floor and deal with problems and bottlenecks before they became crises—another boost to yield and therefore profits.
5. Once Southwest had redefined its served market, marketing's effectiveness increased dramatically.
6. Financial specialists found it much easier to cost individual products and project cash flow.

There was no great leap forward, no giant breakthrough, just steady tactical improvements, all made possible by the general manager's decision to narrow market scope and to adhere to a stable, realistic business strategy. As Southwest Electronics inched backward from the brink of bankruptcy, functional managers began to appreciate why there was harmony rather than feuding along functional borders. Their new boss had provided them with a clear sense of business purpose and a strategic context in which they could see how to be team players.

Southwest Electronics' experiences have generated two important guidelines that many businesses can apply:

1. *Easy solutions to operational problems are often wrong.* Those who try to blame every tactical problem on managers are ignoring the possibility that the cause is either upstream (in another function) or up one organizational level.[3] It is far more sensible to ask *why* functional overload has developed.
2. *A profit-turnaround strategy must be "sold" to each professional before it can be implemented.* The new manager at Southwest did not issue an edict calling for a change in strategy within a few hours of his arrival, because he knew his colleagues would find ways to scuttle it. Instead, he looked for opportunities to persuade his functional

managers that they were currently implementing an un-realistic strategy. He decided to take them on one at a time and try to lift their intellectual sights from the daily crises themselves to the *causes* of these crises.

These accomplishments took much time and a lot of patience. They reflect the qualities of a true teacher rather than those of a turn-around specialist who hacks his or her way out of a profit trap but creates a demoralized management team in the process.

EVOLVING MARKET BOUNDARIES: HOW TO COPE WITHOUT GOING BROKE

Our second illustration shows how valuable it is to make the link between business strategy and functional tactics clear to profes-sionals at all levels within a business. Our source material comes from a new business launched by A. B. Dick Company to exploit an advance in ink-jet printing. It did not flounder like Southwest Electronics. It had its act together *from the very beginning*.

For many years, A. B. Dick Company was a family-run firm. It earned an excellent reputation as a manufacturer of duplicating equipment for offices, churches, and print shops.[4] Senior manage-ment recognized that the duplicating technologies underlying their products were mature. To ward off any erosion in profitability, they recruited talent from leading technical centers and invested in R&D. They also obtained a license to manufacture products based on a nascent ink-jet technology.[5]

New products followed in due course. Each represented solid engineering work, but none provoked much customer enthusiasm. Here was the company's scorecard:

- High-speed facsimile systems: 1 sold.
- High-speed printers for the EDP market: 1 sold.
- Label printers for firms doing mass mailings: fewer than 30 sold.
- Ink-jet printers for communication centers operated by wire services and for large data processing centers: fewer than 200 sold.

As is typical, these failures prompted a reorganization rather than a thoughtful analysis of what had gone wrong. Senior managers seem to have limitless faith in their ability to solve any problem by shifting boxes around on their organization charts.

The firm's CEO created a new-business development component and gave it responsibility for all product innovations based on a single, emerging technology: ink-jet printing. W. R. Stone, the new general manager, was given profit-and-loss responsibility for a start-up business with four functions: product design, manufacturing, marketing, and finance.

The CEO made it clear to Stone that A. B. Dick's board of directors' interest in product innovation had waned and that the corporate treasury had been strained by past attempts to introduce new products. He warned Stone that he had but one time at bat and he was expected to hit a home run.

Basic Postulates of the New Business

Stone's first step was to try to understand why his company's previous attempts at innovation had not succeeded. After talking with the managers who had had a hand in these new products, Stone found a common pattern. His company had failed to appreciate the difference between offering a new product to customers that it had been serving for decades, and offering a new product to a market in which its name was unknown.

Few executives take the trouble to demand a "business autopsy" to uncover the reasons why their new ventures have failed. It is too tempting to attribute their demise to "management error." If that excuse fails to convince, they remind themselves that launching a new business is much like exploring for oil, i.e., sometimes you drill a dry hole!

Stone, however, was motivated to avoid each of the strategic and tactical errors made by those who had preceded him. He invested time and energy in a business autopsy that would lay bare the errors of his predecessors and direct him toward a business design that would assure a handsome profit in record time.[6]

After scrutinizing the strategic choices of his predecessors, Stone concluded that his job was to create a new market rather than serve an old one. He was expected to develop a line of ink-jet printers using an immature, rapidly evolving product technology. Prospective customers had every reason to be dubious about the reliability of ink-jet printers and hesitant about dealing with a new venture with no track record in nonimpact printing.

Nonetheless, Stone was convinced that the risks facing his business were manageable *provided* that he *and all his colleagues* adhered to the following fundamental principles:

1. *Make a realistic assessment of the maturity of the product technology underlying your line of new products.* This principle had emerged from a GE business research team that had drawn Stone's attention to the close link between product technology and market scope.[7] Indeed, this team showed that some high-tech businesses ought to define their served market with one eye on the *state* of their product technology and the other on its *relative* advantage over competing technologies.

In Stone's view, his nonimpact printers rested on an *infant* technology whose full potential was not known. It was quite likely that if his business succeeded in advancing its product technology and perfecting its products, new markets would open up to it. The trick was for everyone in the business to recognize that this new venture faced a market *with elastic borders*. Their challenge was to establish and defend a beachhead in the most accessible market *before products based on competing technologies were available.* They would make a profit *if* they produced attractive products for their *initial* customers and *then* used their newly acquired know-how to move into other markets.

> *Realistically, Stone had to expect some of his early printers to fail in the field. If he did not anticipate reliability problems and find a way to solve them without sustaining a cash drain, his return on investment would be negative for a long time, and his initial customers would become disenchanted with ink-jet printers. Furthermore, A. B. Dick Company's credibility as a competitor would be permanently damaged.*
>
> *That was the bad news. The good news was that A. B. Dick's ink-jet printers exhibited operating characteristics superior to those of impact printers currently in wide use. Specifically, ink-jet printers offered customers the ability to:*

Control, and thus change, markings by digital logic.

Use different fonts and therefore vary the size of markings continuously and randomly.

Use a wide variety of printing speeds (the maximum speed of an ink-jet printer was more than 10 times its minimum speed).

Mark without contacting the medium. This meant that customers could mark moving objects. In contrast, customers who relied on impact printers had to halt their line in order to mark a product or component.

Stone was convinced that these performance characteristics were inherent in ink-jet technology and, at that point in time, were *beyond the range of competing technologies*.[8] They constituted A. B. Dick Company's clear and demonstrable competitive edge. The managerial challenge facing Stone and his functional managers was to capitalize on this competitive edge *quickly* and *prudently*.

Here was a perspective that all *functional managers and* all *specialists had to share. Each had to understand their business's strategic challenge and make an appropriate, timely response that was consistent with the contributions being made by teammates in other parts of the business.*

2. *Sell the first ink-jet printers only to customers who were inclined to tolerate (or compensate for) the immaturity of the underlying technology.* Who were these customers? How could a start-up business with limited resources locate them? American Can Company offered one answer. It sold can stock to large firms that wanted to mark every can with variable information (lot number, date, shift, etc.). These firms would be interested in any new printing device that would enable them to accelerate their production lines. Each firm had full-time maintenance crews ready to go into action if a quality problem developed.

These were exactly the customers Stone wanted to serve! Since they had their own stake in the perfection of nonimpact printers, they were willing to let people from a start-up business into their plants. They were even willing to help Stone's business get the kinks out of its first ink-jet printer.

Note the basic point: a coincidence between the customer's goal and the supplier's goal. This gave Stone and his colleagues a way to cope with field failures using resources under their customers' control!

A Schlitz brewery enabled Stone to test his initial ink-jet printers. Although product reliability problems surfaced, each was solved with the help of A. B. Dick's "partners," namely American Can and Schlitz. A team effort helped Stone to contain the risks inherent in new-business development.

To A. B. Dick Company, at least, this type of team play was relatively new. It had been serving one class of customers for decades. Their working environments were much the same. Engineers were *not* called upon to amend a product after its release. Marketing did *not* view customers as partners in a common cause.

When a firm launches a new business, its general manager must be careful not to allow the mind-set of the parent firm to contaminate his cadre. A start-up business demands a new *mind-set. To be effective and profitable, it must operate from a mind-set that reflects* the *realities of its market* and *the tempo of its competing technologies.*

When Stone and his partners passed this feasibility test with flying colors, they looked for ways to get other breweries to adopt ink-jet printers. Later they made a horizontal move and pursued bottling companies. Each application opened another door. Each contract enabled Stone's business to broaden its knowledge of ink-jet printing and become acquainted with a different industrial environment.

Even in its early years, this start-up business had to adjust to several shifts in its market boundaries. It used each increment in technical know-how to convince a cluster of customers in another market of the advantages of nonimpact printers. Stone could point to ink-jet printers on factory floors. This made it easier for prospective customers to visualize how products from the same technology might apply to their own needs.

Progress was slow, steady, and *profitable*. It had to be. A. B. Dick's board of directors was undisposed to fund any long-term projects aimed at pushing back the "leading edge" of technology. Profits earned from Stone's initial applications were the primary source of subsequent probes of contiguous markets, for example,

> Beverages: metal containers, crowns, and plastic bottles.
>
> Food: glass bottles, labels, cans, cartons, and various other paper-coded containers.
>
> Pharmaceuticals: glass vials, polyethylene plastic containers, cartons, drug containers, and paper labels.
>
> Automotive: parts identification, leaf springs, pistons, car doors, etc.
>
> Electronics: wire marking, integrated circuits, battery coding.
>
> Graphic arts: addressing, business forms, check and document endorsing.
>
> Postal Service: bar coding (for zip codes).

Each of these applications of ink-jet printing required Stone and his associates to enter and analyze a new work environment. At times it was necessary to advance their underlying product technology. The challenge, however, was to nudge the initial market boundaries outward without straining the resources of a medium-size company and without giving the board of directors apoplexy. None of these directors were entrepreneurs like Ford, Edison, Watson, and Sarnoff. Each of them remembered that their firm had had problems commercializing new products in the past.

Even the members of this start-up team had not foreseen the variety of applications of ink-jet printing. At the same time, *they did not make the mistake of being totally caught off guard by success.* Stone had insisted that his product designers look beyond the requirements of their initial customers. He warned them to keep one eye on future applications and to be prepared *to be able to adapt earlier designs rather than starting over.*

Perhaps this is obvious after the fact. But many start-up businesses fail to look ahead. They enter a new market with a single model. They are caught off guard by their own success. Instead of going down their learning curve, they are forced to retreat upward. A. B. Dick Company's new venture did not make this mistake.

3. *A medium-size company cannot capitalize on every opportunity that its advances in product technology open up.*   The EDP
market beckoned A. B. Dick's new venture, but the barriers to
entry were high. First, the parent company had stumbled when it
attempted to enter this market a few years earlier, and it was
unlikely that its customers had forgotten this. Second, this market already was being served by many well-financed firms. To
catch up to these firmly entrenched competitors might take more
resources than a medium-size company had available.

Stone concluded that A. B. Dick needed a partner with a
proven track record in the EDP market and very deep pockets.
He was confident that he could persuade such a firm that the
speed of mainframe computers had outstripped the speed of impact printers.

In the end Stone approached IBM, his former employer. IBM
had a dominant competitive position in the EDP market and
every reason to explore the potential of a new printing technology.

After due negotiation, IBM agreed to sign a licensing agreement with A. B. Dick Company. Each firm had something the
other needed. Each appreciated the value of a business alliance
and the need for interbusiness team play.

The IBM connection aided Stone's parent company in another way: IBM agreed to cross-license certain patents related to
word processing.[9] These might be very valuable to A. B. Dick
Company if it elected to enter the office products market with a
new word processor.

Looking far down the road, Stone could see that the proliferation of word processors would create a demand for fast, silent,
and moderately priced ink-jet printers. Here was a laudable target
to assign to his advanced-products component.

This excerpt from the files of A. B. Dick Company shows
how professionals in start-up businesses can avoid undue functional friction by:

1. *Selecting their initial customers with great care:* Stone
   sought customers who were willing to perform as teammates. They had their own reasons to complement his
   business's efforts to perfect ink-jet printing. All other customers were "off limits."

While some marketing professionals might question such a restrictive view of market boundaries, marketing selectivity did help Stone achieve an adequate rate of return quickly. *This point should be framed and hung on every professional's office wall. Too many professionals emerge from graduate school expecting venture capitalists to provide all the funds needed to push back the frontiers of knowledge. They have not learned* the necessity of building credibility in short but steady increments.

2. *Taking a dynamic view of market scope:* This start-up team viewed its initial contracts as *beachheads.* After consolidating his relationship with one customer, Stone approached others in the same industry. Later he used his initial successes to persuade customers in *adjacent* markets to try his printers. Thus, Stone's view of his served market was dynamic rather than static. Each technical advance and each completed contract expanded his marketing horizon.

3. *Avoiding design myopia:* It is imperative that designers build a degree of flexibility into their initial models. They must not be surprised when new customers insist on tailoring earlier designs to their own environment. When working with evolving product technologies, research and development is never done. Incremental R&D is the price exacted when one enters a contiguous market.

4. *Realizing that other technologies are moving ahead, too:* Each advance of a given printing technology resegments the market. Your competitive edge will be altered by the achievements of scientists in distant fields of endeavor and perhaps by firms that you do not consider your competitors.[10] Therefore, do not be surprised if the ground on which your business rests shifts even though you have not made a single move.

NOTES

1. William Robert Stone is the source of both illustrations in this chapter. Mr. Stone has held positions on the corporate staffs of GE, IBM, A. B. Dick Company, and E. F. Johnson Company. He is now a consultant on business policy questions, especially those related to the commercializa-

tion of so-called "high-tech products." The chapter also elaborates on an article by Stone and Donald F. Heany, "Dealing with a Corporate Identity Crisis," *Long-Range Planning* 17, no. 1 (February 1984), pp. 10–18.

2. Peter F. Drucker, *Frontiers of Management: Where Tomorrow's Decisions Are Being Made Today* (New York: Truman Talley Books/E. P. Dutton, 1986), p. 206.

3. The profit problems of Continental Bank immediately come to mind.

4. In 1979, the company was acquired by General Electric Company, Ltd., of Great Britain.

5. The basic patents were held by Richard Sweet of Stanford Research Institute (SRI).

6. The PIMS start-up database suggests that this period is approximately seven years. See Ralph Biggadike, "The Risky Business of Diversification," *Harvard Business Review*, May–June 1979, pp. 103–10.

7. This research is summarized in Chapter 8.

8. See Bob Stone, "Technology Limits and Printer Design," *Printout Annual,* 1985, pp. 18–27.

9. A. B. Dick Company subsequently entered into cross-licensing agreements with other firms (e.g., Sharp Corporation, Hitachi, and Moore Business Forms).

10. Stone, "Technology Limits." It is also critical to examine the state of the technologies underlying *related* products. For example, data transmission over voice-grade communication lines is not the same as transmission over optical fiber networks. High-speed laser printers presume an advance in the transport of the substrate as well.

CHAPTER 6

A CONSENSUS: THE BEDROCK OF STRATEGY AND TACTICS

We finally had to recognize that one of the vices of the virtue of decentralization is that people don't share ideas.

—Anthony O'Reilly, CEO, H. J. Heinz Company[1]

Many an innovative business strategy has been stillborn because those in charge of implementing it operated from differing perceptions of

- Their business's market boundaries.
- The line of products and services to be offered.
- The business profile to be forged.
- The preferred organizational structure.
- A list of "reserved words," that is, a glossary of key terms to be employed when discussing business policy issues.

When there is no consensus on these fundamental points, managers will be unable to approach strategy development and execution *as a team*.

Who needs a consensus? Answer: *every type of business!* The following example is a stern reminder of what can happen when a CEO and members of his or her corporate staff approach a strategic choice from radically different perspectives.

IS IT A "NEW PRODUCT" OR A "NEW BUSINESS?"[2]

Some years ago, A. B. Dick Company's engineers unveiled a word processor that outperformed products from the number one competitor in the office products market. Their innovation sparked a debate at the company's upper echelons. Some corporate officers were ecstatic. They believed this innovation might serve as the cornerstone of a new business. They urged their chief executive officer to fund a full line of such equipment and assign this product line to a *separate* profit-and-loss center. They arrived at their recommendations with the help of the following criteria:

• *Are our customers different?* Yes! Executives and their secretaries would decide whether or not to replace electric typewriters with word processors. They were members of a customer class that A. B. Dick Company had *not* cultivated in the past.

• *Will the innovation experience a different market growth rate?* Undoubtedly. The demand for word processors in general was expected to increase rapidly. In contrast, the demand for A. B. Dick Company's traditional product line was essentially flat. The strategic options available to businesses facing a rapidly growing market are *different* from those facing businesses that address a stagnant market.

• *Will our competitors differ?* Definitely. If the company introduced this word processor, it would face a new set of competitors.

• *Will we be viewed as a new entrant?* Customers in the office equipment market definitely would regard A. B. Dick as a new, untested competitor.

• *Will we have to develop a different strategy and new tactics?* Certainly. To stake out a position in the office equipment market, A. B. Dick Company would have to follow an aggressive market share strategy. It would also have to adopt tactics that had no counterparts in its established businesses.

• *Will we require different sales expertise?* Most definitely. A. B. Dick Company had built its sales force around high school graduates. The novices' initial job was to service the company's products in print shops, schools, and churches. Their familiarity with print shop supervisors and back-office personnel was, if anything, a disadvantage. Their past assignments had given them no opportunity to learn how to relate to executives and their secretaries.

    A. B. Dick Company's chief executive officer was unmoved by this line of argument. The groove in his mind told him to view the innovation as a "new product" rather than a "new business."

Therefore, he mentally labeled the new word processor as another type of copying equipment and added it to the line of products his existing sales force was selling.

For a time, the new word processor did quite well. Eventually, however, the realities of the marketplace made their presence felt. New competitors penetrated the market, each touting a new model. With its tight funding, A. B. Dick could not retaliate. Its corporate culture did not permit a fast response to threats that originated so far from its core businesses. Other managerial problems preempted the attention of the manager in charge of the new word processor.

> *It is doubtful whether any of the A. B. Dick Company files describes why one of its product innovations failed to establish a firm place in the office products market. Only a new-product autopsy would have revealed the absence of a consensus with respect to the fundamental differences between a "new product" and a "new business."*[3]

The following sections provide consensus-building tools that will help professionals reach a common intellectual platform before plunging into discussions of strategy and tactics.

WHO BUILDS A STRUCTURE FOR A NEW SERVICE BUSINESS?

Normally, general managers are permitted to select an organizational structure that pleases them. If they feel they need advice, they turn to an outside expert rather than to their subordinates. This is hardly the way to foster interfunctional team play.

In the early 1980s, Dr. James F. Sarver had an opportunity to try a collaborative approach to organizational design. He got this opportunity because GE's Lighting Business Group had moved toward a matrix type of organization. It had combined a number of product departments (e.g., Photo Lamp, Miniature Lamp, and Incandescent Lamp) and then transferred many of their engineers to a newly formed engineering department in the Lamp Products Division. Jim Sarver became the new department's first general manager.

Data for Organizational Decisions

Before deciding on a departmental structure, Sarver visited other general managers in his division and asked each of them these questions:

1. What kinds of support do you need from my department?
2. How well are these needs being met?
3. Which engineering activities should be expanded, curtailed, or eliminated?
4. What interface issues do you think might arise between your departments and mine?

Sometime later, Sarver sat down with each member of his staff and their direct reports to determine the status of each technical program underway in his department. He also sought his staff's opinion about the level of resources assigned to these programs and ways to accelerate their progress.

After these interviews, Sarver called for an attitude survey of all of his salaried personnel. He knew this would tell him how people felt about their work and how they were being treated. It would also reveal how they felt about their group's recent organizational changes. A secondary purpose of this survey was to show Sarver how his subordinates interpreted the engineering department's objectives, goals, and project priorities.

The Search for a New Departmental Structure

Both the interviews and the attitude survey indicated that managers in the engineering department regarded the existing organizational structure as inadequate. To start these managers thinking about constructive alternatives, Sarver asked Tom Herlevi, his manager of employee relations, and Bill Vinson, a corporate consultant, to visit each senior manager and obtain his suggestions as to what work the department should perform and how to assign that work to a manageable number of functional components.

Herlevi and Vinson returned with 12 organizational proposals, which they summarized and presented to Sarver and his entire staff. They did not disclose the source of these proposals. This allowed the group to discuss the pros and cons of each proposal.

Sarver sensed that no consensus existed among the managers who reported to him. Therefore, he met with each manager privately to confirm that Herlevi and Vinson had surfaced all of the major organizational options, described them adequately, and presented the rationale behind them.

> *These sessions took a great deal of time.*[4] *Sarver was prepared to invest the time and energy required because he was convinced that if his colleagues helped him develop an organizational structure, they would make it work. This act of faith was justified.*

These lengthy interviews and group discussions eventually produced a consensus. Sarver reflected this consensus in a new organizational structure for the engineering department. He presented this structure to his division manager, along with the names of the individuals he nominated as managers of the four primary functions (advanced technology, design engineering, process engineering, and producibility engineering and support).

Detailing the Approved Design

When his division manager approved the new structure, Sarver was able to turn his attention to two other organizational questions:

- How should we distribute the department's work among the primary functions?
- How should these functions relate to one another?

To identify possible answers, Sarver asked Herlevi and Vinson to take members of his senior staff to an offsite location for two days and develop a preliminary organizational chart. Managers who had not received senior status (and were about to move into what were perceived as less prestigious managerial positions) were invited to attend this meeting. The message to them was clear: We value your ideas; we want your input. Will you help too?

The first day was dedicated to defining the work scope of the primary functions. Initially each new functional manager met privately with a colleague who had had prior experience managing that type of functional work. Each pair exchanged ideas on how best to organize that particular function. Then the new functional managers met as a group. Each presented his recommendations on the kind of work his function should perform and how it might interface with other functions.

These recommendations formed the agenda for a meeting that occupied the afternoon of the first day. Jim Sarver attended this meeting and joined in the discussion, but he was careful not to advocate any particular recommendation.

Organizing the Middle Echelon

On the second day the managers shifted their attention to the components that would constitute the next lower organizational level. These components were labeled *activity centers*. Sarver called for suggestions as to

- The number of activity centers to be formed in each function.
- The scope of work to be assigned to each center.
- The criteria to be used when selecting managers for the activity centers.
- The names of the professionals who were best qualified to head each activity.

Each manager was given an opportunity to express his views on the work to be assigned to the activity centers and to nominate individuals to manage them. Each was urged to comment on the nominees' strong and weak points.

> *Weaknesses need not be fatal. Sarver wanted to find out how his senior managers intended to support nominees while they were adjusting to their new roles.*

Within a very short period of time, the group completed their list of those best qualified for the title of activity center manager.

Professional Staff Assignments

Two tasks remained to be done: assign professionals to one of the four primary components of the engineering department, then assign them to one of its constituent activity centers. These decisions were made in a second organizational meeting, which was attended by the new functional managers and the newly chosen activity center managers.

This session was also conducted in a collegial manner. It began with a series of presentations by each activity center manager. These managers outlined the work they felt should be performed in their centers and named the professionals they wanted to perform that work.

The small group discussions that followed were probably the most constructive part of the meeting. In most instances, the personnel nominations went uncontested. Some of the challenged nominations were resolved when the protesters were assured that a professional assigned to one center was not precluded from assisting another center. Other challenges were settled by "horse trading": I will give you X if you will give me Y. Or you can have Z provided that you promise to permit him to continue his work on project A. In those few instances where two activity managers were unable to agree, the section managers and/or Jim Sarver stepped in to resolve the issue.

Managers left the meeting convinced that they would have a meaningful role to play in the new department. The activity center managers were enthusiastic. *This was the first time in their careers that anyone had ever sought their opinions with respect to functional appointments or to the adequacy of their department's organizational structure.*

The next day, Sarver released his new organization chart and explained to all of his employees what higher management expected from their departments.

The Assimilation Sessions

Since 56 percent of the professionals in the new department now had an immediate manager whom they did not know well, Herlevi arranged a series of "assimilation meetings" attended by professionals in each activity center. His goal was to lay a groundwork for team play within each center and among the centers.

Here is a sample of the nitty-gritty questions that Herlevi surfaced in these meetings:

- What is our mission?
- What resources do we need to fulfill this mission?
- How many resources do we really have?
- Who interfaces with whom within this activity center, with other activity centers, and with other departments and vendors?
- What must we do to both accomplish our mission and fulfill our individual roles?

After the activity center managers left the room, Herlevi asked these questions:

- What do *you* need to know about *your new manager?*
     His career goal?
     His availability for communication?
     His background in our technology?
     His management style?
- What does he need to know *about you?*
     Your individual goals?
     The tools you need to do your work?
     Your strengths and weaknesses?
     The inputs you need in order to make prudent decisions *on your own?*
- How do you want to be managed?
     Do you want your manager to be available? Willing to listen to his staff? Prepared to stand up for it?
     Do you want your manager to give honest and timely feedback on individual performances?
     Do you want your manager to pass on information?

One rarely hears such questions addressed in an *open* meeting. The engineering department allowed such questions because its senior managers wanted to minimize the time lag between the publication of their new organizational structure and the beginning of real teamwork at the middle-manager level.

Imagine how long it would have taken a group of well over 100 professionals to ferret out answers to the above questions on their own and then sift fact from fiction.

Short-Term Results

At that time, no one in the engineering department viewed these organizational choices as either optimal or final. But one thing was clear: It was *their* structure. *Their* fingerprints were on every page. If hidden flaws surfaced at a later date, these managers were prepared to amend their structure. Most of the participants in this collaborative effort at department design would have subscribed to the summary one manager provided: "We ain't in Paradise yet, but at least they asked for our input!"

Jim Sarver monitored these collective organizational decisions. He held monthly roundtable luncheons and invited any managers with an organizational problem to attend and to discuss ways to resolve their problem.

The approach taken by Sarver and his colleagues can be used by any business. This approach will bear fruit *if* general managers will make an upfront investment in team play by

1. Taking the time to conduct surveys and understand the current perceptions of the managers who report to them.
2. Creating a collegial environment in which functional *and* subfunctional managers feel comfortable sharing their points of view.

BUSINESS DEFINITION: A JOB FOR A TOP-LEVEL TEAM

Interfunctional team play requires more than a consensus on matters pertaining to organizational structure. It also requires a consensus on market boundaries and on the structural characteristics to be imparted to the business. The latter requirement is always important for newly launched businesses and businesses in profit trouble. It can also be important in established businesses that appear to have more weaknesses than strengths. The following illustration from the files of a medium-size chemical company explains why this is the case.[5]

The CEO of this company encouraged his division managers to profile each of their strategic business units (SBUs). This directive troubled one division president, because his SBU sold its products in Western Europe as well as in the United States. To arrive at a single market share estimate, he would have to commingle information on two very different markets. This he was reluctant to do; he much preferred to profile two distinct businesses.

This division manager was not trying to be difficult. He understood why his CEO had developed a planning and control system around a modest number of strategic business units. At the same time, he felt justified in challenging this corporate directive. His rationale went along these lines:

> This SBU has provided much of the cash that our parent company needed to execute its aggressive acquisition strategy. We can continue to throw off cash for another three to five years. But after that, we are going to find ourselves in big profit trouble. I have the delicate job of reminding my CEO that he has denied us the investments we needed to stay abreast of our competitors in the U.S. market. We earned attractive profits, but these were siphoned off to other SBUs.
>
> My concern is that a consolidated report on my SBU will mask our true strategic position. It will not draw my CEO's attention to the fundamental changes that have taken place in the U.S. market. Let me share one fact. Four years ago, we faced 30 small competitors. Today we are up against five large, well-financed competitors. Our market share is half of what it once was. Today we are forced to play according to a new set of rules. I must persuade my CEO to reinvest in this business. If I don't, it will be reduced to an also-ran. This cash fountain will dry up!
>
> Luckily, our competitive position in Europe remains strong. There we face less aggressive competitors, and our customers look favorably on our products. Furthermore, we have just spotted a niche in the U.S. market. If we make a number of aggressive tactical moves, we can move in and erect some very formidable barriers to entry. But it will take an upfront investment in product quality and in product development. We will also have to increase the size and expertise of our sales force in order to defend our initial gains.

How can I obtain corporate funding if I meekly adhere to this corporate directive and describe my position in a world market? This will merely reinforce my CEO's current (erroneous) view, namely that my division has no exciting strategic options, that we are indeed only a "cash cow."

Convinced that his analysis was correct, the division manager profiled two "businesses," each with a different strategy. This was not only his right. It was his *duty* to reopen a question that many in the corporate office thought had been settled: Where are my business's boundary lines?

Few financial analysts or outside auditors would dare to challenge the appropriateness of a strategic business unit's boundaries. Indeed, many insiders prefer elastic business boundaries. First, such boundaries free general managers to act quickly when opportunities arise. Second, managers are more comfortable solving nitty-gritty operating problems than they are philosophizing about the nature of their business.

THE BUSINESS DEFINITION PROCESS

Multibusiness firms that used to define their businesses in *qualitative* terms soon discovered that aggressive managers showed scant respect for the market boundary lines specified in business charters. Like the legendary English pirate Sir Francis Drake, they told themselves, "Those who violate a charter may have their knuckles rapped, but if they generate a profit they are not likely to be hung!"

Just how does a CEO preempt such swashbuckling behavior and create a climate that fosters interbusiness collaboration rather than interbusiness feuding? The Strategic Planning Institute (SPI) developed a carefully crafted questionnaire—the so-called PIMS data forms—to help line-of-business managers arrive at a consensus with respect to their market scope, their product line, their production process, and their business's relative competitive position.[6]

SPI insisted that senior managers, not clerks or specialists, answer the questions in the PIMS data forms. To some, this appeared to be an extravagant use of managerial talent. The late Ivon Monk, the chief executive officer of DeLaval Turbine, disagreed. He insisted that the discussions the SPI questions provoked had helped him and his team reach a consensus about their business. The entries they made on the PIMS data forms were only the end points *of a valuable* process.

It is hard to specify a consensus-building tool of comparable effectiveness. Thousands of managers have used the PIMS data forms to reach agreement about the nature of their businesses.

Most of SPI's member companies agree that the business definition process is accelerated when:

• *A process facilitator* (usually an SPI staff member) *chairs each meeting.* The function of the process facilitator is to create and maintain an environment that will encourage the senior managers of the business to challenge traditional answers to questions about their market boundaries, competitors, relative competitive positions, and so on. The outsider is also free to provoke a discussion of market and technological trends that might erode the business's competitive position. This individual is more likely to recognize segments in the served market and inconsistencies in the current approaches to these segments.

• *Meetings are attended by the general manager and all functional managers.* If there are absentees, a consensus is impossible. To minimize the danger that business definition work will falter in the wake of useless semantic debates, SPI furnishes its members with a set of definitions of the most "slippery" terms, such as *customer, product, competitor, market,* and so forth.

• *The high-level team appoints a scribe.* Senior managers are accustomed to dispensing discipline, not accepting it. Therefore, great care must be taken to allow every member of the business definition team to be heard and to have his or her ideas recorded. One way to accomplish these goals is to appoint a team scribe and require him or her to write down on a large easel pad every point brought up. This accomplishes two things: (1) The group can judge whether the words accurately reflect their consensus, and (2) if they do not, dissenters can speak up to amend or challenge the recorded position.

There is a big difference between an oral *and a* written *statement. Managers of exalted rank love to give speeches. Their subordinates smile knowingly at one another and enter no dissent. But when the scribe records the key points and hangs them on the wall of the conference room, these items cease to be part of a speech. They become action items. Each member of the group is forced to register his or her agreement or disagreement.*

Too many businesses tolerate a culture that puts a premium on politeness. Experience shows, however, that the path to a consensus at the top echelon of a business goes through many a vigorous debate.

When the scribe runs out of room, he or she tears off the sheet, hangs it on the wall, and stands ready to fill up a new sheet. By the end of the meeting, the wall of the conference room is covered with paper. The attendees have a visual record of their intellectual journey—a *holistic* view of their business.

To see this as a major contribution to team play at the top echelon of the business, bear in mind the alternative. If there are written minutes of the business definition meeting—and usually there are none—they arrive several days later. If these minutes are inaccurate, there will be few opportunities to amend them.

The Byproducts of Business Definition Work

A number of important by-products emerge from group discussions about business definition. One divisional manager used them to identify those functional managers who had the talent to run an entire business. He watched to see which ones were sensitive to strategic issues of the type that filled his own in-box. He had no trouble distinguishing between managers with tunnel vision and those with a multifunctional perspective.

With the help of SPI's diagnostic software, the process facilitator carefully scrutinizes the data recorded on the PIMS data forms. At the next session dedicated to business definition work, the process facilitator directs the group's attention to the diagnostic messages, which concern such things as:

- Gaps in the data supplied.
- Inconsistencies in the answers.

- Outlandish answers.
- Trends and breaks in trends.

This type of feedback often provokes a discussion that brings the group closer to a consensus.

The End Products: A Business Profile and Performance Benchmarks

SPI's business definition process has two end products. The first is a business profile that *quantifies* the structural characteristics of the business known to be related to business profitability.[7] Such a profile provides functional managers with an *integrated* perspective of their business. It entices them to shed their functional perspective (such as chief specialist of engineering, or marketing, or manufacturing) and adopt the perspective of a general manager, which necessarily is multifunctional. *This in itself is a boon to interfunctional team play.*

The second end product of SPI's business definition process takes the form of a set of business performance benchmarks. For example, SPI member companies can ask for a profitability benchmark. This is defined as the average return on investment that businesses with similar strategic profiles have achieved under "average" management.

The scope of this book does not permit a description of the various methods of generating benchmarks from line-of-business data.[8] However, it is useful to point out the desirability of fashioning a benchmark from cross-functional data. Think, for example, of a manager whose business reported an actual return on investment of 25 percent but learns that SPI has assigned it a profitability benchmark of under 10 percent. The benchmark could be an early alert that the business has serious structural flaws masked by short-term market conditions. This benchmark forces the manager to ask hard questions:

1. Are we actively calling on all the customers in the market we described?
2. Is our position far stronger in one segment of the designated market than in the other segments?

3. Do we really respond to the pricing decisions and promotional campaigns of all the competitors we have identified?
4. Why are we carrying all these fixed assets?
5. Why have we permitted our raw material and work-in-process inventories to rise so high?
6. In view of our major outlays to enhance relative quality, why do so many members of our sales team report that our customers perceive our products as "equivalent" to those of our three major competitors?
7. Why have we allowed our R&D outlays to reach the same level as that of our number one competitor? Certainly there is no direct evidence that these expenditures have elevated our relative quality.

The discussion that follows questions of this type results in a consensus about the structural characteristics these managers wish to impart to their business. It produces a *shared* vision of areas such as the preferred market boundaries, the preferred product scope, and the preferred level of relative quality.[9]

Clearly, professionals in all functional areas need to understand and commit to this shared vision. It forms the bedrock both for *strategic* decisions made by the general manager and for *tactical* decisions made by functional managers and the specialists who report to them.

Several immediate applications of SBI's team-building methods come instantly to mind:

• *Managers of start-up businesses and venture capitalists.* Is there a clear understanding of the market this business intends to serve? Is there a consensus as to the targeted structural characteristics?

• *Managers of a new business.* We have discovered that one of the pivotal assumptions made at the time of launch is no longer valid. We must withdraw from our daily crises and reexamine both the way we have defined our served market and the means we are using to fulfill the promises we made to our financial backers.

• *The new owners of a leveraged buyout.* In earlier years, we were handed a strategy to follow. Now *we* are the architects of strategy and tactics. Isn't it time that we sat down and made certain that we agree on what we are going to do with "our" company? Sure, we have worked together for 10 years, but that does not mean we are all on the same wavelength!

• *Awareness of competition.* There's a new, world-class competitor moving into "our" market. It is time we reached agreement on the rules of the game as it will be played *in the future.* For example, the managers may have to alter their business's profile by

1. Raising the relative quality of their line of products.
2. Drastically reducing their investment in raw materials and other inventories (such as adopting just-in-time ordering practices).
3. Retreating from the low-growth segments of their served market.

SUMMARY

This chapter has emphasized that there is work to be done *before* the senior managers of a business can turn their attention to matters of strategy and tactics. They have some preplanning work to do. They must turn their attention to matters of market boundaries, organizational structure, and the targeted business profile. Many managers have floundered while grappling with these topics because they lacked experience in creating or restructuring lines of business. They have covered up their failures by dismissing preplanning work as too "philosophical" or too "theoretical."

The illustrations in this chapter show the advantages of using a team approach to preplanning questions and of employing an outsider with prior experience in business definition work to help the group reach a consensus on this matter.

NOTES

1. *New York Times,* May 8, 1988, sec. 3, p. 6.
2. This illustration in this section was supplied by W. Robert Stone, a former vice president of A. B. Dick Company.
3. If key players do not operate from the same glossary, they will find it difficult to function as a team. For more on the subtle but important gra-

dations of product innovation, see Donald F. Heany, "Degree of Product Innovation," *Journal of Business Strategy* 3, no. 4 (Spring 1983), pp. 3–14.

4. Time constraints kept Sarver from meeting with professionals at lower organizational levels.

5. This illustration was supplied by Joseph M. Patten, vice president of PIMS Associates, a subsidiary of the Strategic Planning Institute, Cambridge, Massachusetts.

6. The questionnaire also elicits information on a business's revenues, expenses, assets and liabilities. The time span covered is typically 3 to 4 years. This enables SPI to prepare a year-by-year business profile (as well as a composite profile), to detect breaks in historical trends and to observe changes in strategy, tactics and in the competitive climate.

7. See Robert D. Buzzell and Bradley T. Gale *The PIMS Principles: Linking Strategy to Performance,* Free Press, New York, 1987.

8. For example, one can isolate the strategic look-alikes of the business being profiled and treat their average ROI as the appropriate profitability benchmark. This is more meaningful than comparing the business's actual profitability to the average profitability of firms in its industry. The PIMS ROI equation is a second alternative. The coefficients in this model are determined from line-of-business data in the PIMS database.

9. It is never safe to presume that (1) managers share a vision of their business, or (2) they are alert to signals which challenge their strategic purpose. They may go to a management retreat once a year and review their business's progress and plans for the future. But this is not proof positive that they have forged a fresh and viable consensus.

CHAPTER 7

"MAKING THE NUMBER": HOW TO GUT A BUSINESS AND STILL BE A HERO[1]

> Don't focus on what senior managers say. Instead, watch how they move their feet.

Many critics of U.S. firms protest that their performances are based on one flawed consensus: *to produce attractive profits in the short term.* The following managerial statements echo this consensus:

> If we don't make a profit this month, there won't be a long term to worry about!

> Make money and you won't get fired, no matter how badly you miss your other targets (e.g., high service quality).

> Quality of service costs money—money that we'll need in order to make our numbers in the short term.

> Why should I invest in product quality? How can I possibly *make* more money by *spending* more money?

The critics consider this a *flawed* consensus for three reasons. First, managers who implement this viewpoint often rob their business's future in order to advance their own careers. Their consensus holds because every party gets rewarded. Therefore, no one protests. Second, this consensus elicits pious rhetoric at the top echelons. For example, senior managers launch advertising campaigns claiming that "Quality is Job 1." *But they fail to back up their noble words with appropriate changes in the established measures of business and personal performance.* This confuses and frustrates professionals in the middle echelons.

They do not know whether to believe the rhetoric in the business's strategic plan or the stark line items in its financial plan. Finally, the critics of a flawed consensus point out that pressure to make our "numbers" (i.e., our budget/plan) preempts discussions about profit *potential*. Managers do not know (and really don't care) whether their businesses *might have made* even higher profits.

Stockholders, pension funds, and boards of directors essentially have ignored these criticisms. They have not led or even supported the fight to curb the relentless pressure to "make the number this month." They watch silently as managers harvest a competitive position that has taken many years to establish.

This chapter describes an attempt of a modern Don Quixote in the marketing function (whom we shall call Tom Bascom) to change the mind-set of executives in his company and make room for the idea that investments in service quality were quite consistent with "making the number." We will refer to his firm as the "Service Company."

The Service Company serviced appliances manufactured by other businesses in the parent corporation. The demand for such services was fueled by the need to

- Repair or replace products that failed during the warranty period.
- Service "failed products" that were covered by a service contract taken out *after* the warranty expired.
- Service out-of-warranty products when their owners so requested.

Tom Bascom took over the responsibilities of the manager–marketing for service programs. He had been hired because his predecessor had spent millions of dollars on sales and advertising programs that failed to produce any positive results. Bascom received the customary orientation briefing: a tour of a representative regional service center and a mountain of descriptive material on service policies and financial results.

After Bascom dutifully worked his way through this material, his technical engineering background asserted itself. He drew a flowchart recording the sequence of events triggered by a service

EXHIBIT 7-1
Activities in a Regional Service Center

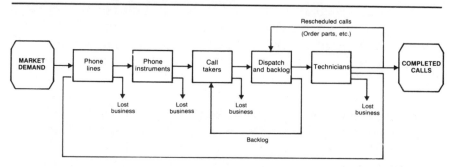

call (see Exhibit 7–1). The flowchart began with "market demand" and ended with "Completed calls" and showed five workstations. On the surface, the work appeared to be straightforward: answer the incoming calls, inform the customer when to expect a response, dispatch the technicians, fix the faulty appliances, and then bill the customers.

Service center managers instructed the people at these workstations to deal with service requests in the following order:

1. Customers with service contracts.
2. Owners of appliances still under warranty.
3. Other customers (i.e., those with failed appliances that were either out of warranty or not covered by a service contract).

At times, customers got a busy signal when they telephoned a center to request service. The groove in the prevailing mind-set read: Service Company *customers will keep calling until a receptionist answers*. But Bascom could find no data on

- The number of times a customer had to call before reaching a receptionist.
- How many customers were dissatisfied with the quality of service rendered by those who took their calls.
- How many customers became so discouraged or angry that they gave up on Service Company and called an independent repair shop.

Concerned by these information gaps, Bascom began to search for records that would provide clues to the effectiveness of a regional service center. He was shocked to find that:

- Service Company's gross revenue (in current dollars) had increased at a healthy rate for the last decade. But when he adjusted the data for price increases and territorial growth, *the trend in revenues was flat.*
- "Quality of service" was purported to be a top priority, but the current system did *not* focus on quality of service. Instead, it focused on profit—on "making the number."
- Managers had little knowledge of the determinants of service quality. More important, they believed that their compensation had nothing to do with quality of service.
- Managers fixed their gaze on three management tools: price, cost takeout, and head count control.[2] These had everything to do with "making the number."

Bascom's orientation period was over. The descriptive material that was supposed to ease him into his new job actually made him very uncomfortable. It convinced him that life in a service business was every bit as complex as life in a manufacturing business.

AN ATTEMPT TO FILL THE DATA GAPS

Engineers are nothing if not persistent. Undeterred, Bascom invested in videotaped focus group research and direct-mail surveys. These materials enabled him to define the customer queues (number of people waiting) that drove a customer's perception of service quality. With this information in hand, Bascom examined those policy statements and procedures already in effect which might affect the length of these customer queues. Were they mutually consistent? Which promoted and which degraded service quality? Bascom then compiled a long list of proposed changes in the way the typical service center dealt with its customers.

Bascom's next step was to determine how much it would cost

to provide more timely service and then to compare this cost with the resulting gain in customer satisfaction and revenue growth.

Each "what-if" question suggested two additional questions. Slowly but surely, Bascom realized that his new job had little to do with marketing work as it is conventionally defined. He could *not* meet his goals by designing a new merchandising program or sales approach. A change in the current pricing policy would not touch the heart of the company's problem. Instead, *he would have to step off marketing turf and deal with the whole product!* In most service businesses, dealing with the whole product means focusing on operations. And changes in operations invariably draw the attention of the manager–finance because these changes impact the bottom line.

The company's newest recruit had to convince managers with 30 years in Service Company that there was a serious flaw in the following logic: If we add personnel to enhance quality of service, our costs will rise and profits will drop—the number will be missed, but the manager will *not!*

Then a light went on. Bascom recalled how mathematical models had helped him in earlier assignments. Perhaps a simulation model would enable him to challenge the conventional wisdom of Service Company's top managers *in a subtle way*. After all, he had used simulation models to mimic production lines. Why not use them to mimic the activities of a regional service center? Certainly a model posed no market or expense risk, and it might provide objective, rational answers to his many what-if questions.

His boss warmed to the idea of simulating a service center, but he offered this piece of sage advice:

> Don't publicize what you are doing. Too many people around here would equate mathematical models with Buck Rogers adventures! However, first try to generate some top-side support for quality of service by briefing our bosses on the results of your recent market research.

Bascom gave the senior managers of service company such a briefing. He told them that an independent customer survey had found that the customer satisfaction rating for their *best* regional service center was in the low seventies.

His audience became very emotional when they heard this. They were unanimous in concluding that Bascom was mistaken and his data flawed.

One can understand why these managers were upset. They knew that their own internal records on quality of service showed customer satisfaction to be in the 90 percent range. Why should these veterans believe this newcomer or his data?

Bascom stood his ground and defended his survey results. He insisted that the company's internal quality-of-service measurement system had been compromised.

After two hours of heated discussion, the audience stopped attacking the data and the marketer's conclusion. They began addressing the real question: If our own system for monitoring quality of service has been compromised, what should we do about it? In the end, they decided to

1. Adopt a new standard for quality of service.
2. Design a new, headquarters-controlled system to monitor performance against the new quality standard.
3. Require the regional service centers to strive to meet the new standard.

Bascom left the meeting feeling exultant. He had been given responsibility for the new system. More important, he felt that his managers had expressed a strong commitment to service quality and would stand solidly behind programs to elevate the company's satisfaction rating. Now he could get on with model building.

BUILDING A MODEL OF A REGIONAL SERVICE CENTER

Bascom silently reviewed the idea of simulating a regional service center. He called on sophisticated modelers in the parent company and asked them if they would develop a model that would help regional managers decide when to add staff in order to meet their new quality-of-service goals. The model would show managers how to balance any increases in expenses and market demand.

To his astonishment, the members of this corporate group were quite unenthusiastic about his chances of success. Some of their complaints:

> Models like yours have never been built for this type of application.
>
> Your design is too ambitious.
>
> Training would be a nightmare—if indeed you could train any operator to use such a model.
>
> Even if you overcame all technical obstacles, you would never be authorized to implement your model.

Bascom responded, "You mean you fellows don't have the technical know-how to help me build such a model?" That innocent-sounding question got the intended response: The experts would lend their full support.

Soon the modeling experts were at a regional service center interviewing managers and employees known to be concerned with enhancing quality of service. Within a few hours, a shift in attitude occurred. The corporate modelers began to share Bascom's vision. They realized the model's potential payoff and embarked on an effort to design a user-friendly model.

Within six months, the modeling team had written 60 pages of Fortran code and checked out their model.[3] From regional center data pertaining to matters such as number and kind of employees, expected call load, and desired level of service quality, the model would generate a printout specifying the staffing requirements implicit in a designated level of service quality. If a center manager picked a leaner staffing level than was called for, the model would display the negative effect of his decision on revenue and income. In short, the model showed the manager the cost of "doing it *his* way."

The model established a link between *business goals* (e.g., service quality, revenue growth, and profitability) and staffing decisions *at the service center level*. Previously the managers had made such decisions instinctively. Now they had a device that could help them make those tough judgment calls on when to "spend money to make money."

VALIDATION OF THE MODEL

Now the central question was: How accurately did the new model reflect the service center's operations? Clearly managers with several years' experience in running a service center were the proper people to answer this question. Therefore, three service center managers from different parts of the country, one of whom had only a few months' experience in service center operations, were brought to headquarters to interact with the model. They were assured that they did not have to accept the model's output if it conflicted with their experiences or management styles. Also, they were free to run the model using their own assumptions.

The Initial Test Results

The first runs generated fresh evidence that the conventional wisdom in Service Company was *incorrect*. Faced with a downturn in market demand, managers did *not* have to cut costs in order to protect profits. In fact, Service Company could boost revenue and net income and increase market penetration *all at the same time*. The trick was to sustain a high level of service quality. These were startling conclusions.

All three managers participating in this test outperformed their budgets. The one with only a few months' experience as a service center manager achieved a 21 percent improvement in revenue and profits over his own plan by faithfully following the model's recommendations. His older, more experienced colleagues, however, were leery of the model's recommendations. They selected a staffing level midway between the one in their own plans and that recommended by the model. So much for experience!

At the end of the validation runs, the three managers recommended that all service center managers receive access to the model and be allowed to use it to fine-tune their staffing decisions.

USING A MODEL AS A CHANGE AGENT

The chief executive officer of Service Company was surprised by the managers' recommendation. He was even more startled when Bascom showed him that a pro forma analysis of company profits indicated that Service Company's profits would have jumped 12 to 20 percent had *all* service centers been run like the three represented in the experiment. This finding convinced the CEO to allow all service center managers to interact with the model.

Most of the managers were skeptical when they arrived at the computer laboratory. They were certain that with all their business experience, they would learn very little from the model.

At the first session, the instructor inquired whether any attendees were willing to wager a few dollars on the upcoming simulation. All quickly reached for their wallets and placed their bets. Then they were asked a series of what-if questions. One example was "What would happen to revenue, profits, productivity, backlog, quality of service, and lost business *if senior managers of Service Company actually acceded to your request for a larger advertising budget?*" Each manager recorded his answer, filled in the model input forms, and then ran the model.

Invariably the model's recommendations proved superior to the seat-of-the-pants judgments made by the attendees! While these managers knew a lot about running a service center, this simulation revealed secrets that had escaped their attention.

However, the designers of the training program had anticipated this outcome. Not wishing to embarrass anyone, they made certain that an attendee saw only the results *for his own service center*. They did not pit one attendee against the others. As the seminar progressed, the attendees began to talk with one another and share opinions about the best way to run a service center.

The instructional staff could not have been more pleased. Line managers in a service business not only were warming up to the advantages of simulation modeling—they were becoming converts![4]

The root of the initial opposition to the model was the service center managers' failure to recognize that they had only a slice of their served market. When their market turned downward, the reduced demand for service nevertheless was many times larger than their own revenue. If they developed the courage to invest in service quality, they would gain *at the expense of their competitors*. They would capture a larger share of a reduced market. In contrast, if they panicked and protected their "number" by slashing their service staff, the opposite would occur: They would drive many of their customers into the arms of independent service businesses.

When the seminars ended, Service Company held a dinner for the attendees. The CEO delivered the graduation address. For an hour and a half, he talked about the state of the business and the need for a higher level of service quality. He even extolled the virtues of the new simulation model. His closing took only three seconds: "Thank you for coming and giving up time with your families. I know you will do a good job when you get back—and remember, *watch your costs*."

A CULTURAL BLOCK

The CEO's closing words captured Service Company's flawed consensus and, in effect, terminated Bascom's valiant and innovative assault on the prevailing wisdom. While the words that fell from the CEO's lips during the first 90 minutes could just as well have been delivered by the speech writer, the three-second closing came from the CEO's heart. They revealed the groove in his mind, the direction he would take if a downturn in the service market occurred.

Tom Bascom missed this fact at the time. The truth dawned on him later when he heard that many service center managers were using the simulation model in a way he had not intended. These astute observers of the CEO's behavior realized that *all* of Service Company's top managers agreed with the CEO on the need to "make the number" and "cut costs." To them, *these were the eternal verities*. All of the inhabitants of the executive suite had absorbed these pearls of wisdom during their first years on the job. They had followed them for years and been rewarded with high-level managerial positions. They were not about to turn their backs on their "recipe for success" and embrace a conflicting recipe spawned by a simulation model. Since these individuals had the authority to approve or reject a service center budget, many ran the model *to discover the required staffing level implicit in their company's de facto harvest strategy.* They would "make their number." They would *not* fight City Hall.

To submit a budget that called for an increase in staff at their regional service centers at a time when industry sales were heading downward would, in the managers' view, expose them to ridicule. This was no way to qualify for promotion! These realists decided to ignore their senior managers' speeches on the importance of service quality. Instead, they watched how their bosses moved their feet and concluded that Service Company:

- Had no genuine interest in growing volume.
- Had no real commitment to service quality.
- Had no interest in maximizing profit.
- Was determined, instead, to make the number this month and every month.

One manager dared to challenge this conventional wisdom. When he took over as manager of the company's least profitable service center, he ran the model and followed its recommendations. Within a few months, his service center ranked with the best in the entire company.

Tom Bascom, the modern-day Don Quixote, had lost the war—he failed to change the mind-set of the executives at Service Company—but he gained the respect of one stalwart manager!

POSTSCRIPT

The marketing department vanished in a "let's-reduce-overhead" drive. The service center managers continued to make their number—by reducing staff. Quality of service plummeted. Independent service firms rushed in to capture customers frustrated by the deterioration in Service Company's service quality. The CEO retired with top honors and was replaced by another advocate of the conventional wisdom. Bascom got the message: He left.

This illustration is typical of the prevailing corporate culture. It is a warning to professionals in every type of business that

1. Managers cling tenaciously to what they learned early in their careers.
2. Managers are reluctant to adopt insights emerging from management tools that were unavailable during their own educational process.
3. Short-term profit performance inexorably crowds out other business goals in some corporate cultures.
4. It is extremely difficult to divert attention from business goals that mirror *past* performance.
5. It is hard to block a de facto harvest market share strategy that is obscured by mere lip service to sales growth and higher quality of service.
6. Managers at the middle echelon of a firm are loath to challenge the mind-sets of superiors who have decades of experience in their businesses and are only a few years from retirement.

Can a firm really mount an effective challenge to the mind-set of an entrenched management team such as Service Company's by dispatching two or three senior managers to a "management retread program" conducted by the faculty of a leading business school? The school-of-hard-knocks would answer: never in a thousand years.[5] If the climate at the *corporate* level is aligned to the same conventional wisdom, it will not support, much less lead, the requisite cultural change process. For this reason, few professionals will read Bascom's diary, pick up his broken lance, and charge the same windmill.

NOTES

1. The material for this chapter was provided by David Krabacker, based on his own experiences in a service business. Before assuming the presidency

of a startup business, he was a senior vice president of Exide Electronics, Inc.

2. Income and technician productivity (number of calls per person per day) were the drivers of a regional service operation.

3. Actually, "the model" became many models. An *input model* described the call-taking functions, complete with phone networks, lines, instruments, usage, buys, time-of-day information, and so on. A *scheduling model* was activated when a service call had to be run. It monitored backlog and promises to customers. An *output model* showed how many technicians would be needed, call productivity, probability of success, parts required, and so forth. All the models contained lost-business recorders that signaled when customers' needs were not being satisfied. After validating these separate models, the modelers linked them into one large staffing/quality-of-service model that mimicked the total business.

4. Business historians would point out that managers in manufacturing businesses had blazed this trail more than 25 years earlier.

5. The reasons are twofold. First, many of those who teach in these programs focus on their *specialty* rather than on how to attack the kind of problem that confronted the marketer. Second, the "graduates" of these programs tend to move on to other companies in a few years.

CHAPTER 8

TIME OUT! WE HAVE TO RESTRUCTURE THIS BUSINESS[1]

> The problems are confused, the solutions contradictory. Yesterday's truth is dead and tomorrow's has yet to be created. No valid synthesis is in view and each one of us holds only one small part of the truth.
>
> —Antoine de Saint-Exupery[2]

The medical profession has established trauma centers for patients who have had a catastrophic experience, such as being severely burned in a fire. Doctors and nurses in these centers help their patients function in spite of their newly acquired physical handicaps.

To whom do general managers turn when their world literally falls apart? What trauma center do they go to? What sympathetic "business physician" listens to them as they describe how their traditional markets have collapsed, their product technology has become obsolete, or a world-class competitor has begun to woo away their customers?

Such managers cannot search for business physicians in the Yellow Pages. Managers are supposed to be smart enough to figure out an appropriate response to any trauma that confronts their business. In reality, however, few general managers find it easy to restructure a business that has been buffeted by gale-force winds. Their chief strength—a broad knowledge of things *as they used to be*—actually *inhibits* their attempts to restructure their businesses. After dealing with nitty-gritty, tactical problems for decades, they cannot see the forest for the trees.

In other businesses, the challenge to reexamine organizational structure and operating procedures originates from another source: technology. The emergence of computers and sophisticated software has presented managers with two options:

- Do we automate/upgrade the information systems we have inherited from our predecessors?
- Do we do something far more fundamental, namely decide which operations deserve to be retained (as "core" or "essential" to our future opportunities) and which should be scuttled?

Typically, such business policy questions are "bucked upstairs." Decisions are made, but the decision makers leave no trail revealing which options they weighed and how they made their choices. For all we know, they tossed a coin, blindly followed their peers, or summoned their favorite consultants and delegated the decisions to them.

The illustration in this chapter advances a more methodical, disciplined approach to business policy questions. It deals with a team effort grounded on the scientific method. The two full-time members of this team were business researchers, but their efforts were buttressed by the team sponsor and scores of middle managers. This team produced an *operational* blueprint detailing how a particular defense business might redefine itself after it had lost a major production contract. We shall de-emphasize industry-specific material in order to highlight the process this team followed. The method described below can be applied to business traumas that are characteristic of nondefense industries (e.g., traumas brought on by deregulation, government edicts, or demographic shifts).

Readers who wish to study our illustration in greater detail will find extracts from this team's file in Appendix B. These excerpts exemplify what is meant by an *operational* business charter, strategy, and functional guidance.[3]

OUR MAJOR CUSTOMER HAS LEFT US!
WHAT DO WE DO NOW?

Years ago, GE had an aircraft accessory turbine department (AATD) that manufactured air-turbine-driven auxiliary power systems for large military aircraft.[4] One day, the U.S. Air Force unexpectedly terminated AATD's largest production contract.

The response to this business trauma was predictable. The manager–marketing was fired. The sales force set out in hot pursuit of every procurement contract. AATD's general manager lobbied the corporate office in the hope of getting a broader product scope. His manager–manufacturing called around to other GE businesses in an effort to locate subcontracts that would help him keep his own shop loaded.

These were laudable, energetic efforts to rebuild sales, but taken together they *did not* add up to a coherent diversification strategy. On the contrary, they led to functional stress. Instead of dealing with one prime contractor, AATD now had a dozen customers. Rather than monitoring one major contract, it had to keep track of many small contracts. Furthermore, each contract had an internal champion who incessantly clamored for more development funding. Each professional seemed to be working hard, but there was no consensus with respect to a turnaround strategy for AATD.

Solid Business Research

Herbert B. Slate, AATD's new manager–business planning, stepped forward with an unusual proposal. Instead of calling for cosmetic changes in business strategy, he asked his general manager to authorize a business research project aimed at developing an innovative response to AATD's business trauma.

Slate got his request. His first step was to obtain the support of a manager of a corporate-level business research component, OR&S Consulting Service. A corporate consultant, Adrian J. Grossman, was assigned to help Slate with his research project.

Before the end of the year, Slate and Grossman produced

- A new charter for AATD.
- A new business strategy.
- Specific guidelines for managers responsible for implementing the proposed strategy.

Following are the highlights of their work (see Appendix B for more detail).

• **Some technologies are more central than others.** All high-tech businesses draw upon product and process technologies that are in the public domain. Some have proprietary technologies. Slate and Grossman reserved the term *central technology* for a product technology that met the following criteria:

1. It was visible in a *sequence* of AATD products.
2. It *differentiated* AATD's products from those of its leading competitors.
3. It underlay hardware systems that had made a *significant* contribution to AATD's profits.

While AATD had considerable expertise in other technologies, only one—its ball piston technology—deserved the status of a central technology.

Surprisingly, there was little formal documentation on the ball piston technology in AATD's file. Few regarded this technology as a valuable business asset. No one justified engineering projects by asserting that they would "advance our central technology."

• **To remain competitive, high-tech businesses must advance their central technology(ies).** Digging into AATD's file, Slate and Grossman were able to document how AATD had advanced the state of the ball piston technology in order to win some procurement contracts. They could even identify the increment of knowledge behind each advance. Here was the element of continuity among contracts that the professionals had lacked before.

The Bottom Line

The findings from this business research project challenged the way AATD was pursuing defense contracts. Slate and Grossman maintained that AATD's first priority was to search for contracts that could be satisfied *without* advancing its ball piston technology. AATD should be alert for opportunities to exploit its "intellectual capital" (i.e., the *past* state of its central technology). Marketing should hunt for prime contractors who would accept products reflective of work that already had been done on the ball piston technology.

In short, AATD had an asset that its financial specialists had over-
looked. Marketing specialists were vigorously pursuing new busi-
ness, but their efforts were not focused. Managers in manufacturing
were not *taking pains to prevent AATD's expertise in the ball piston*
technology from leaking out via the vendor chain.

AATD's second priority was to find customers that desired
to enhance the performance characteristics of their hardware. In
such instances, Slate and Grossman argued, AATD must persuade these customers to *underwrite some or all of the research*
AATD had to do in order to generate systems capable of meeting
their elevated performance standards. Such customer funding
made these contracts doubly desirable. First, the contracts would
further differentiate AATD's product line from those of its competitors. Second, they would cement customers' interest in and
loyalty to AATD's central technology.

Did Anybody Do Anything?

AATD implemented many of the recommendations made by Slate
and Grossman.[5] One recommendation led to a drastic reduction
in the variety of the business's product line. The hardware that
was eliminated accounted for 35 percent of AATD's net sales
billed! For a business confronting a major profit drain, that was a
remarkable indicator of management's regard for the findings.

The manager–marketing used more colorful language to describe the strategy shift at AATD:

The competitive aerospace markets of recent years have taught us
that it is the easiest thing in the world to get into the proposal
business. . . . We determined that we are not going to dilute our
efforts ineffectively through the shotgun proposal technique.
Rather, we are going to concentrate on a few key areas where we
can be truly competitive.

One fundamental and key technology we have in AATD is our
myriad of detailed know-how in pumping fluids at high pressure
with ball pistons. This technology is something we can hang our
hats upon. We have renewed and revitalized our convictions that
the ball piston principle is a sound one and . . . represents better
customer values.[6]

Functional managers also acted on the research findings. For example, they

- Insisted that their engineers distinguish between "claims to have effected a technological advance" (e.g., those based on a theoretical analysis or working model) and a technological advance that had been *confirmed by a customer's order for hardware that reflected the advance.*
- Stopped engineers from "tinkering" with products that were in fact acceptable to the customer as they were.
- Examined contract proposals using the critical concepts fashioned by Slate and Grossman.[7]
- Selected vendors on the basis of *their* particular central technologies.

The last point needs amplification. AATD screened bids by its subcontractors in the hope of finding one that was as determined to advance its own central technology as AATD was to nurture its ball piston technology. They avoided vendors that were long on claims and short on tangible proof of their dedication to their underlying technologies.

The Keys to Success

A number of factors contributed to the success of this project.

The Quality of the Business Researchers.   Managers have been loath to permit operations researchers and management scientists to work on business policy issues. Why did Slate and Grossman get this opportunity? The first reason is that each had a managerial track record and 20 years of practical business experience. Second, Slate was AATD's business planner. By participating in this project, he was not stepping off his assigned turf.

Equally important, Slate and Grossman had complementary skills. Slate had been in the defense industry most of his working life. Grossman had a graduate degree from M.I.T., a thorough grounding in research methods, and several years' experience as a business planner. Both had prior exposure to ill-structured business problems. Both had studied the work of other GE researchers who had successfully tackled and solved poorly defined business problems. Last but by no means least, the personal chemistry between Slate and Grossman was excellent. They had known each other before the project, and each respected the other's abilities. Their mutual trust made it easy for them to criticize each other's work.

Team Sponsors.   John Heldack, AATD's manager–marketing, was the de facto sponsor of the project. He saw the need for this type of business research. He was willing to function as a sounding board for his two researchers. He took the time to listen to their progress reports and to counsel them with respect to implementation. He made no attempt to direct their investigation or to dictate their findings. As the policy implications became clearer, Heldack served as their advocate at AATD's topmost echelon.

Melvin L. Hurni, a corporate officer, helped to fund the project. Politically, his support was useful because his own record in business research was well known to AATD's senior managers.

Contrast this situation with the host of problems that confronted Bascom when he attempted to change the mind-set of the Service Company (Chapter 7). Indeed, he had help from a corporate modeling group, but he had to tackle the behavioral and political problems that surrounded his effort by himself.

Help from Middle Managers.   Physical scientists publish their findings. They invite scientists in other organizations to replicate their experiments and confirm their results. In contrast, business researchers who work on policy issues are prohibited from publishing their results. The data they use are either too sensitive or too proprietary to appear in a journal or book. Therefore, they must find critics *within their businesses*. Business researchers must validate their findings by asking a simple question: *Did any manager act on our results?*[8] Is there evidence that we have *actually changed people's behavior?* If the answer is no, their research must be scored as a failure.

Mixed Support from Senior Managers.   Many of AATD's functional managers—especially John Heldack, the manager–marketing—recognized the policy implications of Slate and Grossman's research. They changed their perspective as to what constituted a "central" and an "ancillary" technology. This was not true for the general manager. He had authorized the project, but he remained aloof from it, claiming that he had "too much on his plate." No doubt this manager was quite busy, but his lack of involvement was widely felt. The project would have proceeded much more quickly had he been willing to (1) help with problem definition, (2) share his ideas on how best to realign AATD, and (3) give some direct feedback on interim research results.

The above example illustrates two major points that are germane to all serious efforts to redefine a business that has experienced a sudden trauma:

1. Business research is practical and beneficial. Admittedly, most of the tools favored by the "average" operations researcher and management scientist are not readily directed at business policy issues. Nonetheless, the scientific method *is* generic. Professionals who are willing to tackle ill-defined business-level problems can help their managers respond to a business trauma. Their success will depend not on their mathematical skills but on their ability to *fashion new concepts,* to challenge the conventional wisdom, and to offer a new way of looking *inwardly* (at the business's expertise) and *outwardly* (to the market). Their challenge is to provide the structural members of a *strategic scaffolding.* While undoubtedly this is the responsibility of senior managers, there is abundant evidence that they need help whenever a trauma strikes.

2. Business research directed at policy issues will *not* be successful if managers remain aloof from the work. Involvement is not merely "nice"; it is essential, because much of the input the researcher needs is in the heads of senior managers. Equally important, senior managers will not comprehend the output of such research if they have failed to follow its month-by-month progress. And they will never rest their decisions on the basis of research that they neither understand nor have contributed to.

MANAGERS AND THE COMPUTER REVOLUTION

Opportunities as well as traumas may require business restructuring. The advent of electronic computers challenged managers to reexamine the nature of their businesses. Few, however, seized this opportunity.

Computers arrived on the business scene in the middle 1950s. Articles about their potential spewed forth in a steady stream. By the 1960s, competitive pressure and aggressive selling by IBM and the "seven dwarfs" produced a surge in the number of EDP centers. Unfortunately, the primary automation targets were labor-intensive, manual financial systems. The motto of the professionals who led the computer revolution was "With our new computer, we can eliminate many clerical positions and provide managers with more data faster and more cheaply."

Little was said about taking a second look at the design of the business. The specialists who designed and programmed computer-based systems thought they could dispense with inputs for senior managers. After all, they were mechanizing existing manual information systems.

When the last manual financial system was automated, the EDP component shifted its attention to the data processing requirements of two other functions: manufacturing and engineering. It was only during the late 1960s and early 1970s that managers of EDP components sensed a problem: They were not *true* members of the management team. All the discussion about management information systems (MIS) was mostly talk.

Simultaneously, managers who had invested in computers, software, and EDP talent became restive when their EDP expenditures reached or exceeded 10 percent of sales. They were forced to question promises made by the advocates of computer-based systems. In company after company, managers began to demand, "Where is all that profit potential you promised?"

Paul A. Strassmann has documented several reasons why senior managers were disappointed with the paybacks on their investments in electronic computers.[9] His findings are, oddly enough, highly relevant to AATD's attempt to restructure its business:

New applications of technology and the desire to acquire the latest equipment follow imitative patterns. Management should recognize these tendencies when embarking on information technology ventures. In the absence of strong leadership . . . little success can be expected. By leadership, I also mean a *strong sense of purpose and a vision* that the leader articulates *about how the results* to be obtained from the technology *relate to the purposes of the business.* If such leadership is lacking the whole point of the venture will become muddled: *relationships among the various participants in the effort will be full of conflict and will stimulate counterproductive behavior. The teamwork needed to deliver good results will be diffused into disjoint acts by isolated individuals.*[10] [Emphasis added]

* * * * *

Organization design, coordination with business strategy, and training to accept new approaches should have the highest priority. This approach contrasts with prevailing practices, which plan for the placement of technology first and only afterwards for organizational adaptation. . . . The choice of technology may thus be almost the last matter to be decided.[11]

* * * * *

The effectiveness of information work can be measured by the value added to the total output of the organization. In the electronic age, work design is reoriented toward maximizing the value added by people rather than by machines. Benefits to the society are maximized through cooperation in eliminating low-value-added jobs and in upgrading people into high-value-added jobs.[12]

The central issue remains: *How is this kind of transformation to be effected?* It is difficult to believe that senior managers are well prepared for or inclined to take on the task of overseeing the transition from low-value-added jobs to high-value-added ones. Have not U.S. managers abandoned many of their manufacturing businesses rather than restructuring them? In moving into the service sector, have they given any evidence of their ability to restructure or redesign their new businesses?

We believe that business restructuring demands a peculiar mix of talent that fortuitously was available to AATD:

- An in-depth knowledge of the business, its technologies, and its procedures.

- Training in the methodology underlying our progress in the physical sciences.

The bottom line remains: *Do managers want to deal with business traumas in an intellectual way?* If they elect to be thoughtful and purposeful in the wake of a trauma, they must be prepared to invest in the requisite (and rare) talent. They must also become personally involved in the work. Saint-Exupery had the right idea: "Each one of us holds only one small part of the truth."

Since managers ultimately have the primary responsibility for restructuring their businesses, they must not delegate this work to subordinates, to consultants, or to pundits on sabbatical from their universities. Rather, they must *lend a hand.*

NOTES

1. The material on business research at AATD, on which this chapter was based, was provided by Herbert B. Slate and Adrian J. Grossman.
2. Antoine de Saint Exupery, *Wartime Writings, 1939–1944* (San Diego: Harcourt Brace Jovanovich, 1986), p. 117.
3. Most business charters have a platitudinous tone, and few business strategies are accompanied by specific functional constraints or functional goals.
4. The product technology discussed in this example is still generating products for GE, although AATD no longer appears on the organization chart.
5. In contrast, many of the technical papers published in *Operations Research* and *Management Science* never had an impact on senior managers. This prompted the Institute of Management Sciences to publish a new journal, *Interfaces.*
6. A presentation by R. Sheehan to a GE audience.
7. We have referred to only two of these critical concepts ("central technology" and "state" of technology). A third was an "ancillary" technology. For a definition, see Appendix B. Many more concepts were developed.
8. Slate maintained a project diary that recorded his conversations with other managers with respect to this project and the actions they took. He called this his "utility log" and stored in it a great deal of departmental lore.
9. Paul A. Strassmann, *Information Payoff: The Transformation of Work in the Electronic Age,* (New York: Free Press, 1985), especially Chapter 9.
10. Ibid, pp. 46–47.
11. Ibid, pp. 200–201.
12. Ibid, p. 244.

CHAPTER 9

VENDORS: FOES
OR PARTNERS?

When I visit established suppliers, I want to spend only a few minutes talking about pricing; the rest of the time I want to devote to
delivery and quality issues.

—Gene Richter, vice president–purchasing,
Black & Decker[1]

U.S. firms traditionally have viewed their vendors as adversaries
rather than as teammates. This is particularly true in industries
where customers buy in large quantities. In exchange, customers
demand a share in the economies of scale their vendors realize.
When a vendor's plant is lightly loaded and filled with specialized
equipment, the purchasing firm will not hesitate to demand
concessions. If a supplier refuses to capitulate, it may discover
that its name has been removed from the buyer's list of approved
vendors. In this manner, vendor turnover becomes a tool for ap-
plying pressure to contractors and subcontractors.

In such an environment, many U.S. manufacturing firms
have avoided long-term relationships with their vendors. In fact,
they have perceived these ties as zero-sum relationships (i.e., for
me to win, you must lose).

At the opposite end of the spectrum are firms that change
vendors infrequently. Some even provide their suppliers with
tools, dies, and consultation services. For example, 3M teaches
its suppliers how to control product quality. In the aircraft industry, contractors that supply major subsystems help their primary
contractors develop orders for new aircraft.

The drawbacks of the traditional adversarial relationships
between original-equipment manufacturers and their vendors
have been widely recognized. For example,

- Foreign governments have insisted that U.S. manufacturers of aircraft engines permit local contractors to perform certain manufacturing/assembly operations.[2] This is collaboration *by government decree*. The goal: to reduce unemployment in the host country.
- The success of Japanese manufacturing firms in reducing their investments in both inventories and warehouse space (just-in-time inventory) is due in part to their close and harmonious relationships with their vendors.

Managers of U.S. firms have quickly perceived the advantages of just-in-time inventory. Those who have walked through Japanese plants have discovered that team play between suppliers and purchasing firms is considered *normal*. Not only do vendors ship high-quality parts and subassemblies; they also find ways to contribute to their customers' cost containment programs.

In contrast, while many U.S. businesses have adopted the concept of just-in-time inventory, they have been slow to elevate their vendors to the status of teammates.[3]

This chapter provides specific illustrations of team play between customers and their vendors:

Illustration	Key Point
Plant modernization	A multifunctional team orchestrates a major change in a production line while the plant remains in operation.
Weapon system acquisition	A government program to accelerate collaboration between builders and deployers of military weapon systems. The shared goal: affordable yet effective weapon systems.
Information system design	A sustained effort to obtain customer buy-in for a new, computer-based system that addresses the operational requirements of a state judiciary.
Linking business strategy and EDP planning	A comprehensive program to close the intellectual chasm between line managers and professionals in a corporate EDP component.

Each example illustrates a determined effort to improve the quality of team play among professionals in distinct organizational components.

GIVING AN OLD PLANT A FACELIFT[4]

Our first illustration of team play between customers and vendors comes from an integrated firm that set out to modernize a complex manufacturing process. There were scores of vendors involved. Some helped with equipment design. Others removed the old equipment to make room for the new.

This illustration focuses not on the content of the work performed by these vendors but on management's decision to employ a multifunctional team *to orchestrate vendors' inputs and minimize downtime of the facility*. The method management used is generic. It is applicable to any project that deals with large numbers of vendors regardless of whether they produce hardware, software, or services.

GE's Lighting Business Group faced a major management challenge when it decided to upgrade a glass plant that made bulbs for incandescent lamps. This decision required the removal of a giant ribbon bulb machine, designing and making a more modern substitute, and installing the new equipment in a plant in Lexington, Kentucky. The job of designing, testing, and manufacturing the new ribbon machine was assigned to a captive vendor— the Manufacturing Technology Programs Department (MTPD).[5]

The schedule for the modernization project was extremely tight, because finished-goods inventory did not provide an adequate buffer during the equipment changeover. Bulbs for incandescent lamps must be stored under carefully controlled conditions, and the amount of such storage space was very limited.

When work began in the mid-1980s, old-timers insisted that management had seriously underestimated the difficulty of modernizing the core of a complex production process while keeping the existing plant operating. The opportunities for error seemed innumerable. For example, design decisions that looked good on paper in MTPD's Cleveland office might not work in blue-grass country. Even if the new equipment arrived on schedule, the old ribbon machine had to be removed from the line. This entailed tearing up the flooring and building a new platform. Hordes of people from different organizations—engineers from MTPD, shop workers from Lexington, architects, outside contractors, and craftspeople from a dozen unions—would be milling about trying to complete their assignments. And the possibility that union members would get into a jurisdictional dispute was chilling.

GE's management conceded that the project was doomed if turf battles erupted. On the other hand, they insisted that the work could be completed on time if every professional functioned as a member of a closely knit team. To this end, GE appointed a new project manager, Dick Divoky. Then it created a multifunctional team to help Divoky anticipate and manage the interface problems endemic to projects that depend on inputs from a large number of organizations.[6]

To the astonishment of all the sidewalk superintendents, the project *was* completed within the assigned time frame and budget. The new equipment was started up at 5 P.M. on the first day. Within two hours, it was producing bulbs of commercial quality. It has remained in service since then.

Senior management was lavish in their praise of the project manager and his team. Dr. Gene Apple, vice president of the Lamp Components and Technical Products Division, told the team he could not remember another project of this complexity both meeting its deadline and staying within its budget.

Keys to Success

Four factors helped the professionals on the ribbon machine team coalesce their talents:

Selection of Action-Oriented Professionals. Each individual appointed to the team felt honored to have been chosen. Each was determined to meet his deadline and bring all of his talent and the resources of his component to bear on the project.

A Positive, Can-Do Attitude.   Team members became convinced that they could overcome any obstacle in their path. This was not the case at the outset, however. Relations between the professionals in the Lexington plant and those from MTPD were strained. For years, the Lexington plant had had to rely on MTPD for technical assistance. The time lag between their requests for help and MTPD's response irritated many plant managers. Therefore, when MTPD announced that it planned to power the new ribbon machine with four motors, the team members from the Lexington plant objected strenuously. They had a ribbon machine powered by four motors in their plant, and the level of glass breakage associated with this machine was excessively high.

The debate over the specifications for the new ribbon machine threatened to go on indefinitely. Headquarters personnel suggested a compromise: Use *two* motors to power the new equipment.

The corporate consultant on this multifunctional team opposed a compromise on the grounds that compromises disappoint *all* parties; there are no winners, only losers. Instead, he recommended that they design tests that would indicate whether or not MTPD's recommended design was optimal.

Such tests were defined and carried out. Unfortunately, each of the contending parties interpreted the test results as favoring its own position!

While the debate was in full force, the manager of shop operations at the Lexington plant arrived at a team meeting. He had been observing the operation of a ribbon machine that was powered by four motors. He reported that the hammer mechanism (which detached bulbs from the ribbon of molten glass) was striking the bulbs *twice* rather than once. If this was the case, the abnormal amount of glass breakage at the Lexington plant could *not* be blamed on the ribbon machine, since the hammer mechanism was actually part of the loader. More important, the debate over whether to use one or four motors to power the new ribbon machine would be moot.

A high-speed camera provided the hard evidence that both debating parties wanted. It proved that the hammer mechanism was the primary cause of glass breakage. Immediately the team authorized MTPD to build a ribbon machine with four motors.

From that day on, the professionals on the team began to think and act as *a single problem-solving unit*. When an engineer from Lexington identified a technical problem, the requisite talent in MTPD appeared within a few days and solved it! When the manager of shop operations took exception to one of MTPD's decisions, he got the following response: "What would *you* recommend, George?"

Before long, the professionals at the Lexington plant were convinced that this multifunctional team had provided them with an informal but effective communication link to their sister department. Past battles with MTPD were soon forgotten.

High-Quality Dialog within the Team. Both the project manager and the team's "process facilitator" paid close attention to the prevailing climate during team sessions. They saw to it that rank did not count. The only authority recognized was the authority of knowledge. If managers dropped into a team meeting, they were politely told: "Leave your managerial hats at the door." The younger team members were encouraged to speak up and challenge the views of their older colleagues.

This openness paid big dividends. As the project was winding down, an equipment designer discovered a way to boost the output of the ribbon machine being constructed for the Lexington plant. But he realized that a change in MTPD's original specifications might delay the installation date.

At the next team meeting, the designer asked if it made sense to implement his design change (and thereby boost output) even though this meant missing the project deadline.

All members of the team agreed that it would not be prudent to miss the deadline. They did, however, instruct the plant architects to modify the new factory layout to allow the department to make the design change at a future date without a serious interruption in work flow.

The designer concurred with this collective decision. Once again his colleagues had proven their openness to new ideas. He conceded the need for business goals to take precedence over equipment optimization.

Inputs from Artisans. Members of the ribbon machine team were equally open to suggestions from blue-collar workers. Therefore, no one was surprised to hear that three nonexempt workers involved in the project had interrupted their summer vacations and driven to the Lexington plant *at their own expense* just to see how "their" project was progressing. One was a welder. The project manager asked him, "Since you are here anyway, how would you like to do a little welding for us?" The welder's response given to this question epitomized the spirit of the entire team: "Half a second. I just happened to throw my work clothes and equipment in the trunk of my car."

Small wonder that Dick Divoky invited the artisans who had helped this team to be present when the new equipment went into production!

The above illustration is a warning not to identify multifunctional teams too closely with new-product development. Such teams are useful in any situation in which

- A project requires inputs from professionals with diverse backgrounds.
- These professionals come from different organizational components.
- The schedule is extremely tight.
- The performances of several businesses will suffer if any schedule slippage occurs.

WEAPON ACQUISITION: A JOINT EFFORT OF USERS AND PROVIDERS[7]

Defense contractors and the military services share many goals and therefore appreciate the importance of collaborating with each other during weapon system acquisition. The obstacles to team play, however, are far greater than those the ribbon machine team at GE faced. The challenges stem from these factors:

- Weapon systems are very complex and require years to develop, test, and install.
- The U.S. Congress provides funds via annual appropriations, a fact that works against multiyear contracts.
- The military services limit the terms of military assignments. Their acquisition specialists come and go.

When Dr. Robert Costello left General Motors and assumed the position of undersecretary of the Department of Defense in charge of weapon system acquisition for all military services, he had already recognized the value of team play between subcontractors (vendors) and their prime contractors (immediate customers). Both have an interest in eliminating non-value-added work. Both seek to avoid excessive overhead. General Motors' vendors would not have been surprised if GM's industrial engineers came to their plants and offered suggestions on how to make their production processes more efficient and their end products more reliable. Such cooperative efforts could have benefited both, because any cost reductions realized would be shared. Perhaps, Dr. Costello reasoned, the same type of team play might be encouraged during weapon system acquisition.

No one denies that weapon systems have cost far more than prime contractors and the government originally estimated. Repeated efforts have been made to improve the quality of these cost estimates, audit the performance of defense contractors, and teach military officers new techniques of program management.

Dr. Costello has encouraged U.S. military services and their defense contractors to reevaluate their roles in the acquisition process and improve their methods of doing business. Here are three primary opportunities for increased team play that can yield the desired improvements:

• **Has the military user defined a realistic and affordable set of military requirements?** Unrealistic requirements trigger expenditures by the contractor. The surest way to reduce the cost of a weapon system is to ensure that the ultimate user has not lost touch with reality.

The infamous $3,200 coffee maker is a case in point. The Air Force had called for a coffee-making device that would perform at high altitudes *and survive a crash of the aircraft*. The underlined phrase doubled the price. More important, no one wants to have to rummage through wreckage to salvage a coffee maker. The user had handed the contractor an unrealistic requirement.

Military weapon systems are complex enough without users calling for features and functions that they really do not need and/ or cannot afford. This is why people in the Pentagon are responding positively to Dr. Costello's injunction: Validate each user requirement.[8]

Timing is all important. At least 75 percent of the costs of a new weapon system are incurred early in the development cycle (e.g., during the "concept exploration" phase of development). This is the best time to search for major cost savings. This is when both contractors and acquisition officers must exercise the greatest diligence.[9]

• **Are we using the most efficient process to develop and produce the weapon system?** Ideally, contractors would inform the military's acquisition office each time they identified a way to improve their current production process so as to reduce costs. There are two ways to elicit such improvements:

1. Offer the contractors a percentage of the savings stemming from their proposals.
2. Send in a team of industrial engineers to analyze and critique the contractors' processes. In short, follow General Motors' example. Go to the contractors' plants and ferret out any non-value-added tasks. Do not settle for cost estimates based on data from an existing but less efficient process. (In the Pentagon, this kind of work is referred to as a "should-cost analysis.")

• **Are government contract regulations and directives part of the problem?** The thrust of this question is to identify unproductive overhead. For example, is the contractor required to make a quality assurance test that is repeated a few weeks later by government inspectors? Are unit costs high because the contract calls for a limited production run and ignores the savings achievable via contracts based on economic ordering quantities and economic production rates? Is the contractor required to generate reports that the government no longer needs?

Contractors would applaud the elimination of government rules and regulations which increase their overhead costs. The intent is *not* to suggest that all constraints be eliminated but to be sensitive to the root cause of contractor overhead. In the Pentagon, this is referred to as "streamlining" or tailoring government regulations to each acquisition effort.

To realize the full benefits of such improvements in weapon system acquisition, both the government and its contractors must become *proactive*. Contractors must be given a financial motive to step forward with a proposal to improve their production processes. The government must be open to evidence that its directives and regulations are spawning needless overhead. Dr. Costello calls this kind of initiative to reduce non-value-added work "could-cost analysis."

The key concepts behind this illustration apply to all types of businesses:

1. A win-win relationship between purchasers and vendors is ideal. Treat vendors like adversaries and they will behave like adversaries.
2. In a team environment, no member has a monopoly on creative thinking, particularly that focused on eliminating non-value-added work and unrealistic assumptions.

CUSTOMER BUY-IN: A CHALLENGE FOR SYSTEM DESIGNERS[10]

In our third illustration, the primary initiative for team building originated with a captive vendor: the director of the first information systems component to offer a state judiciary a computer-based system directed at its operational requirements. This director supervised a small group of system designers and programmers. His "customers" were judges, chief clerks, and administrative officers in various state agencies who dealt with the courts of one eastern state.

In the past, each court was a fiefdom. There were "superior" courts and even "supreme" courts, but the judges on these courts had no direct influence on the quality of information in courts other than their own.

The government agencies and law enforcement bodies that deal with the courts were equally fragmented and also determined to preserve their independence against real or imaginary threats. Since they get their resources one year at a time, their plans generally have a one-year time horizon. A high turnover rate at the upper echelons of these agencies makes it difficult to obtain support for any system project that will take more than one or two years to complete.

The weaknesses inherent in all manual information systems were becoming more apparent and irksome to judges and court administrators in the early 1970s. The data needed for court administration was slow to arrive and sometimes missing altogether. Errors were frequent. Data processing costs were high. Most important, the data came from many manual, stand-alone systems.

In the middle 1970s, a state court administrator appointed a unit to plan for automating the flow of information. He believed that computers could help the courts cope with their ever rising caseload.

The appointment of a new chief justice gave this administrator a chance to lobby for automation throughout the judicial system. He reminded the chief justice that judges and clerks were calling for better and more timely statistics (e.g., on their case backlog and on the average time required for completing a trial). Here was a golden opportunity to demonstrate that computers could handle a task more complex than payroll preparation.

The chief justice concurred and placed automation on the agenda of the very next meeting of judges and court administrators. At this meeting, the administrator described the advantages of an integrated, computer-based information system that would address the *operational* needs of *all* state courts *and* some of the requirements of those state agencies that interfaced with courts (e.g., the police and corrections departments). He assured his audience that computer-based systems would in no way diminish the quality of justice. The administrator closed with a request for permission to establish an EDP component and give it the task of delivering (1) an automated information system and (2) timely statistics that would help judges and clerks improve trial scheduling.

Gamblers clustered around Las Vegas would never have bet on a proposal of this nature. Even Fortune 500 companies were still designing computerized systems one at a time. Their EDP groups were committed to a simpler task: making first- and second-generation computer systems run faster and more efficiently.

For once, these observers were wrong. The administrator got authority to hire an EDP director and establish a small EDP staff.

The Game Plan for a Massive System Overhaul

The new director of information systems immediately set out to establish a partnership relationship with the users of his automated information system. Here were the five main steps in his partner-building process:

1. Define the Requirements. An automated information system entails more than mechanizing data collection and processing the existing manual operations. The EDP director wanted to capture, integrate, and process *all* the information that judges and clerks needed to operate their courts. To achieve this ambitious goal, he had to involve everyone who played a key role in data collection, processing, distribution, and, of course, decision making.

He initiated this involvement by asking the courts and agency heads to make staff available to work with his people. He wanted individuals who were familiar with court procedures and the current manual information systems.

2. Train the "Volunteers." Representatives of the various courts and agencies reported to the director's office ready to begin what they knew would be a long-term project. They had only a vague idea of the project's origins and goals, but they were eager to help.

The director welcomed these people as teammates. He called in his own staff and gave them a simple order: Teach our new friends the rudiments of systems design. Classes began immediately.

Participants in systems design must understand the basic steps in systems development in order to respond intelligently to questions from EDP professionals. This group, however, had to know more than the basics, because they were on temporary duty with the EDP component. Each time they returned to their office, they would be asked a lot questions about their "mysterious project." It was important that they have the knowledge base needed to give accurate answers and to stimulate some early enthusiasm for the end product. In a word, they were being readied for an ambassadorial role!

3. Explain the System Concept.   After his team had learned the basics, the director explained what the new project was all about:

> We are going to *capture operational data at its source, enter them in our computer,* and *convert them into the kind of information your bosses need in order to do their jobs properly.* This means we will be breaking new ground. There are lots of computerized systems that periodically produce information useful to courts and the agencies that deal with the courts (i.e., "batch" systems). We are going to do something much more challenging: develop the very first *on-line* judicial information system.[11] The other 49 states will be looking over our shoulders.

4. Make the First Flowchart.[12]   To make sure that his teammates had grasped the implications of this systems concept, the director put them to work flowcharting the collection, processing and circulation of data in the current manual systems. Who originated which data? How were they entered? To whom were they sent? How were they acted upon? His partners did not have all the answers, but they were willing to put down on paper what they did know.

5. Validate the Flowchart.   When the flowchart was completed, the director sent his partners back to their courts and agencies. They were to interrogate everyone who played a role in data origination, processing, and distribution. Specifically, they were to ensure that the project team was on the right track and capturing the kind of information that judges, administrators, and agency heads really needed. Their interviews pivoted around three simple questions:

- What tasks are you *supposed to be* performing?
- What tasks are you *in fact* performing?
- What tasks do you think you *should be* performing?

The director took these elaborate precautions because he headed the first EDP component to deal with his state's judicial system. He knew his clients were unfamiliar with computer-based systems. Some were skeptical about the project. Others feared that their jobs were in jeopardy. Misconceptions about computers and computer-based systems had to be identified and dealt with, or his ambitious dream would come to naught. The best way to deal with client misconceptions was to send his partners back to their courts or agencies and impress everyone they met with their discipline, rigor, and thoroughness. They were to make it clear that

1. *This project team was working* for them.
2. *No computer specialist was going to dictate what information they would get.*
3. *The relevant data were being captured and protected as they wended their way through the system.*

In a word, the users had to be continually reminded that they were coarchitects *of the new system and* teammates once removed. *At each step in the journey from manual systems to an integrated, computerized system, the users had to be sold and resold on* its value to them.

The director was not being altruistic. He realized that no clients would abandon a manual system that they had designed or maintained for decades and adopt a "mysterious" computer-based system unless they were certain that they would continue to get all the information they needed. He also knew that before clients would surrender data that other *people might find useful, they had to be shown that the new system had fully met their own requirements.*

Staggered Implementation

The new system did not go in all at once. Some of the courts and agencies tiptoed into the computer age; others moved ahead rapidly. This was nothing new to the director. He knew that every organization has its early adopters and late followers. He went out of his way to help his clients with requirements unrelated to the main project (e.g., word processing needs, updating old batch systems, etc.). It was all part of a grand plan: "Let's be helpful wherever we can." What might have seemed a diversion to an EDP professional was actually a means of getting a diverse group of users comfortable with a new breed of professionals.

In the early 1980s, implementation of the new system was well underway. Funding came more easily as module after module went on line. Today judges and court clerks find it hard to imagine how they got along without on-line information.[13]

The key concepts emerging from this illustration are highly relevant to the work of management consultants (whether internal or external consultants), business planners, and advocates of PERT/CPM planning systems. The basic message is one that professionals must learn and continually relearn:

> Your effectiveness lies in the hands of your "clients." Your ideas, however innovative and noble, will *not* take root in an organization without help from your clients. The term *client* is not synonymous with *senior manager*. It includes that host of people who have a hand in data collection, processing, and distribution. Even those in lowly positions may surprise you and sabotage your goals. To prevent this, you must involve your clients at every step of the implementation process. If you are sensitive to their needs and understand their perspectives, you will gain their cooperation and earn their support.

EDP SUPPORT FOR BUSINESS STRATEGY FROM A CAPTIVE VENDOR[14]

Our fourth illustration concerns a team-building method that can help firms with sizable EDP components link the operating plans of these components to business strategy. If these operating plans are not tightly coupled to business strategy, line businesses very likely will *not* deliver on their strategic goals. The cause of this shortfall lies not in the line of business but *in the back office*. The culprit? Poor communication between line managers and EDP managers.

For decades, firms were engulfed in a paper blizzard—the product of their manual information systems. Those who wished to step into the computer age could expect no remedy from an outside vendor. They had to buy the requisite hardware and software and then acquire the experts who could make them work.

The substitution of computer-based systems for manual systems was begun in large and medium-size firms. The executives who ordered this substitution gave little thought to the quality of team play between line managers and professionals in their EDP components. After all, they knew that their EDP staffs would be preoccupied with mechanizing existing, labor-intensive manual information systems (payroll, accounts payable, etc.). These systems supported the work of middle managers and clerical personnel but not senior managers.

Today, however, EDP components are viewed in a different light. At long last, senior managers have begun to take note of the "people in the back office." That raises an interesting question: *How do managers go about linking the efforts of their EDP professionals to their business strategies?*

This became an important question for a large, regional bank holding company. This firm had a sizable EDP component that we will refer to as "MIS." MIS's charter was to provide computer-based information systems, data processing services, and communication systems to its parent company, Midwest Corporation, and its many correspondent banks.

Suddenly MIS's mission became more complicated. The chief executive of Midwest Corporation made a fundamental change in his organizational structure. This shifted the focus from "banks" to "lines of business." The managers who were put in charge of these newly defined businesses formulated aggressive strategies, each of which entailed its own set of supporting tactics.

These developments caught MIS off guard. Most of its professionals had not been asked to participate in the development of the new business strategies. They had had little contact with the managers of these new businesses. Indeed, most of MIS's professionals would have laughed at the very thought of linking their work directly to business strategies.

The manager of MIS had a very good reason to get his staff to pay more attention to business strategies. He had been told that in the future the line managers who had been in the forefront of strategy development were now to establish MIS's priorities. Clearly it was important to rethink the function of MIS and how it related to the rest of Midwest Corporation.

The manager's first step was to convince his own staff of the necessity to effect a change in MIS's own mind-set. He met with his senior and middle managers and told them that it was vital for MIS to prepare a new operating plan. Here were his reasons:

- The parent corporation had restructured itself and the way it intended to market its services.
- MIS's former direct link to the presidents of individual banks had been severed. MIS now had to learn to work with a new set of immediate customers, namely the newly appointed business managers located in the corporate office.
- These line managers were expecting support from MIS in the form of new systems and new communication links. MIS would have to do a great deal of planning on its own just to be able to quote cost and delivery estimates.
- A recent survey had shown that many of MIS's professionals were uncertain about MIS's role in the new organization. They did more than hint that their own managers should provide them with a clearer sense of direction.
- MIS also had a cultural problem. Its former president had insisted that EDP work be centralized. He thought this was the only way that a bank holding company could guarantee data quality and preserve confidentiality. After operating under this mandate for decades, MIS's professionals had slipped into the habit of dictating to their captive clients. MIS, *not its clients,* set project priorities and system specifications. When the projects were completed, MIS informed its customers how much they had cost. Needless to say, some customers were displeased with this kind of behavior, and many were irate over the way EDP costs had escalated.

No one had to remind MIS's management team that their old operating plan reflected this obsolete mind-set and ignored the emergence of new and very aggressive outside vendors.

The staff meeting ended with an agreement that MIS would prepare a new operating plan and use it as a vehicle for (1) linking EDP work to business strategy and (2) challenging the inward focus of many members of MIS's staff and their tendency to sit back and wait for their customers to approach them.

The manager of MIS took the following steps to achieve these noble goals. He decided that . . .

1. *The new operating plan would be written in user-friendly language*. The manager would ban the use of technical terms that peppered conversations in the EDP community. Instead, he would employ the planning concepts and formats underlying the parent company's new planning system. (Here was an interesting role reversal: *Technical people would learn the terminology of line managers rather than demand that line managers learn the rudiments of the language used within the EDP component*.)
2. *The level of detail would be restricted*. Earlier MIS plans had exceeded 100 pages, but few customers ever thumbed through them. The new operating plan would run fewer than 50 pages.
3. *The links between MIS projects and business strategies would be prominently featured*. The new operating plan would cease to be a document for technicians. Instead, it would become a bridge between MIS and its internal customers. Systems designers and programmers would have to turn to other MIS documents for technical information bearing on their projects.
4. *MIS would seek early inputs from its clients*. MIS's customers would be given every opportunity to contribute to the new operating plan *while it was being developed*. For MIS, this was a first. Line managers and EDP professionals were finally speaking the same language and working together. The former we-they relationship had given way to team play.
5. *MIS's senior managers would write the new operating plan*. The head of MIS knew that cultural change had to

begin with himself and those who directly reported to him. Therefore, the members of his management policy committee would co-author the new plan. Then, and only then, would they be in a position to provide their professionals with convincing reasons to support MIS's cultural-change process.

6. *Provide for a "coach."* The manager of MIS arranged for outside consulting support for his various planning teams. At the same time, he made it clear that this consultant would *not* write the new operating plan but was there to serve as a catalyst and teacher.

7. *Make planning a top priority.* The new MIS plan was ready for release in less than three months.

MIS professionals realized that deregulation had produced a new crop of competitors ready and willing to serve the EDP needs of bankers. These competitors were offering new products and pricing them aggressively to establish a relationship with bank holding companies. Time was not an ally of MIS; some bankers within Midwest Corporation already were using outside vendors.

After MIS and its clients had reached agreement on the major projects to be undertaken during the next 18 months, MIS's manager had to share these decisions with all of his people. To do this, he used several standard communication methods. First, he addressed a large meeting attended by all of MIS's senior professionals. He explained MIS's new mission statement, its long-term objectives, and the goals that had to be met in the next 18 months. Then he asked his staff to address each key issue that was confronting MIS in the wake of the recent corporate changes and specify how MIS would respond to it.

> *It is not easy to turn a large EDP component into a team. One thing you should never do is distribute information about top management's decisions in a piecemeal fashion. Those who are not privy to this information will feel left out. Those who are in the know may have a few scraps of information, but they certainly do not have the background information they need to give their specialists guidance. For these reasons, it is prudent to begin the communication process with a general meeting.*

People at the middle and lower echelons of MIS got their first glimpse of the new operating plan a few days later. Since MIS's staff worked three shifts, some of these orientation sessions had to be held in the wee hours of the morning. Each session was chaired by a senior manager who directly addressed the main barriers to implementation.

> *Notice the shift from "general information" to "How does this new operating plan affect your work? What must we start doing? What must we stop doing?" Questions of this type are best fielded by the senior managers in charge of the various components.*

Finally, professionals from each work area sat down to discuss specific work programs. A facilitator from the corporate staff chaired these sessions to ensure that any criticisms about the quality of the information that flowed downward from the top echelons of MIS would surface. The transcripts of these meetings yield more than 800 suggestions.[15]

> *Only in sessions of this type can you discover whether or not the "Indians" are receiving, understanding, and acting on the information transmitted by the "chiefs." The decision to have a facilitator from outside MIS was a recognition of the need to have a free and open dialog.*

The central point in this illustration is that *planning is too important to be delegated to planners*. Professional planners can deliver a solid plan, but they cannot generate an actionable plan *if they work alone*. Too many managers have had to learn and relearn that planning is a *team* activity.

The methods MIS used to link their technically-oriented professionals to business managers can be adapted and applied to many organizations. Here are the essential points:

1. Managers of back-office components must provide their professionals with a context for their technical planning. This often means giving them some understanding of the strategic decisions of their captive clients.
2. Those who prepare technical plans should have a chance to cross-examine the authors of a business strategy. Only in face-to-face sessions will they come to appreciate the

link between their work and business strategy and functional tactics.

3. Operating plans must be prepared by those people who manage the work covered by those plans. Consultants can facilitate their work but ought not to attempt to do the managers' work for them.

4. Never mail the completed plan to subordinates. Instead, submit it to them in person. Then sit down with them and discuss its contents *in terms that are meaningful* to them.

5. Do *not* do all the talking. Try listening to the people who have the power to implement—or to sabotage— the plan. The ideal goal is: Let's regard this document as *our* plan. *Let's live by it!*

NOTES

1. Ernest Raia, article about the 1988 Medal of Professional Excellence, *Purchasing,* September 29, 1988, p. 76.

2. NATO countries have taken a similar bargaining stance when the issue is standardization of weapons and weapon systems.

3. Many firms have drastically reduced the number of vendors they deal with. This has led to greater stability in their relationships with their vendors and to more team play. See "Simpson Industries: Rate All Pertinent Factors but Don't Act Like Big Brother in the Rating Process," *Purchasing,* November 10, 1988, p. 73.

4. This section is based upon extended discussions with Dr. Jim Sarver, Tom Herlevi, and William D. Vinson.

5. This firm (GE) decided long ago that it might sustain a competitive advantage by making its own lamp-manufacturing equipment.

6. Teams of this type had functioned effectively elsewhere in the Lighting Business Group, particularly when the assigned task was complex and surrounded by much uncertainty.

7. This section draws on a paper by Bernard H. Rudwick, "Could Cost Analysis: What Is It? How Should It Be Done?" (Paper presented at the 22nd Annual DOD Cost Analysis Symposium, September 1988.) Prof. Rudwick critiqued the early versions of this chapter and offered many helpful suggestions.

8. And periodically revalidate the specifications of the system.

9. Since the Trident missile is in production, it is too late to question the specifications for missile accuracy. Most of the costs geared to the cur-

rent standards for accuracy have *already been incurred*. No savings would be realized if the military service opted for less accuracy at this late date.

10. This section draws heavily on information supplied by Filomena P. Lupo, currently engaged in systems analysis in Massachusetts.

11. Data from a batch system would have been two days old when it arrived on a judge's desk.

12. This EDP component pursued other projects in parallel. For example, programmers began structuring the database that this integrated system required. Other short-term projects were undertaken to shore up the client's faith in this large, long-term project. For example, word processing software enabled this team to greatly accelerate the publishing of judicial opinions.

13. Only a few years ago, clerks were often unaware of the locations of individuals who had been sentenced by their judges. For all they knew, the prisoner might be next door appearing before another judge!

14. This material is based on work done by Jack W. Kent and this author a few years ago. We acknowledge the insightful critique provided by David Van Lear.

15. Senior managers *did* address the communication problems identified in these sessions, but the nature of their response is not relevant to our main topic.

PART 3

INTERBUSINESS TEAM PLAY: THE IMPOSSIBLE DREAM

It is easier to design corporate hats than it is to get line managers to wear them.

Multibusiness firms pepper our landscape. They owe their origins to many things, including a desire to

- Achieve economies of scale.
- Hedge against oscillations in revenue.
- Realize paper profits.
- At times, enhance the ego of a chief executive.

Whatever the motive, multibusiness firms are firmly entrenched in our culture and will continue to play an important role in our economic affairs. For this reason, Part 3 shifts the spotlight from team play at the line-of-business level to team play at the upper echelons of multibusiness firms.

Team play among senior managers has drawn little serious attention, partly because senior executives have left no paper trails permitting outsiders to scrutinize their decisions or their interpersonal relationships. Outsiders are not allowed to traverse the "corridors of power" and observe the quality of team play there.[1]

Nonetheless, the emergence of world markets and world-class competitors has required U.S. firms to reassess the quality of team play at their topmost echelons. Their corporate staffs are now much smaller. Line managers now have a span of control four times greater than they did a decade ago. The scope and diversity of their portfolios have increased. In light of all these developments, a higher standard of performance is demanded of senior managers as well as a more determined effort to elicit collaboration

- Among line managers in charge of different business.
- Between line managers and corporate staff officers.
- Between managers of new businesses and managers of established businesses.
- Between corporate staff consultants and plant managers.
- Between line managers and their chief executive officers.

What kinds of topics demand this type of team play? Here is a brief sample:

1. How do we transfer expertise from one business to another?
2. How do we establish the profit potential of a contiguous market without making a major investment?
3. How do we accelerate the flow of technical information and managerial know-how within our portfolio?
4. How do we convince plant managers to support our new corporate policy?
5. How do we persuade regional sales managers to support a staff innovation that would add a new service to their product line?
6. How do we put our chief executive officer on the same wavelength as his or her line managers without an avalanche of financial and strategic data?
7. How does this portfolio manage clusters of interrelated businesses?

Part 3 does not offer a sermon on corporate synergy; rather, it reports on a number of explorations conducted by high-level managerial teams. These teams' experiences indicate that team play at the upper echelons of a multibusiness firm is both possible and fruitful.

NOTE

1. General Motors is a notable exception.

CHAPTER 10

TRANSFERRING EXPERTISE: A FORWARD PASS FROM ONE COMPONENT TO ANOTHER

An irresistible piece of business arithmetic:

$$1 + 1 = 3$$

There is something inherently appealing about a medical procedure that removes blood from a healthy person and transmits it to a sick person. Corporate executives would like someone to devise an analogous procedure that would enable them to transfer the expertise of one of their stronger businesses to a business in a weaker competitive position. They can literally taste the profit potential of such a transfusion.

Oddly enough, middle managers have not always welcomed business transfusions. For example, many years ago IBM sought to leverage the technical expertise that had helped it build a dominant position in the office products market. Surely other markets were open to products reflecting the same expertise.[1]

IBM identified two such markets: in-plant print shops and small news centers. Its talented engineers went into action. In short order, they developed the Selectric Composer and the Magnetic Tape/Selectric Composer. Both products reflected IBM's accumulated expertise in electric and electromechanical typewriters.

Unfortunately, these diversification moves by senior management did not succeed. For one thing, IBM's sales force never warmed up to either product innovation.[2] They were convinced that it would be easier, *and more profitable for them as individuals,* to concentrate on selling Selectrics to their traditional customers. Why invest a lot of time and effort to win over new customers when you have all you can do to keep up with orders from old customers?

No marketing textbook suggests that a sales force has the right to pass judgment on the strategic decisions of senior managers. Yet in this instance, IBM's sales force vetoed the move into print shops and news bureaus. There was no raucous debate, no unfavorable publicity. To discern this veto, one had to watch the way feet moved in IBM's sales offices.

In today's business climate, such a veto undoubtedly would be overridden. Firms now actively search for ways to

- Share customer relationships.
- Convert data in private files for the benefit of an entire business.
- Enter contiguous markets using existing back-office expertise.
- Revitalize moribund businesses by getting them to use modern management tools.
- Share technological know-how among businesses.
- Package and share managerial wisdom.

Your firm's success may turn on its ability to leverage expertise in areas other than those listed above. Nonetheless, you probably will find the team-building methods this chapter describes applicable to the managerial challenges facing your portfolio.

CUSTOMER SHARING: A DUTY OF ESTABLISHED BUSINESSES[3]

If you asked 100 line managers to list the strengths of their businesses, perhaps half would point with pride to their close relationships with their customers. But having such relationships is one thing; putting them at the service of managers of newly launched businesses is quite another.

Several years ago, the chief executive officer of a large regional bank set out to leverage the customer relationships of one of its oldest businesses, commercial banking. Specifically, he wanted one of his newest businesses—Corporate Finance—to capitalize on these relationships. Corporate Finance was to offer an abbreviated line of investment banking services to the same customers.[4] It would offer these customers counsel with respect to mergers and acquisitions, private placements, and evaluation of businesses and companies.

The CEO's primary goal was to develop additional fee income and deepen his bank's relationships with middle-market customers (i.e., customers with annual sales between $10 million and $50 million). His secondary goal was to provide specialized counsel to officers in other departments of the bank.

Since the CEO had no entrepreneurs in his talent pool and no specialists in investment banking, he went outside the bank to find a manager for his Corporate Finance unit. He imposed only one constraint on the new recruit: Avoid undue regulatory attention. In all other respects, the new manager was free to

- Select the customers who would make up his served market.
- Choose the types of services he would emphasize.
- Set prices consistent with market conditions.
- Decide when to place bids.
- Fix a level of compensation that would attract and hold a small staff of investment bankers.

Commercial banks rarely give managers of established banking businesses this degree of strategic latitude. This chief executive officer was perceptive enough to recognize that he could not obtain the desired spurt in fee income if he staffed this unit with commercial bankers. He had to dip into another talent pool. This CEO also realized he lacked the knowledge base to give the new people detailed instructions. He was content to specify their unit's objectives and goals and let them decide on tactics. If he linked their bonus to the performance of their particular business (rather than to that of the entire bank), the new unit would quickly close in on its long-term financial goals.

Climate Development

The manager of Corporate Finance knew that it would take a long time to meet his profitability goals if he and his colleagues had to

develop account relationships by themselves. Therefore, he preferred to obtain referrals from commercial lending officers. At the
same time, he realized that bankers talk a great deal about
"cross-selling" but rarely go out of their way to market the products of other businesses in their bank. Therefore, he and his colleagues would have to take the initiative and convince commercial
bankers to support their market entry.

The manager visited each commercial lender and pledged
that he and his colleagues would (1) deliver investment banking
services of the highest quality and (2) allow corporate lenders to
dominate each account relationship. Should a difference of opinion between a professional in Corporate Finance and a commercial banker arise, Corporate Finance would *not* appeal to a higher
authority in the bank or lobby for the CEO's support for its own
point of view.

Privately, the manager called on his staff to project the idea
that Corporate Finance's sole function was to support the work
of lending officers. To elicit this kind of behavior, however, he had
to create a subculture within the bank. Specifically, he was prepared to give each member of his team a voice in determining

- Which transactions to pursue.
- What fee to set.
- When and how to expand the volume of business.
- When to add staff.
- Whom to hire.[5]

When Corporate Finance won a client, the manager designated one of his staff members as "account manager" and made
him responsible for both the nature and the quality of the services
rendered. There was no day-to-day supervision of this account
manager's work.

At the end of each fiscal year, Corporate Finance distributed
its bonus pool in a novel fashion. The manager reviewed the performance of each of his professionals. He then called a staff meeting and announced his recommendation as to how much each
professional should receive. Next, he invited comments and proposed changes. If a staff member felt that his proposed bonus was
out of line with the magnitude of his contributions, he stated his
case to the group.

Note that in doing so, this individual placed himself in a zero-sum situation with his colleagues. For him to receive more, someone else in the unit would have to receive less.

After each staff member had reacted to the suggested distribution plan and the proposed amendments, the group took a vote. This vote reflected a trade-off between the group's desire to retain a colleague's services and the personal penalty one or more team members had to pay in order to accommodate the "plaintiff."

There was one final difference between the prevailing culture in the bank and that within Corporate Finance. The head of Corporate Finance functioned more as a technical leader than as a manager. His subordinates perceived him as *first among equals.* While they knew he had managerial and administrative duties, they treated these as secondary to his primary function: income-generating activities. Whenever a policy question arose, they expected their "leader" to discuss it with them *prior to taking any action.* If there were strong objections to a proposed policy, that policy was shelved.

These organizational practices and customs were deliberately chosen to motivate the professionals in Corporate Finance to create a viable business *in the shortest possible time.* They explain why the new unit broke even in its second year of operation.

To his credit, the manager did something far more specific and useful than describing the culture that prevailed in the bank. He had neither the time, the resources, nor the authority to challenge his bank's culture. He did have the authority and the motive to design and implement a separate culture that met his own team's needs.

Cultural Shock

Needless to say, some bankers questioned the latitude given to professionals on the Corporate Finance staff. They looked askance at the fact that salaries and bonuses in that business were much higher than those earned elsewhere in the bank.

The manager of Corporate Finance answered his critics in two ways. First, he invited them to apply for a transfer to his unit! Second, he pointed out that neither he nor his colleagues were considered candidates for promotion to executive positions within the bank. The higher salaries paid to professionals in Corporate Finance therefore served as compensation for this fact.

The success of Corporate Finance did not sit well with some customers of the commercial lenders, namely firms that competed against Corporate Finance *and lost*. They immediately phoned their commercial banker and berated him. Next, they cornered the bank's chief executive officer and berated him. The latter listened sympathetically and promised to "look into the matter." But when he returned to the office, he made no attempt to constrain his own investment bankers. He merely requested that they keep him informed when their aggressive marketing was likely to create a problem for certain customers of the bank.

A Crisis

Profit pressures throughout a firm can provoke a reassessment of a new business's organizational position. For several reasons, the Corporate Finance unit was relocated at a higher organizational level in the bank holding company. Within a year, there was a new team at the helm of the bank holding company. They had arrived with a corporate restructuring plan in their pockets.

When the professionals who had played a prominent role in establishing Corporate Finance realized that across-the-board budget cuts were in the offing, they concluded that the firm was about to renege on its commitment to investment banking services. When they looked about and found that many other firms were eager to acquire their expertise, they resigned.

The manager of Corporate Finance was unwilling to preside over a halfhearted entry into investment banking. He offered to resign as well. This prompted a reassessment of the corporate decisions that had incited the exodus from Corporate Finance. In the end, this bank holding company agreed to support the venture for three more years. The manager of Corporate Finance was given even more freedom of action and urged to rebuild his staff.

Up from the Ashes

Within a few months, Corporate Finance was back in business. Its manager was able to recruit an even stronger team and rebuild his unit's revenue stream. His product line remained the same: mergers and acquisitions, private placements, and both business and company evaluation.

The number of "deals" concluded increased year after year, and so did fee income. The manager expected applause but got little. Bankers raised their eyebrows when they learned about the size of the bonuses received by professionals within Corporate Finance. They asked themselves why Corporate Finance's professionals qualified for six-digit bonuses when the banks in the same portfolio were taking large write-offs and struggling to make even a minimal return on their assets.

In the end, once again Corporate Finance came under attack. It was repositioned at a lower organizational level. Soon thereafter, the new boss ordered the manager of Corporate Finance to realign his compensation plan.

This decision provoked a second exodus of personnel. Leading the way was the former manager of Corporate Finance.

The successes and failures of this entrepreneur and his team are relevant to any firm that launches a campaign to revitalize its portfolio. They highlight

1. The need to provide a distinct business culture for components that offer a line of services that the established businesses view as "outside the mainstream."
2. How vulnerable a fledgling business is to organizational shockwaves produced by a restructuring of the parent company.
3. The conflicts that emerge when new businesses outperform the "core" businesses within a portfolio.
4. The behavioral problems that arise from an income differential among businesses in the same portfolio.

In such situations, the chief executive officer must either (1) take an active, supportive role in new-business development and for a protracted period of time buffer his or her change agents from profit pressures that engulf older businesses in the portfolio or (2) locate the new service business far from his or her established businesses and forgo any attempt to leverage customer relations.

TURNING PRIVATE FILES INTO A
BUSINESS ASSET[6]

Financial services businesses, commercial enterprises, transportation firms, and newspaper publishers have shown that it is possible to capture and disseminate data in private files. To capitalize on these data, they have invested in elaborate communication networks that link their branch offices to the home office.

Many other firms have *not* tried to leverage the data their professionals accumulate and store in their "private" files. For example, salespersons decide what customer information to collect. Their bosses never think to inquire about the content of these files. There is no sustained effort to motivate salespersons to make their files available to other salespersons and certainly not to professionals in other functions. This is privileged information! No one expects chefs to share their recipes or reporters to reveal their sources. So why should a firm peer into the *personal* databases of their professionals who are in close contact with customers? Let the sales force be judged on the basis of the orders brought in, *not* on the quality or depth of the data they employ to identify attractive customers or conclude "deals."

Customers often challenge this tradition, particularly when two or three salespersons working off of two different customer rosters simultaneously and independently vie for their orders. Such disjointed marketing provokes the question, "Why don't you people get your act together?"

Managers should complain, but they do not. To make sound strategic and tactical decisions, they must have accurate profiles of their customers. Such profiles are hard to construct when key pieces of information are locked up in their subordinates' private files.

This poses two important questions bearing on team play among senior managers:

- How does one get data sequestered in *personal* databases into the new *business* database?
- How can one use such a business database?

A team of professionals at Chase Manhattan Bank, N.A. found answers to both these questions.

The Situation

When large corporate customers began to handle many of their own financing requirements, commercial banks stepped up marketing efforts directed at so-called affluent customers. At Chase, one effort directed at the target market was concentrated in a profit center called Personal Financial Services (PFS).

The senior vice president of corporate planning and development pointed out that there was no consensus as to

Where Chase's affluent customers resided (and migrated to).

What their buying patterns were.

Which of Chase's services they preferred and why.

What new services Chase should consider offering them.

How PFS should customize its approach to the most attractive segments of the affluent market.

Since every bank seemed to be gearing up to penetrate the affluent market, this vice president asserted that Chase needed a better profile of affluent customers. He then offered to provide one person with a marketing background and one management scientist to build a PFS customer database out of data presently residing in the private files of PFS lenders. Such a database would enable PFS to sharpen its understanding of

Customer behavior and preferences.

Influences on customers' purchasing decisions.

Differences among customers (life-style, uses of credit, product preferences, price sensitivity, etc.).

Customer demographics and customers' assets.

Customers' assessments of service quality.

Note that the case for a business database was not *made by lending officers who were in daily contact with affluent customers. These officers concentrated on the sale of particular financial products and services. Their interest ended when a customer obtained the funds he or she had applied for. How* and *where the customer spent those funds were of little concern to PFS lenders. Nor did these officers give much thought to the information requirements of Chase managers who had to chart a business strategy for PFS or define an effective marketing program. Those were someone else's job.*

The Data Base

PFS and Corporate Planning formed a team to develop an accurate profile of affluent customers. After studying a sample of the records maintained by lending officers, the team constructed a questionnaire that identified the data they needed to capture for a PFS database.

Data Collection. They selected a national sample of 2,000-plus private files and began the laborious task of extracting the desired data. They soon discovered that this could not be done via a form letter. In order to collect reliable data, the team had to "get down in the trenches" and help the respondents fill in the questionnaire and reconcile inconsistent answers.

> *This is one more example of the need to distinguish between data collection and data refinement/reconciliation. The quality standards for a business data base are much higher than those for a private data base. Also, one must clearly understand how data elements are linked together.*[7]

Constructing the PFS Business Data Base. Management scientists on the Corporate Planning staff structured a data base to hold the data from this national sample.

Market Segmentation. This Chase team then set out to take advantage of the market segments specified in the Claritas P$cycle Segmentation System.[8] They had no trouble aligning their sample data by these segments (e.g., the percent of Chase customers who were both "up-scale" and "retired"). They also found it instructive to study Chase's penetration of each of Claritas' segments.

> *Those who build private databases must be alert to opportunities to link up to databases built by other firms. Firms like DRI have taken great pains to simplify access to the data they have compiled from*

government and industry sources and to encourage their clients to adapt it to their unique needs.

The results of the team's analysis are proprietary. Suffice it to say that the patterns they found were highly relevant to

- New-product development.
- Advertising and promotional campaigns.
- The choice of regional offices.
- Determining PFS's competitive position by market segment.
- Discovering the ingredients of a differentiated strategy for this profitable business.

Had consultants at Corporate Planning done this marketing analysis "off-line" and then briefed PFS managers, the odds are that some information would have been lost. As it was, this analysis went forward as a team effort. There was no need for an intellectual hand-off and hence no risk of a fumble when information passed between Corporate Planning and PFS managers.

This team's experience is relevant to professionals working in other industries. It is a forceful reminder that

1. Those who maintain personal data often understate the value of "their" data to others.
2. It is the task of managers to

    Define the essential elements of information.
    Reward those who capture such information.
    Emphasize that the chain linking data collection, validation and storage, analysis and interpretation, and dissemination *is no stronger than its weakest link.*

More and more firms are discovering the value of business databases built from transaction data and data in "private" files.[9] For example, companies that issue credit cards now classify their customers by buying pattern. They feed this information to other profit centers interested in (1) early detection of card theft (merchants are warned when a card is being used for a purchase ten times larger than usual) and (2) approaching customers who are prime candidates for high-value services (vacations, insurance policies, etc.) or deluxe merchandise. Each of the above examples reflects an interest in leveraging data. Each requires a *team* effort.

Retail stores have been among the first businesses to energize data obtained at the point of sale. They have converted their cash registers into computer terminals. In this manner, customer's purchase decisions can be instantly fed into the inventory control systems maintained by other profit centers.

Retailers have also demonstrated that information obtained in one marketing area can be of value to stores in other marketing areas. For example, if certain styles proved to be popular with customers in Florida, Arizona, and California during the winter months, their buyers ordered equivalent clothing for their New England stores to sell in April, May, and June.

If and when the factory or office of the future becomes a reality, professionals in different functions and profit centers will routinely share databases.[10] This will give rise to higher-quality team play and provide contributors to joint projects with more timely information.[11] Software firms already are using networks to link programmers assigned to work on different facets of large projects.

GETTING BROAD-BASED SUPPORT FOR
A PROBE OF A CONTIGUOUS MARKET

Executives are understandably cautious about proposals to diversify into a new market. To minimize their risks, they give preference to contiguous markets because

- The image of their firm may have penetrated these adjacent markets.
- Customers in adjacent markets often have requirements that are similar to those of existing customers.
- They can probably utilize many of their current resources.

An officer of a regional bank with an excellent reputation for handling the foreign exchange requirements of large pension funds decided to test the profit potential of a contiguous market, namely one made up of corporations with plants, subsidiaries, and/or vendors located outside the United States. Some of these corporations were being served by large money center banks. Others had only recently recognized the advantages of protecting themselves from oscillations in exchange rates.

The officer recruited a salesperson who had been dealing with top executives of industrial firms. He asked her to propose a way to attract and service corporate accounts. But that was the extent of his guidance.

In a few weeks, the salesperson was back in his office with this message: "I can do it, but I can't do it alone. I'll need the support of our traders and our back office."[12] Here were the main planks in her marketing plan:

1. I will personally track down the attractive corporate accounts.
2. Occasionally I will ask a trader to join me on a sales call. After all, the "product" I intend to sell rests on the expertise of our traders. Their knowledge of specific currencies and of the forces that shape exchange rates is one of our competitive advantages. It is more effective to *exhibit* this expertise than to have me describe it.
3. Quality of service is key to this market probe. Some of the CFOs and corporate treasurers I intend to pursue will have had little experience in international trade. They will require education, handholding, and perhaps some assistance in framing their requests to traders. For this reason, the individuals who handle their telephone calls must be understanding and empathetic. I have been told that in past years, some CFOs have called our trading desk and been told by a trader, "Call back after three o'clock and I'll have time to help you."[13] I recognize the pressures on our traders, but our targeted clients do not. We simply have to bend over backwards to give them courteous, helpful, and effective treatment. No exceptions, ever!
4. You can help me realize this goal by giving our traders a clear incentive to service small corporate accounts in addition to pension funds. Why not broaden their job descriptions and alter the way you measure their per-

formance? That is the most effective way to arouse their interest in customers whom in former years they were told to ignore.

5. I will personally take on the task of helping those corporate officers who are brand new to currency trading. They need TLC, and I will provide it.

6. It goes without saying that the paperwork that a trade generates must be handled with the same efficiency now given to paperwork triggered by a trade for a large pension fund. We certainly do not want a two-tiered back-office system. My clients ought to get the same first-class service that our back-office people now give pension fund managers.

The officer responded, "A solid plan. I'll see that you get the support you asked for. I know you can pull it off. Get cracking!"

Here are the team aspects of this illustration:

- Team membership: *The executive in effect created an informal team consisting of the new salesperson, his traders, and people in the back office.*
- The carrot: *Traders were* not *given a sermon on the value of team play. Instead, their boss's boss informed them that in the future their bonuses would depend on the support they gave to the bank's newest salesperson. If corporate accounts were attracted and well serviced, their bonuses would go up. They would win if the new salesperson won. That kind of communication is crystal clear.*
- Changes in job descriptions: *Traders were also told that they now had to assist with corporate account development and then help service those accounts.*[14]

To old-timers in a very conservative bank, these changes were viewed as shocking, if not revolutionary!

There are two generic concepts in this illustration:

1. *Salespersons with managerial responsibilities.* There are literally millions of salespersons who are thrust into new jobs with a large managerial component: market development. Overnight they pass from being measured on *their solo performances* to being evaluated on the basis of *team* performances. Their teams, however, include professionals who have other work to do. Furthermore, the organization chart says that they will continue to report *to another manager rather than to the leaders of the market development teams.*

2. *Managing from below.* The textbooks say that orders flow downward from the top of the organizational pyramid. But sometimes the flow goes the other way. In this example, the *new salesperson,* not the strategy's original author, drew up the marketing plan. The same type of challenge is there for the asking in every type of business. All that is required is that salespersons

- Be proactive and aggressive.
- Accept some of the responsibilities that textbooks usually assign to managers.
- Be willing to mobilize talent that does *not* report to them.

These skills are in great demand. Unfortunately, they receive little emphasis in our leading business schools.

INFUSING NEW TECHNIQUES INTO A BACKWARD BUSINESS

Knowledge is unevenly distributed in a multibusiness firm. Some profit center managers are quick to capitalize on new management tools. At the opposite end of the spectrum one finds managers who have retired while on the job. They make no effort to upgrade the tools and skill levels in their plants. Their customers are quick to detect this and register their complaints at the corporate office.

When these complaints grow in number and are buttressed by threats ("If you don't take immediate remedial action, we will drop your firm from our vendor list!"), corporate executives must respond. They have four options:

- Demand an instant improvement in current operating procedures.

- Send in a team from another organizational component to point out where improvements are needed and how to achieve them.
- Try to sell the business.
- Abandon the business.

State governments that are actively trying to reduce their unemployment rate encourage firms to select the second option.[15] One Middle Atlantic state went so far as to help finance this option's execution. Specifically, a state agency subsidized an educational program that introduced modern process control techniques to two businesses within its jurisdiction.

Corporate management accepted this offer. It hired a consulting firm—Stochos, Inc.—to design and provide the requisite training in both plants. Stochos's program was built around three important concepts:

1. Quality is *everybody's* responsibility.
2. Even complex statistical concepts can become operational in the hands of managers and workers if

   They are carefully "packaged."
   The concepts are illustrated using *data from the plant*.
   The concepts are presented to *both* managers and production workers.
   The instructor speaks the language of shop people and is committed to making them more effective.
3. Management promises not to overreact to any *future* quality problems or try to place all blame for these problems on workers.

Donald S. Holmes designed and gave all of the instruction in statistical process control. He asked for (1) visible support from the corporate office (the CEO and his consultant on product quality and process control); (2) participation by the plant managers; and (3) access to the entire production force (and no reprisals if they acted according to their new knowledge of process control).

Here were the basic steps in Holmes's acculturation program:

1. An orientation for all plant employees. Holmes launched his program with a talk to *all* managers and employees. He spoke for two hours on two topics: product quality and process control. In the course of this talk, he listed reasons why people in this plant should take both topics seriously. He closed with a brief explanation of a process quality chart.

When outsiders appear on the scene, they must be introduced and their sponsor(s) identified. All targets of the change process should be in this audience irrespective of their level and current commitment to change.

2. A call for volunteers. Holmes then let it be known that he was looking for "a few good men" to spend eight hours with him studying the quality problems that plagued their plant. He also promised to show them the roots of these problems. He got his volunteers and met with them and their managers.

Job one was to rebuild worker morale. The plant had knowingly shipped products that failed to meet customer specifications. Naturally, workers were upset by this cavalier attitude toward quality control. They were also concerned about their job security and a possible plant closing prior to their retirement dates.

Holmes gave the workers a reason to believe that their production processes could be brought under control. He advised them not on process control techniques but solutions to particular problems. The volunteers soon began to appreciate their consultant's 30 years of practical experience and his ability to show them how to solve any of their process control problems.

3. Recruitment of worker-management teams. Holmes was now ready for module 3: special help for six worker-management teams who would tackle *particular* process control problems in the plant. All the workers on these teams were volunteers. They agreed to meet with their consultant once a week.

One of Holmes's goals was to demonstrate, *using plant data,* the existence of tools with which to solve the process control problems. He wanted his teammates to watch product quality improve as the team applied these tools to their own production data.

Another of Holmes's goals was to persuade his new teammates to record instances in which they thought their process had gone "out of control." Many had stopped making entries in their quality records, because their managers ignored the fact that products were out of control.

4. An effort to prevent managers from scuttling the change process. The fourth plank in Holmes's change program confirms the value of outsiders as change agents. After the quality teams had begun to address process issues, two new quality problems arose:

Problem 1: Quality dropped. Management reacted predictably: "Find the worker responsible and fire him!"

Holmes intervened. He reminded the managers that they had promised that if quality went out of control at some future date, they would allow him to study the quality records and isolate the reason. The managers granted his request, and he was able to convince them that there had been no worker negligence. No worker was fired.

Problem 2: A shipment valued at $150,000 was returned by a customer with a note saying "quality unacceptable." The managers in the plant were shaken by this and began to search for the workers who had last touched that shipment.

Once again Holmes intervened, claiming that the managers had promised that he would be allowed to study the quality control records. These records included a note written by a blue-collar worker: "I wouldn't ship this lot to my worst enemy!"

Management admitted their culpability. The blue-collar members of Holmes's teams began to believe in process control. At the same time, they were concerned that only 25 percent of the work force was learning what they were.

Holmes assured them that the rest of the work force eventually would come around to their way of thinking about process control. While not on the quality team, those workers surely were watching.

Today this plant ranks among the best in the firm in process control.

Think of the many businesses in middle America that need an equivalent intellectual infusion. The steps for imbedding new concepts and new management tools are clear:

1. Find a gifted and dedicated teacher who is problem rather than technique oriented.
2. Initiate a change process with this outsider's help.
3. Show corporate support for local quality enhancement efforts.
4. Don't talk about potential quality problems. *Solve the ones at hand.*
5. Train a team of workers and managers to use the same tools. This may require four to eight weeks of on-the-job consulting and training. It always requires a lot of patience and a deep commitment to workers who agree to help change the mind-set of their business.
6. Take measures to protect workers who use the new concepts and tools from reprisals by local managers when or if their process goes out of control.

MOVING KNOW-HOW AROUND WITHIN A PORTFOLIO

Every chief executive officer yearns to see his or her professionals who work thousands of miles apart share information. The personal contact may take the form of brief questions:

Have you ever encountered a problem like . . . ?

Do you know where I can get information on . . . ?

Can you refer me to someone who is an expert on . . . ?

Do you know anyone who has had firsthand experience with equipment that . . . ?

The classic ways to handle such inquiries are

- Establish an information clearinghouse or reference library.
- Arrange a conference or seminar for those interested in a particular topic (e.g., robotics, software that simplifies simulations of manufacturing processes).
- Form user groups (The first such groups targeted the needs of managers who used a particular type of computer hardware or software.)

Akio Morita has written about Sony's annual "technology fair" and monthly R&D meetings. The latter are attended by all top executives and division heads.[16]

> We will have to try to put all of the great engineering power of our company together and use that as one system. . . . Knowing how to make the best use of your engineers will be the test of whether a company will succeed in the coming age. . . . Technological management will be the key to success for companies anywhere in the world in the coming years.[17]

It is regrettable that U.S. executives have spent so much time calling for a "level playing field" rather than imitating Sony's steps to foster team play among engineers.

Firms that cannot afford to sustain their own technological networks do the next best thing: They attend meetings of professional societies or go to symposia organized by consulting firms. Others are lucky enough to find clients or vendors who will take the initiative and disseminate information that bears on a topic of interest.[18]

Often a corporate staff component takes the lead in exchanging technical information. For example, FMC created a corporate component to advocate quality enhancement. The manager of this component convened a quality conference in Tucson, Arizona, where he made every effort to applaud existing seminal quality enhancement projects; share information on these projects' payoffs; and emphasize that hourly workers were ready, willing, and able to take on some of the tasks traditionally reserved for specialists in quality control units.

Without strong corporate support, technology sharing is difficult to achieve or sustain. The Bright Stik team was able to leverage the technological know-how of the Major Appliance Group with respect to ultrasonic welding and molding of plastic parts because of GE's long tradition of favoring interbusiness dialog.[19] There was in fact a corporate infrastructure that helped GE businesses locate relevant pockets of technical expertise and facilitate information sharing.

Smaller firms that wish to avoid "reinventing the wheel" turn to consulting firms when they want access to state-of-the-art technology. Thus, they buy into an informal technology network.

The ultimate form of technology sharing was described in Chapter 8. There we saw an illustration of different lines of business in the same portfolio exploiting one product technology (the ball-piston technology).

Imagine the value of an early warning system that would enable R&D professionals and engineers to monitor changes in "technology share," that is, the relative standing of each of the major technologies underlying shipments in a given industry.[20] This tool would emerge quickly if the federal government formulated an explicit industrial policy.

PACKAGING AND SHARING MANAGERIAL WISDOM

For more than a decade, Fred Borch, the former CEO of General Electric, subsidized a research project aimed at identifying and codifying the "laws of the marketplace." He asked himself, "If Macy's can learn from Gimbel's, why can't I alert my newly appointed general managers to management decisions that are likely to (1) enhance business profitability or (2) lead their business straight into profit trouble?

Borch's corporate research team uncovered stable patterns in line-of-business data furnished by GE's departments.[21] These data were stored in a corporate database. In-house consultants stood by to help general managers capitalize on the insights of GE's most successful businesses and to prevent the strategic boners typical of imprudent or inexperienced managers. In 1972, this methodology was made available to other firms.[22]

SUMMARY

The message of this chapter can be summed up as follows: U.S. firms are *not* farming as well as they might and have not made the kind of comprehensive, sustained effort to leverage the skills and knowledge that the professionals in their various profit centers possess. Managers have overlooked the fact that the early proponents of decentralization also invested in a corporate infrastructure that would facilitate exchange of information among profit center managers.

The emergence of a world market demands a firm commitment to asset sharing. The word *asset* must be broadened to include

1. Customer relationships.
2. Private data.
3. Back offices.
4. Managerial tools and techniques.
5. Technical knowledge.
6. Managerial wisdom.

Without such a commitment, the term *corporate synergy* will remain an empty buzzword. Fortunately, many of the tools firms need to encourage interbusiness team play have been developed *in this country* and are available for cloning. All it takes is a level of effort equivalent to that which went into establishing quality circles.

NOTES

1. This illustration was provided by William Robert Stone.
2. There were other forces at work. For example, customers grew nervous when they saw that IBM had no follow-on products.
3. This illustration was provided by Walter Maurer.
4. The Glass-Steagall Act prevents banks from offering a full line of investment banking services.
5. Note the similarity to the culture that prevails in many large law firms.
6. This section is based upon an interview with Gerald Weiss, a senior vice president of Chase Manhattan Bank, N.A.
7. Data can be dropped into a private file without attending to how it relates to existing or future data.
8. The Claritas P$cycle System is marketed by Jonathan Robbin. The segments were defined with the help of government data.
9. They are also purchasing access to databases built by others (e.g., those sold by Data Resources, Inc.).
10. In the 1970s, GE made an effort to compile and sell "manufacturing lore" accumulated by hundreds of plants.
11. Personal databases often contain obsolete data.
12. Particularly, the professionals who follow up on a particular trade and make certain that all of the paperwork is done and done right.

13. Traders operate under great pressure when the exchanges are open. They watch many currencies, track other traders, and make risky decisions within a very short time frame.
14. She took care to schedule joint marketing calls in a manner that accommodated "her" traders' primary responsibilities (interbank trading and trading for pension funds).
15. They have an explicit industrial policy aimed at keeping plants in their territory open and turning out competitive products.
16. Akio Morita, Edwin M. Reingold, and Mitsuko Shimomura, *Made in Japan: Morita and Sony* (New York: E. P. Dutton, 1986), p. 246.
17. *Ibid.*
18. 3M invites its vendors to courses on product quality. GE has allowed Capital Resources Management, Inc., to market its educational software on cash management.
19. See Chapter 3.
20. The terminology was suggested by Dr. Paul Nowill. A step in this direction has been taken by some industries. For example, tire companies began to collect and distribute industry data about the inroads made by radial tires.
21. This team was headed by Dr. Sidney Schoeffler.
22. Initially via a business research project—the PIMS Project—at the Harvard Business School, later via the Strategic Planning Institute, Cambridge, Massachusetts.

CHAPTER 11

THE ODD COUPLE:
LINE AND STAFF

The two greatest lies ever told:

STAFF CONSULTANT: We have come here only to be helpful.

LINE MANAGER: We are so glad you came. Stay as long as you like.

Tension between "line" and "staff" is hardly a new phenomenon. Line managers talk as though they preferred that their corporate staffs be liquidated. Why? Because if this were done, there would be no more assessments to cover the cost of staff programs!

Many chief executive officers tolerate this kind of tension because they acknowledge the validity of pooling certain work. For example, pooled purchasing leads to volume discounts; research is pooled because research talent is in short supply.

This chapter opens with two situations in which staff people were able to persuade line managers to respond positively to their programs. The steps they took to elicit high-quality team play worked. The chapter closes with a look at a segment of corporate life that needs more team play: capital appropriations.

A TEAM EFFORT TO PUT TEETH INTO
A CORPORATE QUALITY POLICY

Firms that manufacture paperboard and packaging materials have capital-intensive production processes. Market growth is slow, and it is hard for a firm to convince customers that its boxes differ significantly from those offered by its competitors. In this type of industry environment, one does not expect to find many businesses with above-normal levels of profitability.

We look at one such firm that had more than a score of plants scattered throughout the United States.[1] It had a broad product line that it sold to more than 10,000 customers engaged in the manufacture of durable and nondurable goods. We will refer to this firm as "Box Company."

The chief executive officer of the Box Company asked his corporate marketing staff for ideas on how to improve the firm's profit performance. Three professionals within corporate marketing had learned that the PIMS research team had uncovered a strong, positive link between business profitability and product/service quality.[2] Intrigued by this finding, they soon convinced themselves that a corporatewide quality enhancement program might enable their firm to exceed the industry's (low) profit norm.

Their boss, the senior vice president of marketing, agreed that such a program might be helpful provided the company could obtain reliable plant data on the level of relative quality.[3]

The chief executive officer was willing to sponsor a corporate quality enhancement program and even to fund a market research study of his customers. Corporate marketing was handed the job of designing a questionnaire on relative quality, selecting a market research firm to conduct the interviews, and orchestrating the implementation of the market research findings.[4]

Corporate Marketing resisted the common practice of contracting for a market research study and then mailing the survey results with a cryptic note saying, "There's some good stuff here" or "I hope you find this useful." Instead, they set out to generate some grass-roots support for their firm's goal of increasing relative quality and profitability. Following were the main elements of their program:

1. Sell "quality" to plant managers. The first step was to get the attention of plant managers. They were an unusual group of people. Since they had been accustomed to operating with little or no supervision from the corporate office, any attempt at a "hard sell" would have been self-defeating. Corporate marketing decided on another approach: It would send three staff consultants to visit plant managers and invite them to (1) propose questions for the new customer survey and (2) nominate customers and prospects to be contacted. The individuals who issued this invitation were personally acquainted with the plant managers and spoke "shop language." They were careful to represent the quality enhancement program as an "experiment" and made no promises about short-term, dollar-and-cents payoff. Most important, the plant managers were informed that they, not the corporate office, would decide which market research findings merited a response.

2. See how other managers were investing in product quality. These visits were followed up with a barrage of clippings on quality enhancement from business journals. Particular emphasis was given to testimonials by other managers on the link between quality and profitability.

3. Get the support of division managers. A separate effort was made to win the support of the division managers to whom the plant managers reported. They too were invited to frame questions for the market researchers to pose to customers and prospects.

When the plant managers learned firsthand that their own managers were proposing questions for the quality survey, they had an additional reason to get behind the corporate program. They could see that it was definitely not just a brainchild of corporate marketing.

4. Involve the CEO. While questions for the market survey were being framed, corporate marketing was looking for ways to involve their chief executive officer in the campaign to elevate relative quality.[5] They began by asking him to write a letter to each prospective interviewee. They explained why they were taking the survey and how they would use the information collected.[6]

Corporate marketing gave their CEO a second assignment: to record his reasons for launching a corporatewide quality enhancement program. His remarks became part of an audiovisual presentation given to employees in every plant.

An officer of the company was asked to attend this presentation and field questions from the audience. There were plenty of questions. This was the first time employees had seen this type of top-down communication. Their feedback was very positive.

5. Determine how customers rated the quality of products and services. Before long, a survey instrument reflecting inputs from more than 50 Box Company employees was ready for the market research team. Even before the last interviews were conducted, plant managers were telephoning corporate marketing to inquire how much longer they would have to wait to see the results of "their" survey. In their eyes, the survey team was their agent, charged with the responsibility of obtaining answers to "their" questions.

The customer response exceeded all expectations. Data were obtained from a majority of Box Company's current customers and 38 percent of the designated "prospects." More than 60 percent of the respondents identified themselves. Many phoned or wrote the CEO of Box Company to amplify their answers to the survey questions.

This market survey shattered a cherished belief of many Box Company managers, namely that "a box is a box is a box . . . ". The customers pointed out many opportunities for product differentiation.

6. Turn the responses into action. After tabulating the responses, the consultants in corporate marketing turned their attention to action programs at the plant level. The team that had sold plant managers on the need for a quality enhancement program was reactivated. Their new assignment was to (1) present to each plant manager the responses of his customers and prospects and (2) discuss possible responses.

The consultants applied no pressure. They unveiled no "preferred response." Instead, they made it abundantly clear that each plant manager had control over the nature, timing, and tempo of his plant's reaction to these results.

7. Avoid mustering peer pressure. After they returned to the corporate office, the consultants wrote up their notes on the private sessions and mailed a copy to their host. Other plant managers were not privy to market research information obtained from firms that were not in their served market. Corporate marketing bent over backwards not to appear to be a corporate clearinghouse for tactical moves adopted by or being debated in other plants. The goal was to obtain a *free* response from each plant rather than a standard collective response.

Most of the plant managers responded positively to the insights gleaned from the market survey. Here are two brief illustrations.

• The plant that received the highest quality rating from customers had a return on investment (pretax and preinterest) of only 7 percent. Its manager immediately recognized the inconsistency between his rate of return and his quality rating. For years, he and his sales team had (wrongly) believed that their product was a "commodity." The survey made it clear, however, that many customers held a different view: They appraised product quality as superior because of the service that was rendered along with the product.

The manager of this plant decided to raise his selling prices. Some of his colleagues thought this was the height of folly. Yet within three years, the plant's return on investment soared to 24 percent—very respectable return for a capital-intensive business. More important, shipments from the plant did not fall off after the price increases were announced.

• Another plant manager was so intrigued by the information in the survey report that he called on each of his respondents. They made him aware that the common carrier who delivered his boxes and cartons was unreliable. This manager had been concentrating on ways to control product quality in house and therefore failed to realize that his customers expected him to monitor the quality of the *delivered* product. It was a simple matter to change common carriers and thereby eliminate this overlooked drag on product quality.

The chief executive of Box Company had his own reasons for being pleased with the quality of teamwork between the staff consultants in corporate marketing and the plant managers. Three years after the first survey was taken, those plants offering products that customers rated as high quality realized an average return on investment of over 20 percent. In contrast, plants that failed to utilize the information supplied by their customers had rates of return on investment far below 20 percent. When subsequent market surveys confirmed that their perceived relative quality remained low, these plants were either sold or assigned a new management team.

Box Company's recipe for success is easy to replicate:

1. Deal with line managers one on one.
2. Select consultants who speak shop language.
3. Give line managers a chance to be involved at every stage of a joint program.
4. Allow line managers to tailor customer information to their particular situations. If a certain customer's response seems "strange," invite the critic to visit the source and get the reasons behind the answer.
5. If line managers need assistance in formulating responses to customer information, "get down in the trenches" with them. Help them develop customized responses *with which they will be comfortable*. Never insist on a single, corporate-favored response.

INNOVATION: A CHALLENGE FOR BOTH STAFF AND LINE MANAGERS

Staff consultants can have a sudden "inspiration" at any time. Their problem is that line managers rarely warm up to their ideas. The reasons are always the same:

We are too busy.

There's not enough money in the budget.

Our customers will never go for that idea.

We must first deal with a crisis.

Behind these standard excuses lurk deep reservations about staff innovators. Champions of new products and services come and go. Quite a few do not deliver on their rosy projections. Small wonder that line managers do not rush to implement their ideas. Having said this, we concede that line managers are among the first to complain about product obsolescence and to call for new ways to cope with turbulent markets and/or aggressive competitors.

The next two illustrations emphasize that both staff and line managers share responsibility for the pace at which innovations are converted into viable products and services. The first comes from a manufacturer of medical devices that we will call MD, Inc. The source of the innovation was a corporate marketing component that we will call "the unit." The second illustration comes from a firm with an enviable record of erecting businesses upon completed R&D work.

Bidding on a Problem Bugging Immediate Customers[7]

MD, Inc., has been manufacturing medical devices for over 30 years. It has a direct sales force that calls on specialists in several branches of medicine. R&D people at the corporate level continually upgrade MD's product line. Customer service and customer education have always been priorities.[8] The combination of high-quality products and high-value services has created a close bond between MD and its immediate customers.

In recent years, market and industry forces have diverted physicians' attention from their patients to their "business." The reasons are familiar. Hospitals have instituted programs designed to slow down the increases in health care costs. Some of these programs have reduced physician income. Patients have become less pliant. Some have abandoned their family doctors and taken out membership in health maintenance organizations or physician groups that offer prepaid plans. Others have turned away from invasive medicine and toward unconventional forms of treatment. If they elect to have surgery, they "shop around" before selecting a surgeon. On the supply side of the equation, an oversupply of physicians in certain parts of the country has fanned the fires of competition.

Finally, physicians are being deluged with paperwork, and increasing numbers are being subjected to peer reviews. Many doctors now ask themselves: Is this why I went to medical school?

Jodi Harpstead, the manager of Professional Services, a small marketing component at MD's headquarters, was instructed to study the turbulent market facing doctors and see if she could spot market opportunities lurking amid the chaos. She did just that and returned to her manager with a novel idea:

I think we should offer a new line of services related to "practice enhancement," a subject close to the hearts of our traditional customers. They are deeply concerned about their practices. Why not ride to their rescue? I am sure we have much information in our files that would be useful to them, and we could broker other information pertinent to growing a medical practice. The turbulence that is bugging our customers need not stand in the way of practice enhancement. The techniques we will suggest will be consistent with the ethical norms of our customers.

Harpstead expected opposition to her proposal from several sources:

- Colleagues who were straining to master information on MD's latest additions to its line of medical devices.
- Salespeople with a pronounced technical orientation were unaccustomed to mastering new material about a line of *new services* (e.g., giving seminars on practice enhancement; advising doctors on how to improve their public image; compiling and analyzing demographics and market trends that affect patient load; helping to improve the quality of services they give patients and their families.
- Senior managers who were proud of their firm's profit performance and would find a dozen reasons not to divert resources from product technology and reliable hardware to a line of services unrelated to hardware.

Nonetheless, Harpstead and her colleagues persevered. They set out to recruit a team of "believers" and, with their help, demonstrate that the doctors on whom MD, Inc., called would welcome suggestions on how to shore up their practices in spite of market turbulence. We will summarize the main elements of Professional Services' internal marketing program for *a single* service in its proposed line of services, namely a seminar in practice enhancement. The service did not offer just one seminar. It was equally innovative in its efforts to stimulate interest in the other new services in the proposed market basket.

1. Obtain a small amount of "seed" money from corporate management to develop a pilot seminar program. Test it in one district. Harpstead and her staff avoided two errors often made by creative staff people: (1) spending a lot of time developing an elaborate, detailed plan and (2) calling for a major investment in additional staff and in market research to substantiate their claim that customers would indeed be interested in their idea.

> *Harpstead's unit elected to keep a low profile. They contented themselves with feedback from top management that went along these lines:*
>
> > *That sounds like a good idea.*
> >
> > *Our customers might find that helpful.*
> >
> > *Develop some hard evidence and we will take a second look at your proposed line of services.*

2. Think small—at first. This corporate marketing unit could not get "air time" at sales meetings to tell the field about their proposed seminar (much less to talk about their entire line of services). Every sales meeting was reserved for discussions about MD's new hardware. Therefore, the unit broached their idea of a pilot seminar to district managers one-on-one. With an untested seminar design, it was not practical to think about reaching every customer of MD, Inc. Best to start small, beginning with a hand-picked, friendly audience.

3. Do an in-house quality check. Harpstead's boss had been a district sales manager. He agreed to critique the proposed seminar and the "advertising" material the unit intended to use in its internal marketing campaign. Better to correct any flaws *before* approaching line managers.

4. Select partners from the disposed. Every firm has a small group of managers who welcome change and are willing to scuttle ancient practices and procedures. These people are called the "early adopters." Typically, these individuals are either young, new to their positions or confronting aggressive competitors in their market. Their openness is in sharp contrast to the defenders of the status quo who argue: "If it ain't broke, don't try to fix it!"

Harpstead and her colleagues concentrated their internal selling effort on the early adopters rather than on managers who were under great time pressures or were convinced that the best way to improve profits was to introduce new medical devices. In marketing terms, the unit segmented their internal market. They would approach and work with those line managers who were open to innovations. With their help, they would accumulate the hard evidence needed to convince the defenders of the status quo.

5. Select the physicians who would attend the pilot seminars with the greatest care. Line managers were asked to nominate physicians to attend the initial seminars. Harpstead and her colleagues visited these doctors and found they were eager to attend a seminar on practice enhancement. Their enthusiasm was contagious. Slowly but surely, MD, Inc.'s sales force became interested too.

Harpstead's unit was very deliberate about this indirect form of internal selling. The process was reinforced by

- Minimizing the work line managers had to do to launch the seminar program. Ninety-five percent of the work would be done by the corporate marketing unit.
- Stressing the value of the seminar as a *marketing tool,* as a weapon line managers could use to win new customers, solidify relations with key accounts, or deter brand switching. The seminar came to be regarded as something owned by line and staff managers.

6. Gather at an appropriate watering hole. Because specialists in all fields of medicine are averse to roughing it, the pilot seminars were held at a well-known vacation resort.

7. Invite outsiders to speak at the seminar. Time was of the essence. Professional Services decided to rely mostly on outside consultants to deliver the first seminars. Each consultant had a reputation in practice enhancement. Each knew a lot about the concerns of doctors and how to address them. Their messages had already been carefully packaged, pretested, and rehearsed. For Harpstead's unit, this meant a short payback period for their "seed" money and a good chance to win rave reviews.

8. Listen carefully to customer feedback, and get line managers to listen, too. Customer feedback was collected at each seminar, analyzed, and incorporated into the design of the next seminar. This feedback was shared with line managers, along with profuse thanks for "a great seminar."

The character of the internal marketing effort by Harpstead and her colleagues changed after the initial seminars. Members of the unit realized that physicians were in a better position to persuade the early adopters and their bosses that practice enhancement was a topic whose time had come. Therefore, they let the attendees at the pilot seminars convince MD, Inc., to add innovative services aimed at helping doctors bolster their practices. After all, they realized that line managers are more likely to listen to customers than to staff consultants!

9. Perform aggressive follow-up. After the pilot seminar, line managers began telling their colleagues about the impact of the seminar on customer relationships. At regional and district sales meetings they reported that this new service had helped them recapture accounts and solidify their customer relationships.

Before very long, Harpstead was being asked to arrange for "her" faculty to speak at dinners and meetings attended by MD's senior executives. Within months, more and more managers in the firm seemed to be talking about practice enhancement. In fact, line managers began to refer to the new seminar as "*our* new marketing tool." This convinced Harpstead and her colleagues that their innovation had taken root. It was time for them to once again visit physicians who had attended the initial seminars and market complementary services that would help them boost the quality of patient care. *These new services were unrelated to MD's medical devices.*

Every firm has a corporate staff, and many staff consultants develop innovative ways to respond to market opportunities. But all too often, staff consultants proceed as if they had to market their innovations *by themselves*. Line managers do not respond, partly because they did not call for the innovations, and partly because they perceive that they will complicate their own programs. Small wonder that a "we-they" relationship—rather than a team relationship—develops between line managers and staff consultants.

The above illustration is a reminder that innovations by staff consultants must be sold *in house* before they can be sold to customers. Like it or not, an effective sales approach aimed at line managers is a critical early step in the development of any new product or service. The greater the degree of novelty, the greater the need for *creative* internal marketing.

While the senior managers at MD, Inc., were delighted with the unit's early success, they did *not* see these new services as the foundation of a new business. Their mind-set was still dominated by hardware. To observe the kind of team play needed to erect a new business on an innovation proposed by a staff component, we must tap the files of another company.

A Corporate Nursery for New Products

Firms interested in leveraging their R&D work must either launch new businesses or sell their patent rights. Those that perceive a business latent in their R&D results sometimes transfer the result to a "product section." This is a small organizational component whose sole job is to erect a new business on completed R&D. Its success depends on high-quality team play. There are four distinct teams:

- A small cadre of managers and specialists who must solve a host of technical problems related to the new product and its production process. Then it must develop a marketing plan.
- The cadre plus a "host" department that offers these professionals a temporary home and logistical support.
- The general manager of the product section and his or her division general manager and champion.
- The cadre and their counterparts in established businesses.

We will illustrate the above points with the help of an example from the product section that added Noryl to GE's line of polymers.[9] Any firm that wishes to erect a new business based on a new product, service, or material can follow the same process.

Here are the main steps GE took.

1. Appoint a cadre. Innovation is a full-time job. It is *not* work to be fit in when specialists have free time on their hands. GE appointed a general manager to head the commercialization of Noryl. It gave him a cadre of specialists with engineering, manufacturing, and marketing skills to help him move Noryl from the laboratory into the marketplace. One of the specialists had participated in the basic research that produced Noryl.

Three points are worth noting:

- The cadre was *small.*
- A scientist left the lab to help convert the innovation into a marketable product. This provided a hedge against any loss of information during the transfer from an R&D center to a line organization.
- Senior management did not give this product innovation to an existing department lest it be neglected or given only tepid support.

2. Select a leader who knows both science and business. Noryl's general manager had several advanced degrees plus prior managerial experience in a *line* organization. Both factors were critical. First, there were many engineering problems to be solved. Second, hands-on business experience would ensure that each member of the cadre operated from a profit orientation *from the outset.*

> All too often innovations are steered to market by scientists who are forced to learn about business as they go. This need for on-the-job training unduly lengthens the development cycle.

3. Provide the cadre with a temporary home. The Noryl cadre was located in an established profit center that served as a corporate nursery for promising product innovations. It provided the cadre with office space along with administrative and logistical services, leaving them free to attend to their primary job.

> The intent was to relieve the entrepreneurs (innovators) of chores and worries associated with facilities, housekeeping, and logistics. Their sole job was to make a profit, and quickly. They were in a race to market. To win this race, they had to create a safe, efficient production process and confirm the existence of a sizable, profitable market for their new product.
>
> Every scientist has faith in his or her innovation. The task of a cadre of a product section is to prove that this faith is justified. That is a difference that makes a difference.

4. Provide a carrot. New businesses funded by venture capitalists reward their cadres with valuable stock options. GE, however, did not follow this practice. The members of the Noryl team had to be content with much less. If they were successful, their product section would be upgraded to a stand-alone department. They would then become prime candidates for the top managerial positions in the new department.

5. Call on established businesses to lend a hand. Members of the Noryl team had the right to call on professionals in any GE department who could help them solve their product and process problems. To encourage the leveraging of technological knowledge, division general managers regularly brought their managers to remote conference centers for "cross-fertilization." Their goal was to foster enduring personal relationships among the attendees. Then, when the attendees returned to the office, they hopefully would feel free to send up an S.O.S., confident that another manager would share his information or experiences *on demand*. Even young engineers did not hesitate to make *direct* contact with managers in a distant department and ask for their help. They were programmed to expect knowledge to flow freely across organizational boundaries rather than through traditional channels.

Many European firms discourage such freestyle behavior. Rigid class boundaries require that information move along the prescribed bureaucratic paths. Young engineers speak when they are spoken to. Camaraderie is not encouraged.

6. Find a product champion and political adviser. Prior to the 1980s, GE's corporate officers were former salesmen, electrical or industrial engineers, or financial specialists. Given this fact, how could Noryl's general manager hope to liberate funding for his team? The judge and jury who dispensed capital appropriations did not have training or experience in chemical engineering or research. Therefore, they could not understand the symbols and notation system he employed to describe his new polymer. They had no "feel" for its market appeal.

Noryl's general manager looked to Dr. Charles Reed, his division general manager, to solve this problem. Dr. Reed had a doctorate from M.I.T. He understood all the technical challenges facing the Noryl cadre. His position in the corporate hierarchy gave him a chance to study the political factions that waxed and waned in GE's executive suite. Whenever the Noryl team needed an additional infusion of capital, Dr. Reed choreographed their approach to the corporate trough. If he felt the members of GE's corporate office were preoccupied with weighty corporate problems, Dr. Reed would scrub the Noryl presentation. He preferred to unveil Noryl's request for additional capital when the odds for a favorable vote were higher.

> *A major obstacle to product innovation work is the fact that the people performing it often must obtain funding from executives who have no feel for their work. Their internal bankers are not visionaries. The innovators need an intermediary who understands them, their profit goals, and their product development work. This combination is infrequently found in a talent pool fed by Ph.D. and D.Sc. programs.*

7. Proceed one step at a time. In the chemical industry, it is customary to build pilot plants and use them to generate data related to plant safety and efficiency as well as to confirm estimates of market potential. For example, one U.S. auto manufacturer was sufficiently interested in Noryl's attributes to accept shipments from its pilot plant one barrel at a time! This was a signal to the Noryl cadre to begin thinking of upscaling from a pilot plant to a large production process.

> *In the previous case, Harpstead viewed her first seminar as an experiment. She used it as a chemical engineer might use a pilot plant, namely* to produce information under carefully controlled conditions. *Like Noryl's team, she wanted to*

Study a "process" in operation.

Flush out its imperfections.

Be ready to intervene if "glitches" appeared.

8. Infuse operations with a strategic vision. Every member of the Noryl team understood that GE's cluster of chemical businesses had to conform to a niche strategy.[10] Rather than going head to head with the giants of the chemical industry, they would concentrate on proprietary, specialty chemicals. Each business in this cluster was expected to generate a stream of earnings that would reinforce their CEO's wavering faith in high-quality specialty chemicals. To do so, their product innovations had to have superior qualities and be supported by a dedicated group of application engineers. "Me-too" products and incremental improvements were *not* acceptable.

All too many fledgling businesses operate with a flawed mindset. Their managers fail to recognize the need to exceed the quality standards of established vendors. Too many concentrate their attention on making their products work or meeting industry standards.

In contrast, Noryl's cadre understood that they had to develop information that would persuade their internal bankers that they could control their product and process quality, carve out a profitable niche, and defend it against all competitors. Lacking this kind of evidence, they would not have qualified for the funding they needed to move to the next stage of business development. High *relative* quality was the foundation of their price structure, their profit performance, and their sales growth. Without it, they could not develop customer loyalty or erect a viable business.

This illustration is a reminder that a technological advance is no guarantee of business success. To produce profits *quickly* requires high-quality team play, a realistic strategy, a "patron" with some influence over corporate funding, and a manager with as much respect for the laws of the marketplace as for the laws of science.

Banks, financial services firms, hospitals, and physicians all need to develop, test, and market new products or services. Often their success hinges on their ability to elicit inputs from individuals who do not report to them and their ability to obtain a stream of funding from administrators without prior experience in new business development and a shallow understanding of the nature of their innovation. The Noryl experience emphasizes the need to:

1. Separate business development from day-to-day operating work.
2. Start with a minimum investment in fixed capital.

3. Recruit a small number of highly dedicated professionals drawn from the relevant specialties.
4. Have these professionals work cheek to jowl, thus eliminating the need to exchange information via bureaucratic communication channels.
5. Convince the professionals that they must

> Race to the market.
> Produce differentiated rather than "me-too" products.
> Be spartan (no fancy offices).
> Earn each successive increment in funding (rather than act as if they have a private line to a Santa Claus with deep pockets).

6. Find a spokesperson and champion who has the power base and personal relationships to

> Speak up for the innovators if the faith of the suppliers of capital begins to waver.
> Keep technically oriented innovators on a sound strategic course that will generate significant profits *quickly*.

THE LEFT HAND VERSUS THE RIGHT HAND: LINKING CAPITAL APPROPRIATIONS TO BUSINESS STRATEGY

Access to the corporate treasury is a concern of both line and staff managers. In most medium-size and all large companies, requests for capital appropriations get mired in a long and tedious process. Usually this journey begins when a general manager defends a proposed business strategy before one or more corporate officers. Aggressive strategies require sizable commitments of new capital. Usually, these take the form of new plant and equipment, new warehouses, or new sales outlets. Supporters of such strategies do not offer specific information as to *how* the implied increment in investment will be spent. Few planning systems require more than a general statement of the tactics that will be used to implement the proposed strategy.[11]

If the proposed strategy is approved, the nitty-gritty operational planning begins. Scores of specialists and consultants will be drafted to prepare detailed tactical programs. For example, if the new strategy calls for additional output, where will it be produced? What manufacturing processes will be used? Which control systems will be needed?

Senior managers and members of the corporate planning staff have no hand in such analyses. This is operational planning, the domain of general managers and functional specialists.

After operating plans are written, the general manager gets caught up in a third planning process, capital appropriation review.

We are not concerned with the details of capital allocation or the criteria used in appraising a request for new capital. We will merely note four things:

- There are three distinct planning processes, each with its own forms, exhibits, scope, and cadre of specialists.
- The specialists who work on a capital appropriation rarely, if ever, see a copy of the strategic plan that triggered their work.
- Corporate staff managers are allowed to comment on a request for capital before the request is approved. Usually they concentrate on aspects of the request that concern their specialty.
- One corporate consultant—usually someone trained in finance—follows the paperwork after it arrives at its corporate destination and makes sure that it is complete and contains all the required signatures.

Clearly this whole procedure emphasizes discrete contributions, *not team play*. There are scores of specialists from the various functions but *no multifunctional team*.

Some chief executives recognize the danger that the output of these three distinct planning processes will be uncoupled. In some instances, they position in their corporate planning department the consultant who shepherds capital appropriations through the corporate labyrinth. Their intent is to hedge the risk that the analysis behind the request for new capital is inconsistent with their earlier strategy discussions with line managers.

TRW addressed the tension between strategy development and capital budgeting in a more formal way.[12] In 1987, TRW began using a new resource allocation process. Basically, senior managers now decide whether to allocate capital to a sector or group *at the same time they are evaluating their strategy and the supporting action programs*. Managers at lower organizational levels will be authorized to determine *how* those resources will be utilized (what equipment to purchase, what plant site to select, etc.) In short, TRW now has a "one-stop approval mechanism" for action programs, annual capital budgets, and annual expense budgets.

Senior managers will continue to monitor strategy implementation as seems advisable during the year. For example, their approval will still be necessary if there has been a major change in a business unit's resource requirements. Their sanction will also be needed if a group or sector manager wishes to make a high-risk investment or a major acquisition.

Businesses that have no approved strategy must seek the chief executive officer's approval with respect to both the amount of capital and the way it will be spent.

The details of TRW's new resource allocation system are not germane to a book on team play. What *is* important is to integrate strategic decisions and allocations of new capital. Firms that allow a time interval of 12 to 18 months to develop between a decision to approve a business strategy and the decision to allocate the capital needed to implement that strategy invite tension between two different and largely independent planning systems.

NOTES

1. This material was provided by Jim Haag and Edwin DeVilbiss. Sally Huysack provided comments on an early draft.
2. See Sidney Schoeffler, Robert D. Buzzell, and Donald F. Heany, "Impact of Strategic Planning on Profit Performance." *Harvard Business Review* 52, no. 2, (March–April 1974), pp. 137–45. See also Robert D. Buzzell, "Product Quality," *PIMSLETTER* 4 (1978).

3. The concept of relative quality was explained in Chapter 4.
4. There was some discussion about creating the position of vice president–product quality. Nothing came of this because of the hostility of plant managers to "corporate interference." It seemed more prudent to rely on the expertise of corporate marketing. Each of its consultants had worked in a box plant and was on a first-name basis with each plant manager.
5. The customers' perception of the quality of a plant's product line, vis-à-vis that of the lines offered by that plant's top three competitors.
6. Most of these respondents had never received any direct communication from the CEO of Box Company.
7. Jodi Harpstead provided the material for this section.
8. Medical researchers are quite prolific. Physicians must update their knowledge base continually and stay abreast of changes in products and product technology.
9. This illustration draws on information provided by the late Dr. Robert Finholt, a product section manager, client, colleague, and friend.
10. We will discuss business clusters in more detail in Chapter 12.
11. Of course, there are exceptions. Businesses with access to the PIMS database may obtain from it estimates of the increment of investment per dollar of value added that are associated with a given change in market share.
12. This information was provided by Robert L. Saslaw, until recently TRW, Inc.'s director of planning.

CHAPTER 12

THE LACK OF TOP-DOWN TEAM PLAY: A PROBLEM THAT DEMANDS A SOLUTION

> *CHIEF EXECUTIVE:* You would not believe the revenue projections that cross my desk. They are off the wall! I plead with my line managers, I threaten them, but in most instances my advice falls on deaf ears. I can't seem to get them to produce strategic plans or budgets that have a half-life greater than two months.

> *LINE MANAGER:* Once again I have to crunch numbers for the corner office. I submit a strategic plan and a budget that never seem to please anybody up there. What a waste of resources!

The definition of *top manager* depends on one's perspective. In the management literature, the term stands for a chief executive or chief operating officer. But in multibusiness portfolios, there are intermediate echelons with titles like *sector manager, group executive,* and *division manager.* Whatever one's definition of *top manager,* the quality of the dialog that takes place between the top manager and the line managers who report to him or her is vitally important.

This is a much neglected topic despite the abundant evidence that top-down team play leaves much to be desired. Both parties work for the same firm, eat in the same executive dining room, and call each other by first name. Yet they do not operate on the same intellectual frequency. The infrequent meetings between business managers and their CEOs are *not* used to communicate or reemphasize a corporate vision. Instead, they are more like sessions that managers of stand-alone businesses might have with their bankers. The primary emphasis is on measures of financial performance. This explains why top-down team play is the rarest of all types of team play and the hardest to sustain.

To rectify this situation, it will be necessary to

- Develop a shared perspective of the link between corporate strategy and business strategy.
- Adopt a more standard and more compact way of organizing information on the status of lines of business.
- Give more than lip service to the interrelationships among related businesses.

If such changes are not made, the quality of top-down team play will deteriorate further due to (1) a sharp increase in the size and diversity of corporate portfolios; (2) the sheer complexity of the task of overseeing a diverse portfolio; (3) a failure to invest in tools that could facilitate a constructive dialog between the two parties; and (4) decentralization. Meanwhile, there is no indication that the traditional obstacles have eroded the strong, aggressive personalities found in the top positions, the premium that senior managers place on loyalty and obedience (and their low tolerance of criticism from below),[1] the conflict between corporate goals and personal agendas, or incentive systems that pit managers against one another.

Clearly the barriers to top-down team play are formidable. Nonetheless, we have assembled the fruits of a number of efforts to lower these obstacles. Even incremental improvements are significant, particularly in firms that have slashed their corporate staffs by 40 to 60 percent and simultaneously quintupled the span of control exercised by line managers.

This chapter will *not* appeal to top managers who are rapidly closing in on their long-term goal of a trio of staff members: a lawyer, an accountant, and a janitor. Nor will it appeal to line managers who are determined to keep their bosses in the dark about what happens in their businesses. The chapter *will* appeal to those CEOs and line managers who are, at least occasionally, open to a plea for more top-down team play.

COPING WITH VOLUMINOUS FINANCIAL DATA: TOOLS FROM CHASE MANHATTAN

A torrent of financial data flows forward from line-of-business managers to the corner office. Most of it arrives via a management information system (MIS). Since 1970, some data have traveled via a parallel system: the strategic planning system.

Charles M. Neul and Deborah A. Smith, two vice presidents on the corporate planning staff of Chase Manhattan Bank, have produced a graphic model and a mathematical model to help senior managers cope with information overload. Their work was triggered by a request by Chase's president to his chief financial officer: It is time to improve the way our lines of business measure productivity.

Neul and Smith began by studying the productivity measurements called for by Chase's MIS. None of these measurements could be linked directly to profitability, nor did they permit comparability across lines of business. Since the system used a number of unrelated measures, managers were never sure what was wrong in the business or what to fix. Finally, managers who made investments to boost productivity had no way to determine if their investments had paid off.

To rectify this, Neul and Smith fashioned three measures of productivity:

- Labor efficiency (value added/number of employees.)[2]
- Capital efficiency (investment per employee).[3]
- Operating efficiency (income before overhead per dollar of value added).

They chose these measures because they could tie them into return on investment[4] and construct them from concepts familiar to every manager.

A Productivity/Profitability Grid

Neul and Smith believed that certain patterns of productivity with corresponding levels of profitability occur naturally.[5] Using two of their productivity measures—labor efficiency and capital efficiency—as axes, they created a two-dimensional grid as shown in Exhibit 12–1. They divided the grid into four regions (see Exhibit 12–2) based on combinations of each of the two measures being above or below a certain level. They hypothesized that if the productivity patterns in each region differed and thus affected ROI, they would observe significantly different ROI levels among the four regions given a large sample of businesses in each region.

The PIMS database of 2,600 lines of business was used to test this hypothesis. The results supported their theory (Exhibit

EXHIBIT 12–1
A Productivity Grid

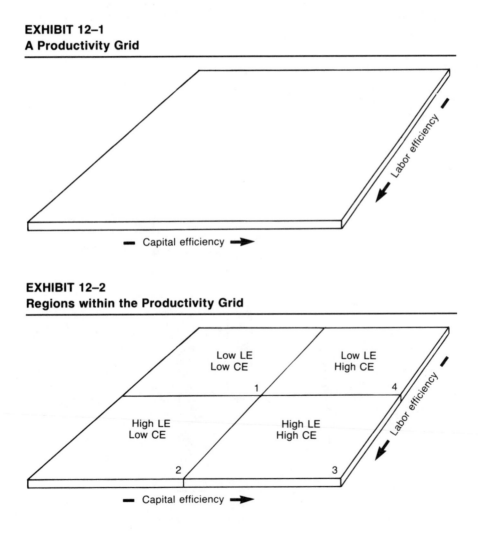

Capital efficiency ➡

EXHIBIT 12–2
Regions within the Productivity Grid

Low LE Low CE 1	Low LE High CE 4
High LE Low CE 2	High LE High CE 3

Capital efficiency ➡

12–3). Average operating efficiencies and ROIs differed significantly among the four regions. In a structural sense, then, a business's regional membership provided a good guide to the business's potential profitability.

When Neul and Smith analyzed 28 Chase businesses by placing them in their productivity grid, they were quickly able to diagnose different productivity problems and opportunities among the businesses. After seeing their initial results, their president directed them to do a more detailed study of several businesses with the help of the managers who ran those businesses, in order to validate their "top-down" findings. This they did and got complete validation in every case.

EXHIBIT 12–3
Return on Investment and Operating Efficiency for Four Productivity Patterns

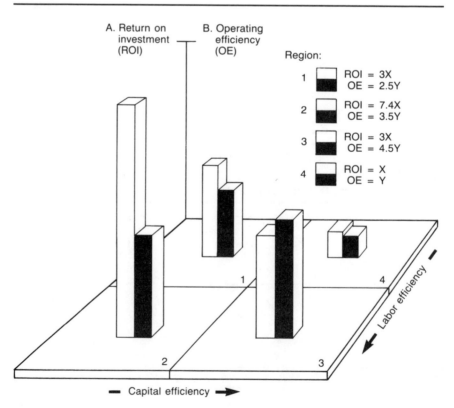

Neul and Smith wanted to see whether this way of looking at labor and capital productivity would provide any new insights for other chief executive officers. The CEO of a manufacturing firm offered data on more than a score of his lines of business. However, he did not tell Neul and Smith the names of these businesses.

Much to their surprise, Neul and Smith discovered that most of this CEO's businesses piled up in region 1 of Exhibit 12–3 (low employee efficiency and low capital efficiency). They were also surprised that only a few stellar businesses were responsible for most of this portfolio's profit.

When they looked at the "drivers" behind their ratios, they spotted other things that a CEO might miss if he or she were looking at budgets from a score of businesses. Here are two illustrations.

The "Fat-Growth" Pattern in a "Fast-Growth" Market. Several businesses in this portfolio were serving fast-growth markets. While they reported a growth in net income, their investments were growing even faster. Consequently, the return realized on their investment dropped. More important, the managers of these businesses had *not* converted their growing value-added stream into greater labor efficiency.

The CEO had obtained basic data from these businesses that would have revealed the "fat-growth" pattern, *but he had not put the pieces of this puzzle together.* ("Fat-growth" refers to the behavior of managers who get careless when sales come easily.) Indeed, he (and others) had applauded these managers for the growth they had achieved. The point was that this was not *productive* growth. The CEO had *not* asked his managers why they had allowed the number of employees to grow so fast. He had *not* asked them why their ROIs were dropping and what they were doing to reverse this trend. His attention was diverted by the fact that these businesses had ROIs above the corporate average.

Neul and Smith emphasized the main point: *These so-called stars of this CEO's portfolio were fading.* Rapid market growth had made the managers complacent. They had missed a golden opportunity to erect barriers to entry and get ready for the inevitable shakeout.

A Former Star Performer.   One business fell into region 4 of Exhibit 12–3 (low labor efficiency and high capital efficiency). A few years earlier, this business had been one of the most profitable in the entire portfolio. Yet it had allowed value added to stagnate while it added large increments in investment. The result was a lower operating efficiency and ROI.

Neul and Smith asked this chief executive officer, "Why are you investing so heavily in a business that has posted no gains in employee efficiency or been able to reverse the downward trend in value added?" Their question went to the heart of the business dynamics—to the "drivers" *behind* their measures of business performance and productivity. CEOs who fail to ask questions like this in effect abdicate their right to "oversee" the performances of their lines of business. Their lack of attention to the trends *behind* measures of business performance sends a clear message to astute line-of-business managers:

> The boss is too busy to understand what is going on at the profit center level.

> The boss is *not* a teammate. He is preoccupied with what happens at the board of directors level.

The above are only a few snippets from an extended discussion that Neul and Smith had with this chief executive officer. He thanked them for giving him a "new perspective" of his portfolio and for using their productivity-profitability grid to help him integrate information that had been available *but not previously assimilated* in a comprehensive and useful manner.

Encouraged by this exchange, Neul and Smith enhanced their analysis of the performances of Chase businesses using what they had learned from this outside application. Opposite the name of each business they put a red or green square to show whether ROI was moving up or down, respectively. This was the first time Chase's CEO had seen so much critical information packed into a two-page graphic view.

The final step was to use the grid to track the productivity performance of Chase and its peers (i.e., other money center banks). "Relative productivity performance" furnishes an ideal context for a discussion between line managers and their CEO.

First, they can see how competitors are reacting to similar environmental changes. Second, they get a graphic picture of the impact of different strategies on productivity performance.

A Resource Allocation Model

One of a chief executive's key functions is to allocate new capital. Each line-of-business manager waxes eloquent on why he or she should have access to the corporate trough. Those who have reported low labor productivity and low capital productivity in the past use this as a reason to persuade their CEO to grant them a "productivity booster" (i.e., more investment per employee). The CEO, therefore, faces a complex decision. He or she realizes that the line managers are inclined to view the future through rose-colored glasses. The CEO cannot fund all projects. Which businesses should be funded? Which businesses should be expected to provide funds for other profit centers?

Neul and Smith modified a linear programming model to help Chase's president answer such questions. It was based on the productivity performance data developed for each business. They showed the president how he could take data already coming forward via his budgeting process and

1. Prioritize line managers' claims for new investments.
2. Quantify the portfolio's ability to fund the capital requirements of its "best" businesses.
3. Quantify the cost of remaining in a particular business (e.g., one that had long been in profit trouble).
4. Quantify the effect of various funding scenarios on corporate and individual business performance.

Here was a model that Chase's president could use to *prepare for a dialog with line managers*. It helped him understand the implications of the budgets that littered his desk. It helped him execute a triage analysis, that is, fix his attention on his "winners" (clusters of businesses that are good investment opportunities), "cyclical businesses" (those in temporary profit trouble), and "losers" (those that had severe profit problems that had to be addressed before receiving another infusion of corporate capital). Finally, this model was a question generator. It surfaced issues that deserved a place on the agenda for any meeting between the CEO and line managers.

Line managers could use the same model to

1. Prioritize the product lines that were contending for resources that had been made available to that business.
2. Substantiate a business's claim for additional corporate resources despite a temporary deterioration in its market environment.
3. Illuminate the profit implications of investing in one product while not investing in others.

Neul and Smith do not claim that their productivity grid and resource allocation model addresses every topic of interest to line managers and CEOs. They do maintain that these tools put both parties on the same wavelength and help them avoid "information overload." They provide a context for reporting business performance and for viewing the firm as a whole. Chase's line managers can use the very same concepts and the same model that the corporate officers use. If something is missing from the corporate portrait, line managers can surface that item and discuss it. *There is no need to jump to another intellectual frequency.*

The Teams behind the Two Models

It took five distinct teams to build the Chase models.

Team 1. Chase's senior vice-president–corporate planning provided Neul and Smith with a type of work environment rarely found in large firms. In this milieu, they had the time to do business research, examine new ways to look at accounting data, and experiment with a variety of models. There were no absolute deadlines, and few other major projects were assigned them during this research period.

Team 2. Chase's president listened patiently to a stream of progress reports from Neul and Smith, who had a chance to display their interim results and confirm that their models were relevant to issues important to the bank's top managers.

Team 3. Early in 1988, Neul and Smith received a chance to test their models on a wide range of Chase businesses. Line managers liked what they saw and recommended that the president encourage the use of the model bankwide.

Team 4. As the project neared completion, Neul and Smith prepared for an intellectual handoff to corporate budgeting. They were careful to keep their colleagues in corporate budgeting informed on the progress of their research. Neul and Smith were happy to turn over to them the software containing their LP model and to define the data needed to run it. At the same time, they made it clear that they had no interest in running this model regularly. While they were willing to give their opinion on the proper use of this model, their primary interest was research, not budgeting.

The harmonious relationship Neul and Smith established with their colleagues in corporate budgeting contributed to the success of this research project. In other firms, the relationships between strategic planners and financial planners has been anything but harmonious.

Team 5. The team play between Neul and Smith was of the same caliber as that between Slate and Grossman described in Chapter 8. Their differing backgrounds enhanced each other's strengths. The fact that Neul had spent four years at the bank and Smith only one did not prevent them from forming a partnership of equals to conduct their business research and test its relevance to any improvement in top-down team play.

Underlying Neul and Smith's approach are a number of principles with broad applicability across businesses

1. *Work first with the data at hand.* It is easy for business researchers to call for new data. Normally line managers resist such requests because they feel they have their hands full just meeting the current information requirements. Researchers and staff consultants will encounter less resistance if they focus on squeezing insights out of *available* data.

2. *Keep it simple*. Neul and Smith did not subscribe to the motto of many management scientists and operations researchers: *When in doubt, favor complex/sophisticated models*. Whenever Neul and Smith are criticized for the simplicity of their grids, they respond:

> We intended for them to be simple. That is why we chose productivity measures built from terms familiar to every manager. We did not try to dazzle our clients. We believed that it was necessary to meet them *on their turf*. We subscribe to the motto of Slate and Grossman: of what value is a model that's never used?[6]

STRATEGIC DATA: TOO MUCH AND TOO LITTLE

Many of the strategic plans written in the 1970s and early 1980s were packed with information on market, industry, and competition. Only the most dedicated chief executive officers managed to work their way through these tomes. There were obstacles at every step. For one thing, line managers did not share a common language. What one manager called an *objective* another manager called a *goal*. A pivotal business decision (e.g., diversify into market X) was called a *strategic move,* but so was a trivial change in a tactical program (e.g., begin advertising on TV). Some strategic plans were fashioned from inputs from all functions. Others consisted only of financial data.

Firms that persisted with strategic planning tried to standardize language. This was not an easy job. Each new manager brought along his or her own intellectual baggage. In a matter of months, these managers would begin lobbying for the terminology that they had mastered in their former companies. Few colleagues cared enough to interrupt them and hand them a copy of the glossary of terms adopted by their current firm.

A number of GE consultants were forced to address these problems when they were commissioned to examine an important corporate issue: What do we do about our struggling computer business? In the process of addressing this problem, the consultants briefed the sponsors of their analysis using a standard framework (see Exhibit 12-4).

EXHIBIT 12–4

A Framework for Linking Corporate Strategy, Business Strategy, and Functional Tactics

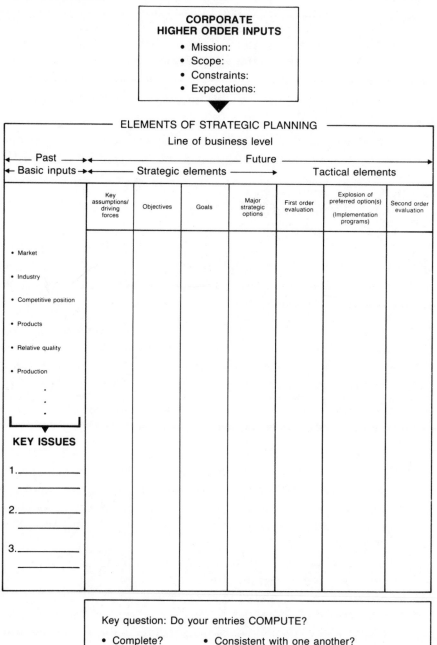

	Key assumptions/ driving forces	Objectives	Goals	Major strategic options	First order evaluation	Explosion of preferred option(s) (Implementation programs)	Second order evaluation

CORPORATE HIGHER ORDER INPUTS
- Mission:
- Scope:
- Constraints:
- Expectations:

ELEMENTS OF STRATEGIC PLANNING
Line of business level

Past — Future
Basic inputs — Strategic elements — Tactical elements

- Market
- Industry
- Competitive position
- Products
- Relative quality
- Production

KEY ISSUES

1. _____
   _____
2. _____
   _____
3. _____
   _____

Key question: Do your entries COMPUTE?
- Complete?
- Accurate?
- Consistent with one another?
- Match plans of related businesses?

A number of chief executive officers have adopted this framework and require their line managers to follow it when giving presentations on business strategy. They have found that it acts as a break on the fast talkers, the poets, and the dreamers who have not sufficiently thought out the strategies they are recommending. This format structures the dialog between CEOs and line managers. Specifically, it

- Initiates the dialog with a reference to the link between corporate strategy and business strategy (the higher-order inputs).
- Requires line managers to begin with the "Basic Inputs" (see column 1 of Exhibit 12–4).

Too many line managers begin their dialogs with their CEOs with a rosy account of all the great programs they intend to work on in the future. They gloss over the fact that some of their past strategic and tactical decisions have been flawed or unimplemented.

These basic inputs include all of the structural characteristics of the business (market share, investment intensity, relative quality, etc.) that business research has shown to be closely linked to profitability. These deserve a prominent place in discussions between CEOs and line managers. They remind top managers of the important distinction between the properties of the business *and the* personal characteristics of its managers. *As Joseph Patten has warned, "CEOs must not expect a jockey [the manager] to win the Derby if they give him a nag [a poor business] to ride!"*

- Draws attention to *related* data elements—for example, by linking a downward trend in market share to other entries such as an undifferentiated product line; an increase in the sophistication of customers accounting for 50 percent of sales; entry of a major competitor from another industry, or a high management turnover.

  This is quite different from having separate paragraphs on each of the above points in a strategic plan.
- Surfaces gaps and inconsistencies in the information presented.
- Protects the top manager against information overload and forces line managers to think about the essential elements of the information. Note that there is a place for identifying the key issues facing the business. Immediately the eye is

drawn to how the managers will react to these issues in the future.

If all line managers adopted this framework, CEOs would find it much easier to absorb and interpret what they were saying. They would also be more likely to note where the plans of one business affected those of another.

We believe that top managers have every right to specify the key topics to be covered in their exchanges with line managers and the sequence in which to present them. After all, general managers have had no trouble adhering to standardized accounting practices, so why not expect them to organize voluminous strategic data into a compact, standardized format?[7]

Managers who are accustomed to writing lengthy strategic plans buttressed by scores of exhibits and appendices will protest that it is impossible to cram into one tabular display all the information bearing on a business's past and future strategic positions. This task is indeed difficult, but it is not impossible. We believe that any general manager who cannot convey the strategic position of his or her business and the strategic options using this framework is probably not ready for a serious dialog with the CEO.

HOW INTERBUSINESS RELATIONSHIPS COMPLICATE TOP-DOWN TEAM PLAY

The first corporate planning systems required line managers to forward strategic plans on their lines of business. They did *not*, however, require that chief executive officers reciprocate. There was no formal corporate plan and, hence, no rigorous way to determine whether or not business strategies were adequately aligned to corporate strategy.

Furthermore, corporate planning systems did not make any provision for a strategy for *related* businesses, such as businesses that

- Addressed *contiguous markets* (e.g., automobiles sold to rental car firms and automobiles sold to individuals).
- Offered *competing* products or services (e.g., cameras that required film that was laboratory processed and cameras that produced photos almost instantaneously).

- Produced products that depended on *substitute* technologies (e.g., laser printers and ink-jet printers).
- Offered products and/or services that were part of a "chain" (e.g., hardcover books, paperbacks, book clubs, books recorded on cassettes).[8]

It is hard to miss such interbusiness links. Yet most planning systems do *not* deal with them explicitly. They leave it up to the chief executive officers to take account of interrelated businesses the best way they can. Line managers are reminded every so often to "wear their corporate hats" and urged not to be "parochial" when developing strategies for their own businesses.[9]

Such platitudes are rarely taken seriously in firms that measure line managers solely on the basis of their short-term profit performances. Since few general managers have seen any advantage in leading a movement to reform their firms' measurement and bonus systems, many marketing opportunities are ignored. To pursue them would require a consensus about a shared strategy and a great deal of team play across business borders.

Consultants on GE's corporate staff have searched for ways to encourage team play among managers of related businesses. Here is a brief summary of three of the methods offered to GE's corporate office.[10]

1. An integrated strategy for a "business cluster." A *business cluster* is a group of businesses so closely related that senior managers rightfully demand that line-of-business managers get together and develop a single strategy.[11]

Entrepreneurs do this instinctively. Their strategic decisions are made with an eye on their impacts on several (related) businesses. For example, David Sarnoff's vision for RCA included program origination, distribution, *and* equipment for viewing programs in the average home. Had his line managers produced separate strategic plans for businesses that were linked in this functional manner, Sarnoff would have thought them mad.

In contrast, GE's management selection criteria produced more administrators than entrepreneurs. The company invested in equipment for program origination, distribution, and reception (TV sets and TV tubes) but delegated responsibility to managers of *separate* departments. Each submitted plans, but these were reviewed *one at a time* rather than *as a set*.

GE's planning development staff tried to persuade the corporate office that its decision to create strategic business units had not gone far enough. Therefore, this staff recommended that the group executive responsible for several GE departments serving the communications market call for a *single,* integrated strategy covering all businesses participating in the home entertainment market (e.g., those selling studio cameras, transmission equipment, and TV sets). To complement these traditional products, the staff made a case for a new venture (Tomorrow Entertainment) to (1) produce TV programs and (2) capitalize on GE's technical capability to project TV images on large screens and establish ad hoc networks to pull in programs for large, specialized audiences (e.g., political fund-raising dinners).

This proposal was not fully implemented. Integrated strategies demand that senior managers assume the role of team leader and take many risks that accompany entrepreneurial decisions. Few senior managers want interbusiness team play badly enough to place their careers on the line in the manner of a Marconi or a Sarnoff.

2. An arena analysis. An *arena* is a set of related markets. For example, a transportation arena would encompass customers who purchase automobiles, buses, trains, ships, aircraft, and pipelines as well as the equipment, services, and, at times, the information systems, control systems, and software necessary for sustaining such products.

Few businesses attempt to offer all the products and services that the customers comprising an arena require. Nonetheless, it is useful to conduct an arena analysis to enable executives to quickly update their information as to

- Trends affecting the customers who make up the set of markets so that the executives can appraise the arena's overall attractiveness.
- Where their businesses have taken positions in the arena and how strong the positions are.
- What their competitors are doing and what strategic moves they may be contemplating.
- Outside forces affecting the arena (changes in tax laws, government regulations, import ceilings, etc.).

An arena analysis will also provide a scenario for at least the next five to ten years and a list of the strategic options available to all competitors. The final section contains an appraisal of the strategic options open to the executive who called for the analysis.

A well-executed arena analysis will

1. Identify future profit trouble.
2. Highlight changes in the odds for business success.
3. Uncover threats to the firm from an unexpected quarter.
4. Detect technological trends that undermine the viability of a solid business or create new market opportunities.

The worst fate that can befall a chief executive officer is to discover that the bulk of his or her established businesses fall in an "unattractive" arena and that the most profitable product lines are about to come under severe profit pressure (e.g., due to deregulation, the collapse of oil prices, an industry shakeout involving scores of undercapitalized firms).

Those who conduct an arena analysis attempt to challenge grooves in the mind-sets of corporate officers such as:

We must stay in business X even if it is losing money.

Our "core" business is steel. We simply must invest $1 billion to meet foreign competition.

The only role of our credit business is to finance the purchase of our own line of computers.

The quality of an arena analysis does not depend on its length or the volume of statistical data compiled. A well-done arena analysis can convey a great deal of significant (qualitative and quantitative) information in 20 to 30 pages. Top managers will not read anything longer. They (rightly) expect the authors of an arena analysis to pour over the raw material and the boring statistics and then display the *significant* strategic messages.

3. A strategic map. Firms that operate with a skeletal corporate staff can resort to another tool to foster interbusiness team play: a strategic map. This is a graphic plot of the products and services that the firm offers to a set of related markets. Exhibit 12–5 is a partial listing of the products and services offered to

EXHIBIT 12–5
Fragment of a Strategic Map for the Health Care Arena

DEGREE OF COMPLEXITY (value added)	OFFERING		CUSTOMER (OEM, WHOLESALER, RETAILER, CONTRACTOR, CLINICAL LAB, TRAINING INSTITUTION, DOCTOR/DENTIST OFFICE, INDUSTRIAL CLINIC, NURSING HOME, GROUP PRACTICE/CLINIC, HOSPITAL, HEALTH MAINT. ORGANIZATION, PATIENT)
	Equipment and Supplies	Services	
HIGH Systems	Turnkey Installations (e.g. operating room system, radiology suite, I.C.U.)	Health Maintenance Organizations / Hospital Chains	
MEDIUM Sub-systems: Professional Equipment, Supplies and Services	Equipment Sub-systems (e.g. remote control x-ray, monitoring unit, automated clinical lab) / Professional Equipment (e.g. x-ray, nuclear camera) / Professional Supplies and Kits / Prosthetics / Drugs: Ethical Proprietary / Facility Construction / Radioisotopes	Multiphasic Testing Center / R&D Consulting / Management Services / Medical Info. Services / Training / Publishing / Equipment Services / Food Services / Financial Services (leasing, mortgages, accts., rec.) / Business Info. Services / Insurance / Pharmacies / Mortician Services / Ambulance Services	
LOW Nonprofit Products and Services, Components and Materials	Nonprofit Equipment (e.g. beds, chairs) / General Hospital Supplies (e.g. bandages, gowns) / Lab Reagents / Basic Chemicals / Land	Facility Maintenance / Para-Professional Manpower Services / Wholesaling / Retailing and Renting / Laundry Services	

Source: Adapted from a report prepared by Roger Yepsen, former consultant in GE's planning development unit.

various classes of customers making up the health care arena. It can be used as a checklist by firms thinking of entering this arena and by firms that might wish to redirect their resources from one customer class to another.

A strategic map is a business analog of situation maps that military commanders have used for decades to depict the deployment of their troops and the movements of enemy forces. Its content is dictated by the strategic issues confronting a particular executive rather than by the interests of his or her staff. A strategic map might display

- The status of a portfolio (In which markets do we compete? What do we offer these markets? What is the market share rank of each business?).
- The degree of integration (does this firm offer materials [e.g., plastics], parts [wiring devices], assemblies [compressors], discrete products [appliances] and systems [electric kitchens]?).
- Changes in business strategy that increase business risk, such as

    A market shift (e.g., selling appliances in the Common Market as well as in the U.S. market).
    A product shift (e.g., from selling a discrete product, such as a telephone for end users, to a small system, such as a mobile radio system for cab and trucking companies).
    A shift in product technology (e.g., from bias to belted-biased tires and from glass-belted radial to steel-belted radial tires).
    Competitors' diversification moves.

- A competitor's entry into "your" market or into a market adjacent to the one your firm serves (e.g., a Japanese firm that entered the U.S. market with a copier for large businesses is now rumored to be preparing to expand its line to include copiers for homes and small businesses).

Strategic maps will appeal to executives who want to

Understand the forces *behind* the numbers that appear on their income statements and balance sheets.

Be forewarned about risky business strategies (e.g., those entailing a jump from one market to another).

Be alerted to the strategic intentions of their competitors, especially those of raiders from a distant industry in which there is considerable excess capacity.

Spot profit threats that already have registered in one or two businesses but might engulf the entire portfolio in a few years.

4. Strategic maps do *not* belong in a file. They should be displayed on the wall of the CEO's office, where they will be a visible reminder to line managers that "no business is an island unto itself."

Clearly, strategic maps will have little appeal for executives whose arsenal of management tools consists of only an income statement and a balance sheet.

CALL FOR ACTION

Teambuilding *ought* to be a priority for U.S. firms. Unfortunately, it has *not* been. Adversarial relationships have been the core of our managerial practices. We have swallowed the myth that internal competition is the best way to achieve peak efficiency and effectiveness.

U.S. consumers do *not* subscribe to this myth. Just watch their buying habits. Daily they proclaim their preference for products made offshore—those fruits of national cultures that emphasize team play, collaboration, and joint performance.

Something ought to be done, right? Various examples of that "something" are most revealing:

- "Give us a level playing field . . ."
- "Try quality circles. That will address the root of our problem, an indifferent and recalcitrant work force."
- "Give up on manufacturing. Our workers are inefficient, undermotivated, overpaid. Let's be content to just put our own label on goods that firms in the Far East make for us. That will permit us to give our full attention to *service* businesses."

- "We have lost market share because our labor costs got out of line in the postwar period. It's time to rewrite those sweetheart labor contracts. We'll demonstrate our hard-nosed realistic attitude by closing our older plants and bargaining hard with the unions in our newest plants. If they try to block our efforts to slash unit costs and boost yield, we'll give them a 'take-it-or-we-close-the-plant' ultimatum."

So much for team play, U.S. style. Such arguments permit us to explain away our erosion in market share *by blaming everyone else*. Who? The government—for failing to keep out foreign, higher-quality products. The unions—for making "unrealistic" demands. It is *so* convenient to have a scapegoat, particularly when a complex managerial problem turns up in our in-box. It proves that we have

- Noticed that there is a problem.
- Offered a solution which requires *no effort on our part*. (Let George solve it. It does not matter who George is. The trick is to pin the responsibility *on someone else*.)

Now the evidence is rolling in that the lack of team play has a *managerial* root. Just examine the performance of Japanese firms that moved into plants in this country, hired our "lazy, undermotivated" workers, *and proceeded to turn out high-quality products*. Managers from another culture have shown that it is possible to convert U.S. workers who were impregnated with an anti-management philosophy into *team players* and produce cost-effective, high-quality products.

This is most unsettling to U.S. managers, who will have to either find a new scapegoat or make a dramatic shift in the hallowed managerial practices that have led to the "hollowing of America."

The response made to this challenge will interest many other stakeholders: The federal government—which would like to reduce the trade deficit. Our state governments—which cannot remain solvent if their pockets of structural unemployment continue to grow. Our young people—who aspire to something more than flipping hamburgers in McDonald's. Most especially, our minority groups—who find it all but impossible to make it in a high-tech society.

How does an entire society discard its myths and erase the grooves in its mind, *quickly*? That is indeed a formidable challenge because, in complaining about U.S. managers, we are actually complaining about *our society as a whole*. We have a predilection for instant gratification, for taking care of ourselves and turning away from festering problems (the environment, the erosion of our infrastructure, the sad state of our education system). Most important, in our fantasy world, we have told ourselves that:

- We don't have time for the pain.
- A problem we don't face will go away by itself.
- A shallow solution that can be explained in a 60-second sound bite is better than a complex, realistic solution that requires careful attention for 60 minutes.
- We can find a specialist for every problem that comes our way.

Alas, this is all fantasy, and it has been mirrored in the behavior of our managerial class. Do you really doubt this? How then do you account for

- Executive salaries which run into seven digits (in spite of inept performances)?
- Managers who walk around with the equivalent of a Sony Walkman headset that plays only one song, all day, every day? ("The bottom line, that is all that counts! Make 'the number.' Worry not about the 'little' people who pay the biggest penalties for our managerial boners.")
- The take-over mania?

Our bottom line is simple: *It does not have to be this way*. We *have* an arsenal of teambuilding tools but we have not been motivated to use them. They take time, they require effort, and worse, they might require an upfront investment—which, as we all know, is a threat to next month's profits, the metric we live by, our passport to higher salaries, more perks, more of everything.

Fortunately, some of the teambuilding tools described in this book can be put to work without waiting for our managerial class to be reborn or reoriented. If we do not get leadership from executives or from general managers of line-of-business, you and I can make a difference, by our own actions. Reform has to start someplace. Why not with "Indians?" Some day, some place, an "Indian" with an appreciation of team play and possessing team-building skills may become a "big chief."

Let us hope that this happy day comes soon, because our world-class competitors are becoming more formidable each and every day. Time is *not* on our side.

NOTES

1. How many top-level managers do you know who would subscribe to Saint-Exupery's sentiment: "If I differ from you, far from wronging you, I enrich you"? See *Wartime Writings,* 1939–1944 (San Diego: Harcourt Brace Jovanovich, 1986), p. 118.
2. For a bank, value added was defined as total revenue less cost of funds less outside purchases.
3. In this bank, the controller's allocation of capital was employed as proxy for "investment."
4.

$$\text{ROI} = \frac{\text{Labor efficiency} \times \text{Operating efficiency}}{\text{Capital efficiency}}$$
$$= \frac{(\text{Value added/Employees}) \times (\text{IBO/Value added})}{\text{Investment/Employees}}$$
$$= \text{Income before Overhead/Investment}$$

5. Measured by pretax return on investment.
6. See Chapter 8 for a discussion of this work.
7. At one time, GE's CEO was given back-to-back briefings by a corporate staff consultant. The latter took pains to follow a consistent format in each of his presentations.
8. "National Geographic Expands Its Television Horizons," *New York Times,* June 20, 1988, sec. 9, p. 8.
9. In firms like IBM and General Motors, the number of businesses in the portfolio is relatively small. Senior managers can reasonably be expected to address such interbusiness trade-offs.

10. The decision to fold two or three departments into one strategic business unit was intended to avoid excessive internal competition. One staff consultant went so far as to develop an input-output model to track the effect of one department's decisions on other departments (the so-called "brother-sister relationship").
11. For more detail on business clusters, see Donald F. Heany and Gerald Weiss, "Integrated Strategies for Clusters of Businesses," *Journal of Business Strategy* 4 (no. 1, Summer 1983), pp. 3–11.

APPENDIX A

THE CONTRIBUTIONS OF A QUALITY MAP TO TEAM PLAY DURING NEW-PRODUCT DEVELOPMENT

Definition of a Quality Map

A *quality map* is a graphic model used by professionals on a multifunctional team to make explicit and understandable the linkages between their technical decisions and two business goals: customer satisfaction and business profitability. Exhibit A–1 is a slice of a quality map for Bright Stik, the GE lamp system discussed in Chapter 3.

Functions of a Quality Map

The primary purpose of a quality map is to help professionals from various functional areas integrate their respective contributions to new-product development or quality enhancement. A secondary purpose is to offer a strategic context to specialists working in the middle and lower echelons of a business. It reminds them to make their contributions with one eye on customer satisfaction and the other on business profitability.

EXHIBIT A–1 Fragment of a Quality Map Developed by a Multifunctional Team Charged with Commercializing a New Product (Bright Stik)

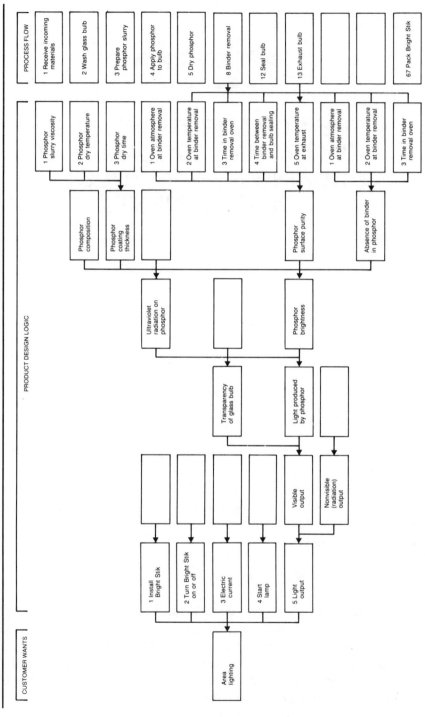

HOW QUALITY MAPS FULFILL
BUSINESS NEEDS

Quality maps address five important business needs:

1. Avoid New Products with Too Many Bells and Whistles. A quality map forces product designers to focus on those customer wants that the multifunctional team has listed. It minimizes the danger that they will design a new product they feel their customer *ought to want.*

2. Be Alert to the Downstream Effects of Technical Decisions. A quality map exposes the dangers which attend solo performances. It helps specialists comprehend the impacts their decisions will have on their teammates who make their contributions to new-product development at a later time or in a remote functional area.

3. Get Everyone to Contribute. A quality map encourages professionals to comment on the decisions and trade-offs being made in *another* function. Typically, specialists are reluctant to do this. They recall their professors' admonition, "Stick to your own knitting." But in team meetings professionals are, by definition, equal in power, creativity, and insight. The whole purpose of a multifunctional team is to encourage a *broad* perspective. Therefore, with all eyes fixed on a *shared* quality map, manufacturing's representative will be comfortable pointing out that an engineering decision unduly complicates his or her work and might extend the development cycle.

Designers are more open to such comments when they are made *early* in the product development cycle. They may even concede that there is an array of design options that might yield the same end product characteristic. Normally, people in manufacturing would never be told about these options, particularly if they spoke up after product and process specifications were finalized.

Readers who have never been concerned with the details of product innovation work may not appreciate the novelty inherent in the above sentence. The fact is that in many businesses, product designers do *not* bother to document the intellectual path they took to arrive at their recommended design. The few who do would not think of inviting their colleagues in manufacturing to critique the options they are contemplating. According to the rules of behavior in businesses organized along functional lines, engineering completes the design of a new product and passes on to manufacturing only the *end result* of their thinking: product and process specifications. As attendees at "quality colleges" are taught, these specifications are to be treated with reverence. They are *not* offered as points of discussion or as a subject for negotiation. Quite the contrary. Product designers have worked too long and too hard to welcome any suggestions from another function that might send them "back to the drawing board." Rather, they tend to assume that any criticisms from manufacturing spring from a dubious allegiance to existing processes and an unwillingness to try anything new.

4. *Avoid Unnecessary Investments in New Equipment, Jigs, Dies, and Fixtures.* A quality map is an invitation to product designers and manufacturing engineers to pool their personal databases early in the development cycle. If they work together, they often can minimize the need for additional capital outlays.

5. *Think about Profit at the Outset of the Development Cycle.* A quality map moves financial analysis *from the very end* of the product development cycle *to the very beginning*. For example, any design decisions that "gold-plate" the new product stand out like a sore thumb, since they cannot be linked to any of the specified customer wants. Profit considerations take precedence over any tendency to advance the "state of the art." Cost reductions made with the help of a paper model are positive proof that specialists are bringing a *business* perspective to bear on their functional work.

APPENDIX B

AN OPERATIONAL BUSINESS CHARTER, BUSINESS STRATEGY, AND FUNCTIONAL GUIDANCE

Every professional sports team has a playbook that lists complex offensive and defensive plays. These playbooks are constantly being updated and modified in light of new information on the resources and intentions of "the enemy."

The three exhibits that make up this appendix (Exhibits B-1, B–2, and B–3) are taken from a playbook prepared by two of GE's business researchers, Herbert B. Slate and Adrian J. Grossman, in GE's Aircraft Accessory Turbine Department (AATD). Their research was summarized in Chapter 8. We hope the reader will view the details of these exhibits as their authors intended, namely as carefully crafted statements of (1) business scope, (2) business strategy, and (3) constraints that top managers impose on functional tactics (i.e., the "higher-order inputs").

Professionals with operating experience will realize at a glance that these exhibits reflect a lot of thought. Each word has been carefully chosen. There are no platitudes, no pompous phrases of the type so often found in policy statements prepared by general managers or their public relations staffs.

EXHIBIT B–1
A New Charter for AATD

AATD should be viewed as a design-manufacturing business resting upon specific component technologies. These technologies are diverse, complex and changing.

AATD's market consists of a limited number of customers with highly-specialized requirements which are shaped by higher-level, system decisions over which AATD has little or no control.

EXHIBIT B–1—*Concluded*

AATD is a manufacturing business. It offers its customers *hardware systems* rather than discrete parts or components. These systems are customized. Therefore, to keep them aligned with their customers' rapidly escalating requirements, AATD must continually advance the product technology(ies) upon which they rest.

Each of AATD's customers invests heavily in scientific and engineering programs which are intended to improve overall system performance. The technological advances resulting from this R&D activity impact the relative quality of the products offered by businesses making up our industry.

To remain a qualified vendor, AATD must also invest in R&D. Specifically, it must advance the state of those component technologies which differentiate its product line from those of its leading competitors.

Other hardware components are required to complete the systems AATD offers. These components can be purchased from state-of-the-art vendors.

AATD competitors are sophisticated and well funded. They are developing and aggressively exploiting markedly different technologies in order to produce products for the same set of customers. Consequently, AATD can not relax its efforts to defend and extend the technological expertise which differentiates its products from those of its competitors.

Spare parts for installed hardware systems are an important source of profits for AATD and for an extended period of time.

EXHIBIT B–2
Planks in the Proposed Business Strategy

- Develop and exploit those applied technologies upon which rest those primary components of AATD's hardware systems, i.e., its "central technologies."
- Invest in a limited number of central technologies which
    Yield products applicable to numerous, durable market opportunities.
    Have upside potential, i.e., there is a chance to advance their "state."
    Have an edge over other competing technologies.
    Will attract company and customer research funding.
- Advance the state of each central technology by expending AATD's own creative effort so as to be able to satisfy (or anticipate) changing market requirements.
- Understand and use (but do *not* advance) those applied technologies underlying minor components of AATD's hardware systems. Refer to these technologies as "ancillary technologies."

EXHIBIT B–3
Strategic Constraints on Functional Managers

1. *Guidelines for the R&D Function:*
   - Since AATD's customers regularly escalated the performance standards of the hardware systems they purchased, the department's R&D staff *must continually add to its expertise in a central technology.*
   - AATD's scientists must be proactive rather than reactive, i.e., they must try to *anticipate* future states of their "central" technology(ies).
   - Should a central technology become mature, AATD must acquire mastery of another technology germane to its work. AATD ought *not* fund R&D projects tied to a technology which has lost its status as a "central" technology.
   - AATD can only afford to invest in a few central technologies. Each of its R&D projects must be closely linked to business goals. AATD's scientists and engineers have no license to pursue "pet" exploratory projects unrelated to a central technology. The department ought not to bet its future on serendipity.

2. *Guidelines for the Manufacturing Function:*
   - Every effort must be made to safeguard AATD's proprietary position in its central technology. Therefore, all products and components reflective of such a technology *must be manufactured in house.* Manufacturing ought *not* subcontract production to outside vendors. This might give them access to proprietary data and possibly tempt them to become a competitor of AATD.
   - Manufacturing must acquire from a preferred vendor all hardware that is ancillary to its own primary hardware components. A preferred vendor is defined as one who is interested in *advancing* a technology which AATD has classified as an "ancillary technology."
   - The Manager–Manufacturing is authorized to manufacture components made from an ancillary technology *provided* it is profitable to do so.

3. *Guidelines for the Marketing Function:*
   - AATD's salespersons are to pursue contracts related to AATD's expertise in a central technology. Thus, they are not to view themselves as order takers.
   - The preferred sales opportunity is defined as one which calls for hardware systems which can be assembled from components reflective of a *past* state of AATD's central technology. Therefore, each salesperson must be familiar with the state of the central and ancillary technologies underlying each of the components in AATD's hardware systems.
   - While salespersons may return with sales opportunities which will require AATD to advance its central technology, only the general manager can authorize the investment of resources needed to effect such an advance.

REFERENCES

Books

Abell, Derek F. *Defining the Business: The Starting Point of Strategic Planning*. Englewood Cliffs, N.J.: Prentice-Hall, Inc., 1980.

Abell, Derek F., and John S. Hammond. *Strategic Market Planning:* Problems and Analytical Approaches. Englewood Cliffs, N.J.: Prentice Hall, Inc., 1979 (especially Chapters 6–10 and Appendix A).

Barzun, Jacques. *Science: The Glorious Entertainment*. New York: Harper & Row, 1964, pp. 26–27.

Bilby, Kenneth. *The General: David Sarnoff and The Rise of the Communications Industry*. New York: Harper & Row, 1986.

Bloom, Allan. *The Closing of the American Mind: How Higher Education Has Failed Democracy and Impoverished the Souls of Today's Students*. New York: Simon and Schuster, 1987.

Buber, Martin. *I and Thou*. A new translation, with a prologue and notes by Walter Kaufman. New York: Charles Scribner's Sons, 1970.

Buzzell, Robert D., and Bradley T. Gale. *The PIMS Principles: Linking Strategy to Performance*. New York: Free Press, 1987.

Cousins, Norman. *The Healing Heart: Antidote to Panic and Helplessness*. New York: W. W. Norton & Co., 1983.

Crosby, Philip B. *Quality is Free: The Art of Making Quality Certain*. New York: McGraw-Hill Book Co., 1979.

Day, George S., *Strategic Market Analysis: Top-Down and Bottom-Up Approaches*. Marketing Science Institute, Research Program Working Paper, Report 80–105, August 1980.

Deal, Terence E., and Allan A. Kennedy. Corporate Cultures: The Rites and Rituals of Corporate Life. Reading, Mass.: Addison-Wesley, 1982.

Drucker, Peter F. *The Effective Executive*, New York: Harper & Row, 1966.

————— . *The Frontiers of Management: Where Tomorrow's Decisions Are Being Shaped Today*. New York: Truman Talley Books/E. P. Dutton, 1986 (especially Chapter 24, "The Information-Based Organization").

————— *Management: Tasks, Responsibilities, Practices*. New York: Harper & Row, 1973.

Garvin, David A. *Managing Quality: The Strategic and Competitive Edge*. New York: the Free Press, 1988.

Geneen, Harold, and Alvin Moscow. *Managing*. Garden City, N.Y.: Doubleday, 1984.

General Electric Co. *Organization and Policy Guide No. 20.7*. Business Charters, 8-15-59.

————. *Using the "Added Value" Concept to Throw New Light on Business Relationships, Opportunities, Requirements*. Engineering Services ENS-R-105, 9–56.

————. *Cybernetics: The Next Step in Management*, 1952.

Grossman, Adrian J. "Inner-Directedness in Planning" (Chapter 7). In *Modern Industrial Management*. Edited by S. Benjamin Prased. San Francisco: Chandler Publishing Co., 1967, pp. 143–74.

Hall, E. T., and M. R. Hall. *Doing Business with the Japanese*. Garden City, N.Y.: Anchor Press/Doubleday, 1987.

Hamermesh, Richard G. *Making Strategy Work: How Senior Managers Produce Results*. New York: John Wiley & Sons, 1986.

Hayes, Robert H., and Steven C. Wheelwright. *Restoring Our Competitive Edge—Competing through Manufacturing*. New York: John Wiley & Sons, 1984.

Hickman, Craig R., and Michael A. Silva. *Creating Excellence: Managing Corporate Culture, Strategy, and Change in a New Age*. New York: NAL (New American Library), 1984.

Hopkins, David S. "New-Product Winners and Losers." Research Report no. 773. New York: The Conference Board, 1980.

Kelley, Robert E. *The Gold Collar Worker: Harnessing the Brainpower of the New Work Force*. Reading, Mass.: Addison-Wesley, 1985.

Krause, William. A. *Collaboration in Organizations: Alternatives to Hierarchy*, New York: Human Sciences Press, 1980.

Mahler, Walter R., and Stephen J. Drotter. *The Succession Planning Handbook for the Chief Executive*. Midland Park, N.J.: Mahler Publishing Co., 1986.

Martel, Leon. *Mastering Change: The Key to Business Success*. New York: Simon and Shuster, 1986.

McCormack, Mark H. *What They Don't Teach You at the Harvard Business School*. Toronto: Bantam, 1984.

Morita, Akio (with Edwin M. Reingold and Mitsuko Shimomura). *Made in Japan: Morita and Sony*. New York: E. P. Dutton, 1986.

Naisbitt, John, and Patricia Aburdine. *Re-inventing the Corporation: Transforming Your Job and Your Company for the New Information Society*. New York: Warner Books, 1985.

The New York Academy of Medicine. "Clinical Education and the Doctor of Tomorrow", by David E. Rogers, M.D. Final chapter from *Proceedings of the Josiah Macy, Jr., Foundation National Seminar on Medical Education,* November 1988.

Nicolson, Harold. *Diaries and Letters, 1930–64.* Edited and condensed by Stanley Olson. New York: Atheneum, 1980 (especially pp. 250–53).

Ouchi, William G. *The M-Form Society: How American Teamwork Can Recapture the Competitive Edge.* Reading, Mass.: Addison-Wesley, 1984.

————— . *Theory Z: How American Business Can Meet the Japanese Challenge.* Reading, Mass.: Addison-Wesley, 1981.

O'Toole, Patricia. *Corporate Messiah—The Hiring and Firing of Million Dollar Managers.* New York: William Morrow, 1984.

Peters, Thomas J. *Thriving on Chaos: Handbook for a Management Revolution.* New York: Alfred A. Knopf, 1988.

Peters, Thomas J., and Robert H. Waterman Jr. *In Search of Excellence: Lessons from America's Best-Run Companies.* New York: Harper & Row, 1982.

Porter, Michael J. *Competitive Advantage: Creating and Sustaining Superior Performance.* New York: Free Press, 1985.

————— . *Competitive Strategy: Techniques for Analyzing Industries and Competitors.* New York: Free Press, 1980.

Raelin, Joseph A. *The Clash of Cultures: Managers and Professionals.* Boston: The Harvard Business School Press, 1984.

Reich, Robert B. *Tales of a New America,* New York: Times Books, 1987.

Roberts, Edward B., ed. *Managerial Applications of System Dynamics* (especially Chapter 4, "Strategies for Effective Implementation of Complex Corporate Models"). Cambridge, Mass.: MIT Press, 1979, pp. 77–85.

Rudwick, Bernard H. *Solving Management Problems: A Systems Approach to Planning and Control,* New York: John Wiley & Sons, Inc., 1979.

————— . *Systems Analysis for Effective Planning.* New York: John Wiley & Sons, Inc., 1969.

Salisbury, Harrison E. *The Long March—The Untold Story.* New York: Harper & Row, 1985.

————— . *A Time of Change: A Reporter's Tale of Our Time.* New York: Harper & Row, 1988.

Salomon Brothers Inc. *Technology in Banking: A Path to Competitive Advantage.* May 1985.

Schein, Edward H. *Process Consultation: Its Role in Organization Development.* Reading, Mass.: Addison-Wesley, 1969.

————— . *Process Consultation: Lessons for Managers and Consultants.* Vol. II (OD Series). Reading, Mass.: Addison-Wesley, 1987.

Sloan, Alfred P., Jr. *My Years with General Motors.* Eds. John McDonald and Catherine Stevens. Garden City, N.Y.: Doubleday, 1964 (especially Chapters 3 and 4).

Strassmann, Paul A. *Information Payoff: The Transformation of Work in the Electronic Age*. New York: Free Press, 1985.

Strategic Planning Institute. PIMSLETTERs on Business Strategy. Cambridge, Mass.: SPI (various years):

No. 1   Schoeffler, Sidney. "Nine Basic Findings on Business Strategy," 1977.

No. 3   _____ . "Market Position: Build, Hold or Harvest?" 1977.

No. 11 _____ . "Good Productivity versus Bad Productivity," 1979.

No. 21 Gale, Bradley T. "Productivity Benchmarks," 1980.

No. 30 Buzzell, Robert D., and Mark J. Chussil. "The Full Potential of a Business," 1983.

No. 32 Gale, Bradley T. and Ben Branch. "Beating the Cost of Capital," 1984.

Report on "Look-Alikes," 1980.

Touche Ross International. *The Impact of Technology on Banking, World Summary, 1985*. Eds. Thomas H. Hanley, James M. Rosenberg, Carla A. D'Arista, and Neil A. Mitchell. 1985.

Articles

Business Week

7–4–83   "The Competition Besieging ITT in Telecommunications," pp. 46–47.

4–29–85 Beam, A. "A Troubled Polaroid Is Tearing Apart 'the House that Land Built,' " pp. 51–52.

1–20–86 Byrne, John A. "Business Fads: What's In and Out," pp. 52–55ff.

8–4–86   Nussbaum, B. "The End of Corporate Loyalty," pp. 42–45.

8–18–86 Bianco, A. "Jerry Tsai: the Comeback King," pp. 72–77.

11–24–86 "Deal Mania . . . The Restructuring of Corporate America" (Special Report), pp. 74–77.

6–13–88 F. A. Miller. "How Amex is Revamping Its Big, Beautiful Money Machine," pp. 90–92.

6–27–88 J. B. Treece. "Putting a Dent into the Taurus Image," p. 55.

7–4–88   Dwyer, Paula, and Staff. "Top of The News" and cover story: "The Defense Scandal—The Fallout May Devastate the Arms Industry," pp. 28–32.

9–12–88 Byrne, John A., and Staff. "Caught in the Middle," pp. 80–89.

Fortune

6–13–83 Dreyfus, J. "Handing Down the Old Hands' Wisdom."

7–4–88   Curran, John C. "Companies That Rob the Future," p. 84ff.

Harvard Business Review

Schoeffler, Sidney, Robert D. Buzzell, and Donald F. Heany. "Impact of Strategic Planning on Profit Performance," March–April 1974, pp. 137–45.

Gluck, Frederick W., and William N. Foster. "Managing Technological Change: A Box of Cigars for Brad," September–October 1975, pp. 139–49.

Leavitt, Theodore. "Marketing Myopia," September–October 1975, pp. 26ff.

Hobbs, John M., and Donald F. Heany. "Coupling Strategy to Operating Plans," May–June 1977, pp. 119–26. (Reprinted as Chapter 21 in *Strategic Management*. Ed. Richard G. Hammermesh. New York: John Wiley, 1983).

Shapiro, Benson P. "Can Marketing and Manufacturing Coexist?" September–October 1977, pp. 104–14.

Vinson, William D., and Donald F. Heany. "Is Quality Out of Control?" November–December 1977, pp. 114–22.

Biggadike, Ralph. "The Risky Business of Diversification," May–June 1979, pp. 103–10.

Gale, Bradley T. "Can More Capital Buy Higher Productivity?" July–August 1980, pp. 78–86.

Hauser, John R., and Don Clausing. "The House of Quality," May–June 1988, pp. 63ff.

The Journal of Business Strategy

Heany, Donald F., and Gerald Weiss. "Integrating Strategies for Clusters of Businesses," Summer 1983, pp. 3–11.

Heany, Donald F., and William D. Vinson. "A Fresh Look at New Product Development," Fall 1984, pp. 22–31.

Heany, Donald F. "Businesses in Profit Trouble," Spring 1985, pp. 4–12.

Harvard Magazine

"Needed: Better Ways to Train Doctors," May–June 1984, pp. 32ff.

Inc.

Richman, Tom. "What Business Are You Really In?" August 1983, pp. 77–86.

"Information Strategist: Paul Strassmann," March 1988, pp. 27–38.

Long Range Planning

Stone, W. Robert, and Donald F. Heany. "Dealing with a Corporate Identity Crisis," February 1984, pp. 10–18.

New York Times

7–20–86   Durmak, John. "Camera: Tape Tells the Story in Canon's New System," p. 43.

3-6-88   Deutsch, Claudia H. "Kodak Pays the Price for Change," Sec. 3, p. 1.

6–20–88   Shenon, Philip. "Weinberger Says Bribery Inquiry May Show Reforms Are Necessary," Sec. 1, p. 1.

7–3–88   Markoff, John. "American Express Goes Hi-Tech," Sec. 3, pp. Fl, F6.

10–2–88 Weaver, Paul H. "My Sojourn at Ford—Life among Motown's Machiavellis" (Business Forum).

11–27–88 Teiger, David A. "Work Together—Even When Apart," Sunday Business Section, p. F2.
Keidel, Robert W. "Going Beyond 'I'm O.K., You're O.K.,' " Sunday Business Section, p. F2.

The New Yorker

Newhouse, John. "A Sporty Game: Betting the Company," June 14, 21, 28, and July 5, 1982.

Newsweek

Easterbrook, Gregg. "The Revolution in Medicine," January 26, 1987, pp. 40ff.

Planning Review

Heany, Donald F. "Porter's Competitive Advantage Revisited," January 1986, pp. 27–29.

1985 Printout Annual

Stone, Bob. "Technology Limits and Printer Design," pp. 18–27.

The Wall Street Journal

5–2–83 Foster, Richard. "To Exploit New Technology, Know When to Junk the Old." Manager's Journal.

8–1–84 Seib, Gerald F. "Costly Rivalries: Pentagon Has Trouble Winning Cooperation between the Services," pp. 1ff.

INDEX

A

Adversarial behavior patterns
  in committees, 33
  entrenchment of, 10
  among managers, 196
  reasons for, 14–22
  in vendor relations, 146–47
Apple, Gene, 149
Arena analysis
  results of, 232
  use of, 231–32
Asset sharing, 194
Assimilation sessions, 111–12, 165
Attitude surveys, 108

B

Back-office technology
  in business strategy, 165
  importance of, 57
Bloom, Allan, 83
Blue-collar workers
  on multifunctional teams, 151–52
  outlook changes for, 10
Borch, Fred, 193
Business autopsy, 97
Business charter example, 245–46
Business clusters
  defined, 230
  strategies for, 230
Business databases, 180–84
  quality control for, 182

Business definition
  balanced input in, 116
  byproducts of, 117–18
  consensus methods, 116–17
  diagnostic software for, 117
  difficulties in, 113–14
  end products from, 118–20
  language barriers to, 116
  process, 115–17
  process facilitator for, 116–17
Businesses
  conventional wisdom within, 133
  dominant function in, 16
  external changes and, 21
  functional organization, 18
  goals, 23
  high-tech, 16, 138
  information exchange within, 180, 207
  mature, 16
  organizational design, 143
  organizational flux in, 19–20
  performance measurement for, 118–19
  restructuring of, 135–45, 157–60
  sales department in, 17
  shared strategic context in, 25
  subcultures within, 176–77
  symptoms of dysfunction in, 27–28
  takeovers, 21–22
  traditional organization of, 14
Business organization
  activity centers within, 110
  team approach to, 107–13

Business organizational design,
107–13
Business problems
creative approaches to, 60–61
incremental approach to, 95–96
multifunctional team approach to,
34–40
research on, 142
solutions through reorganization,
97
team sponsorship for, 38–39
Business profile
forward planning with, 120
uses for, 118
Business research principles,
225–26
Business strategy
business definition and, 119
capital appropriations and, 212–14
changes in, 234
clarity in, 228–29
EDP components in, 160–66
example of, 246
excellence as a goal in, 210–11
financial plan within, 123
focus for, 86, 99, 138–39
functional tactics, 166
implementation of, 85
importance of consensus in, 105
information requirements in, 182
need for, 93
pertinent questions within, 112
planning framework, 227–29
for related businesses, 229–30
research within, 137–42
retreat as, 94
staffing decisions in, 128
Business trauma
from computerization, 143–45
functional stress and, 137
handling of, 135–36
importance of leadership during,
144–45
team approach to, 145

C

Capital allocation
lack of team approach to, 213
model for, 223–24
Capital efficiency, 218–26
Central technology
defined, 138
importance of, 138
Change
computerized agents for, 130
ideal agent for, 5
outsiders as agents of, 190
resistance to, 189–90
Claritas P$cycle Segmentation
System, 182
Clout, 38, 59, 61
Collegiality
and innovation, 209
in multifunctional teams, 151
among professionals, 110
in team play, 109–11
unusual approaches to, 176–77
Committees, adversarial behavior
patterns in, 33
Computerization impact on organizational design, 143–44
Consultants
back-up for, 189–90
restrictions on, 37
role of, 36–37, 53, 164, 166
selection, 201
skills required, 37–38, 52
Corporate synergy, 194
Costello, Robert, 153–55
Cost reduction
in development cycle, 154, 244
product requirements and, 153
through regulation streamlining,
154
team approach to, 154
Cross-selling, 176
Customers
changing needs of, 83

Customers—(*continued*)
  databases regarding, 180–84
  disjoint marketing to, 180
  versus end users, 51
  establishing, 89
  product input from, 199
  quality control input, 70–72
  satisfying, 160, 163
  sharing of, 174–79

D

Data leveraging
  customer files, 180–84
  team approach, 184
  technical data, 192–93
Discrete products versus systems,
  77–81
Disneyland, 79
Divoky, Dick, 149, 152
Drucker, Peter F., 8, 10, 29

E–F

Early adopters, 204
End users versus immediate
  customers, 51
Financial data, 218–26
Flowcharts, 158
Ford, Henry, Sr., 26, 74
Forecasting total demand, 61

G–H

Grossman, Adrian J., 137–41, 245
Heany, Donald F., 45, 233, 242
Heldack, John, 141
Herlevi, Tom, 108–11
Holmes, Donald S., 188–90
Home banking, 80
Hurni, Melvin L., 141

I

Iacocca, Lee, 9–10
Innovation, 201, 207–12
Interfunctional team play and organization structure, 107–13
Internal marketing
  direct, 196–201
  indirect, 201–6
Intrapreneurship, 175–79, 185–87,
  202–7

J–K

Japanese management, 11
Just-in-time inventory
  achievement of, 147
  and vendor relationships, 147
Knowledge worker
  defined, 10
  nature of, 29

L

Labor efficiency, 218–26
Leadership
  background requirements, 208
  styles of, 177
  worker morale and, 188–90
Leveraged buyouts, 119–20
Linear thinking, 64–65

M

Management decisions, 193
Management information systems
  (MIS)
  integration of, 160–66
  utilization of, 143–44, 157
Managers
  attitudes of, 19
  care and feeding of, 201

Managers—(*continued*)
  crucial role of, 236–38
  ego trips by, 20
  line versus staff, 196
  organizational tinkering by, 19–20
  relationship with professionals, 112
  revolving-door effect and, 19
  strategic constraints on, 247
  strategic decisions by, 89
  team play among, 170
  turnover in, 19–20
Market boundaries
  contiguous, 184
  elastic, 115
  fluctuation in, 101–3
  perception of, 105
  product technology and, 101–2
Marketing
  goals in, 174
  internal, 196–207
Marketing segmentation, 61
Monk, Ivon, 116
Morita, Akio, 1, 10–11, 192
Multibusiness firm troubleshooting, 187
Multifunctional teams
  appropriate uses for, 34–35
  benefits of, 46–48
  building, 35–40, 157
  coalescence, 151
  collegiality in, 151
  versus committees, 31–34
  consultants with, 36–38
  defined, 31
  enhancing effectiveness of, 39–40
  to foster innovation, 207–12
  guidance of, 54
  handling of, 56
  ideal uses for, 152
  informal, 184–87, 203–4
  for new-product development, 42–51
  office space for, 208
  participant selection criteria, 35, 149–52

Multifunctional teams—(*continued*)
  problem-solving strategy, 36
  rewards for, 209
  sponsor obligations, 39, 56
  volunteer workers on, 189

N

Nay-sayers, handling of, 57–59, 128, 159, 203–4
Neul, Charles M., 218–26
New businesses
  criteria for establishing, 106
  customer targeting by, 102
  customer views of, 89
  definition process for, 119
  forward planning in, 101
  functional stress in, 89–92
  mind-set for, 100
  versus new products, 106
  professionals within, 89
  risk containment for, 98–100
New-product teams
  benefits of, 46–47
  business decisions by, 50
  efficiency in, 41–42
  marketing information within, 47–48
  quality map use by, 241–44
Non-profit institutions, 41
Not invented here factor, 54

O

Operating efficiency, 218–26
Organizational structure, collaborative approach, 107
Organization charts
  benefits in ignoring, 187
  as detriment to team play, 14

P

Patten, Joseph, 228
Peer pressure, 199

Peer review, 17–18
PIMS database, 219
PIMS data forms
  diagnostic software for, 117
  use of, 115–17
Planning, team approach to, 165–66
Process, connection with product, 56
Process control, 188–90
Process facilitator, 116–18, 151, 165
Product, connection with process, 56
Product differentiation, 199
Product image, 51–56
Production process enhancement, 57–59
Productivity
  measures of, 218
  profitability and, 218
  relative performance, 222
  trend measurement, 221–23
Productivity/Profitability Grid, 218–23
Product line expansion
  business sense in, 49–51
  designer's perspective on, 49–50
  examination of, 139
  personal computers and, 77
  and product structure, 76
  product technology and, 98
  purposeless, 77
  salesforce attitude toward, 173–74
  team approach to, 49–51, 211–12
Product migrations, 79–83
Product quality; see also Quality control
  customer perception of, 68, 70–72, 200
  defined, 67
  failures in, 65–66
  peripheral issues, 200
  product-related attributes, 68, 71
  service-related attributes, 68, 71
Products
  effects of computerization on, 81
  redefining, 82–83

Products—(continued)
  relationship to services, 68, 71, 74
  services as, 82
  versus systems, 77–81
  unrealistic requirements for, 153
Product spectrum, 77
Product technology
  market boundaries and, 101–3
  product line expansion and, 98
Product variety
  excessive, 75
  linear thinking about, 74–76
  team approach to, 74–75
Professionals
  collegial evaluation of, 110
  information sharing by, 191–94
  personal objectives, 14, 20
Profitability benchmarks, 118–19
Profits
  conventional wisdom, 122, 132–33
  potential, 123
  pressure toward, 178

Q

Quality circles, 10, 66–67, 194
Quality control
  for business databases, 182
  multifunctional responsibility for, 73
  standard approach to, 66
  worker morale and, 189
Quality enhancement programs
  grass-roots support for, 197–200
  parameters for, 191
  plan for, 67, 73
  profitability and, 197
  team approach to, 74, 197–200
Quality map
  defined, 241
  functions of, 44–45, 241
  nature of, 44
  uses for, 243–44
Quality profile
  nature of, 68–70
  procedure for, 70

R

Reed, Charles, 209–10
Relative quality
  enhancement of, 198
  internal versus external views of,
    70, 74
  nature of, 68
Reserved words, 105
Resource allocation model, 223–24
Retreats, 109–11, 209

S

Saint-Exupery, Antoine de, 145
Sarnoff, David, 230
Sarver, James F., 107–13
Service businesses
  back-office technology, 57
  business strategies for, 125–26
  performance measurement, 124
  quality control in, 66
  team approach for, 41
Service quality
  data analysis of, 124–30
  mathematical modeling of, 127–30
  standards for, 127
  team approach to, 79
Sheed, Frank, 14
Simulation modeling, 127–30
Slate, Herbert B., 137–41, 245
Smith, Deborah A., 218–26
Specialization and team play, 14, 22
Sponsors
  backbone in, 179
  importance of, 141–42
  leadership styles, 178
  obligations of, 39, 56, 179, 204
  problem-solving clout of, 38–39
  selection, 209
  visible backing from, 198
Staff development, 191–92
Staggered implementation, 159–60
Stone, W. R., 97–103

Strassmann, Paul A., 143–44
Strategic business units
  definition for, 114
  elastic boundaries for, 115
  scope for, 231
Strategic data unevenness, 226
Strategic map
  nature of, 232
  uses for, 234–35
Strategic Planning Institute, 67,
    115–19
Strategic scaffolding, 142
Systems
  designs of, 157
  versus discrete products, 77–81

T

Team play; *see also* Multifunctional
    teams
  barriers to, 14–29
  collegiality within, 109–11
  effect of turnover on, 19
  face-to-face communication in,
    164–66
  fostering, 113, 164
  horse trading within, 111
  interbusiness, 99–100, 102, 147,
    155, 169–70
  interfunctional, 113–20
  language barriers to, 15–16, 25
  linear thinking and, 46, 64–65
  in multibusiness firms, 169
  in new-product design, 41–51; *see
    also* New-product teams
  peer pressure and, 199
  performance measurement in, 17
  reasons for, 5–6
  during takeovers, 21–22
  top-down, 216–17, 229–30
  traditional organization and, 14
  trends in, 235–38
  within world competitors, 8
Technology sharing, 191–93, 209

Top-down team play
  areas for, 217
  barriers to, 217
  interbusiness relationships and, 229–30
  need for, 217
  scarcity of, 216–17
Turnkey contracts, 80

V–W

Vendors, team play approach to, 147
Videotex, 80
Vinson, William D., 45, 108–11, 242

Worker-management teams, 189
Worker morale
  boosts for, 191
  leadership and, 188–90
  quality control and, 189

Y–Z

Yepsen, Roger, 233
Zero defects
  desirability of, 66
  emphasizing, 10
  pitfalls in, 68